THE STRANGER'S HOMECOMING

THE STRANGER'S HOMECOMING

A House in the Alto Minho, Portugal

Igal Sarna

Translated from the Hebrew by Yifat Doron

Signal Books
Oxford

First published in 2022 by
Signal Books Limited
36 Minster Road
Oxford OX4 1LY
www.signalbooks.co.uk

A catalogue record for this book is available from the British
Library

ISBN 978-1-8384630-5-2 paper

Cover Design: Tora Kelly
Typesetting: Tora Kelly
Cover Images: Orit Morad
Printed in India by Imprint Press

Contents

Preface to a Home vii

1 Lisbon, a Dead King on a Horse 1

2 A House in the Net 17

3 Hereinafter "the Estate": Candemil, Vila Nova de Cerveira 25

4 Poland, Palestine, Portugal 37

5 Senhor Franco and his Sad Daughter Marília 51

6 The Business Class Carpenters 67

7 The Marco Silva Universe of Old Objects 81

8 Zé Paolo and the house of Granny Ermelinda 197

9 Conversations with Horses 113

10 The Longest Dry Spell in Ninety-Nine Years 147

11 Tiago: Under a Miracle Sky 167

12 The Round Window that Sailed from Jaffa 209

13 The Baba Schulz Ashram and 360 Parrots 229

14 The Lost Princess of Alto Minho 259

15 The Mystery of the Vanishing Glass Harp Player 281

16 Cow Shed Dreams 299

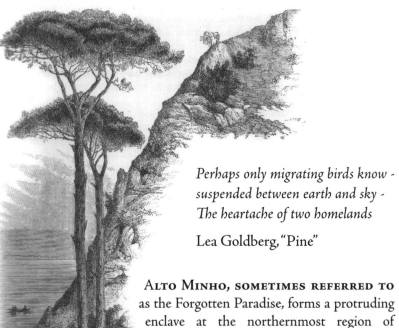

Perhaps only migrating birds know -
suspended between earth and sky -
The heartache of two homelands

Lea Goldberg, "Pine"

ALTO MINHO, SOMETIMES REFERRED TO
as the Forgotten Paradise, forms a protruding
enclave at the northernmost region of
Portugal, stretching over an area
larger than 2,200 square kilometres.
Roughly a quarter of a million
Portuguese inhabit the region in
small yet well-bordered properties
across land that has been much
divided. Sectioned between the
Minho and Cávado rivers, the Alto Minho is
mountainous, densely forested and rich in water
and vegetation. The inhabitants are devout folk
who eat a lot of bacalao and lamprey, drink *vinho*
verde, and finish off a meal with aguardiente.

The town of Vila Nova de Cerveira with its villages, one of
which is Candemil, lies to the north of the region, on the banks of
the Minho, where it flows to the Atlantic Ocean. Until the relatively
recent construction of a network of motorways, the Alto Minho
lived out of sight, in relative peace.

The symbol of Vila Nova is the deer. I have yet to see a live one.

Preface to a Home

WHY PORTUGAL? I AM OFTEN asked this question by friends and random strangers - or more specifically, why the Alto Minho? Why not a classical destination like Greece or Spain, or a vibrant city such as Berlin? This book should provide a lengthy answer to that question. It was inspired by my personal journey during these first years as a stranger in a foreign land, and out of a curiosity and familiarity which grew over time. It was written during random hikes on old country roads, sheltering in the ancient hallways of ruined mansions, inside the courtyards of long-abandoned houses surrounded by a barbed wire of wild raspberry, forbidding entrance to any and all.

All my life I have been the one asking the questions: as an opinionated boy, as a sceptical adolescent, and for most of my adult years as an investigative journalist. For the better part of my thirty-five-year career I sought out solutions to mysteries the world over, such as the one haunting my youth. I was born in a house replete with the secrets of my parents, survivors of a war that did away with most of their relatives. Forced to abandon their beloved Europe, they made their escape; yet secretly continued to long for their old *patria*. It was a forbidden longing, for how were they to miss a home which nearly destroyed them?

My mother and father clung passionately to their new Mediterranean homeland. They started a family and built a life but continued to reminisce over the land of their youth, with its great expanses of water and forestland, mud and fog, old buildings and snow laden rooftops. My mother grew up on a poor farm and my father in a small town on the banks of a magnificent river.

My childhood memories are shrouded in the fog of pre-war Europe: its secrets and forbidden attractions are entwined with the rage - the desperate clinging of my parents to their new refuge, Israel, where they viewed themselves as pioneers.

Daily life was harsh: further weighed down by the feeling that they had no other option. My child's ear grew more attuned to hushed conversations than to normal speech. I used to know my country like the back of my hand. Indeed, it is as small as the palm of a continent - but bursting with angels and demons; with new and ancient graves. As an investigative journalist for the weekend edition of a daily, I investigated the land and its people in depth, and so became acquainted with the underground currents that ate at its foundations. I watched closely as it changed, and at a certain moment I came to the realization that I had become an alien in my own home. A longing for stability - inherited from my parents, coupled with an alertness to danger - called on me to move on. To emigrate.

For many years I fantasized about building a retirement home on a certain Greek island, which I remembered fondly from a trip taken in my youth. But as the situation escalated into a crisis the thought of some place more distant than the Mediterranean occurred to me. Together with my partner we considered the Iberian Peninsula at the edge of Europe as some form of compromise between the warm climate we grew up in, and frosty Europe. It stood in stark contrast to the sweltering Tel Aviv where I grew up and raised two children.

It is possible the answer also lies in my family roots. It may be that my great grandparents are from the Iberian Peninsula. As many Israelis are now finding out, Jewish ancestors migrated to central Europe following the Jewish expulsion from the Peninsula at the end of the fifteenth century.

Orit and I began our quest in Spain, passing through sweltering Andalusian towns, avidly taking in the scent of jasmine. We considered staying. But there was a moment, almost palpable, like the sound of an iron cog clicking into place, when a longing for homecoming and peace swept over me. It happened on the banks of the River Minho, which called to my mind the river from my father's tales, next to thick forests such as those that loomed in my mother's stories, and by the ocean which facilitated the escape of many refugees from the war.

But the main answer as to "why the Alto Minho" lies in everything which I will attempt to describe in this book: the encounter with Portugal and its northern region, this unique land lying under a miracle sky, the melancholic and generous Portuguese with their secrets, their mysterious, abandoned houses and the modest daily beauty of their landscapes. Living here at the westernmost tip of Europe, I feel my heart open to a forgotten paradise close to a place once referred to as the edge of the world. Here, God is an extremely devoted gardener, and life runs almost to the rhythm of a pair of oxen harnessed to a wooden plough, its wheels made of iron hoops; and global greed has yet to sink its teeth into this welcoming land.

Lisbon, a Dead King on a Horse

"Visiting the city for the first time, you feel as though
you have been there your entire life."

Enrique Vila-Matas, *The Vertical Journey*

1

Among all the dark, glossy taxis waiting at Lisbon airport, it was a dingy yellow Vauxhall that immediately lunged at us as if it had been lurking in wait. Upon receiving the designated address, its elderly driver dashed off energetically in the maddening heat, windows rolled down, swearing at other hapless drivers.

"Loco!" he would scream at anyone attempting to overtake him; that is until we hit a traffic jam. "Traffic," he chuckled. Striving to locate the alleyway where we hoped to find our rented room, he engaged in lengthy debates with other drivers, until finally racing on, zigzagging between cars, traffic jams and squares. "Fuck! Shit!" was the extent of his charmingly broken English. Finally, we rode up a steep hill before miraculously stopping in front of the right house on the Rua de São Gens.

During the first night in Lisbon, Orit was woken by a nightmare. In her dream we were desperate to return to the city we had come from but could not recall which city it was. The dreamscape was weird. She found herself in a building, climbing up to the roof. We lay there by an old concrete swimming pool as other people came to lie and rest beside us. It felt like a return home, back from our time-lapse. Yet we no longer formed part of Time itself. "It was like speaking a language you once knew but had forgotten and you kept stumbling over words," she said.

My sometimes sad, forever joyous lover: the Portuguese city overwhelms her, throws her into confusion. My wise *amada*, whose curls are like a wild forest, who single-handedly rescued herself from a ruined family life at a young age, is now gloomily enchanted with the city of Lisbon. It is as if *fado* forms the long-forgotten score for a childhood she has never had. "Since we first arrived, I have been restless. My spirits seem to rise and fall in rhythm with the undulating streets." The town casts its random mood swings upon her. All around us are secret passages, the decaying houses of the dead, locked doors, dark spaces and curtains eaten away by time swaying like moths' wings through open windows.

"Here, I feel as in no other city." A pervading sense of absence is coupled with dramatic shifts in her emotional state. She searches for the right words: "a crumbling city in technicolour, ruins disguised as palaces, bare-bones returning to the earth, exposed iron veins, a life among ghosts." It is both a carnival and a cemetery. Everything that was and is no more.

I read to her from the Spanish Enrique Vila-Matas, who described Lisbon in *The Vertical Journey* as "a labyrinthine city, with high points overlooking exhausting sights, and the empty eternal truth of the sky, sad and captivating unlike any other. An aerial city that, like a snake, seems to emerge from its old skin. Visiting the city for the first time, you feel as though you have been there your entire life." My beloved says: "Lisbon stirs my depths, bringing to the surface things best left untouched."

At the Café do Monte near our rented rooms in the Bairro da Graça, they serve excellent espresso coffee. Sitting there, we witness the comings and goings of the owner and his family, neighbours, workers and friends. We feel like guests invited into their living room. The dark-skinned bartender is called Demis Bambi. His mother is Jamaican, but he takes his name from his Angolan father. He has lived in Lisbon for nearly twenty years "because people here are friendly and genuine". The café proprietor's son is his godchild.

Like many places here, the small café is decorated a crimson red, calling to mind the internal organs of some animal. Scattered around are children's toys as if the family lives here. An Almodóvar poster hangs next to Tom Waits and Fernando Pessoa; artistic and practical life is assembled in no particular order: children, umbrellas, empanadas, an orange sponge cake and a coffee to wake the dead. An old woman with twisted rheumatic hands insists on finishing an entire cake all on her own. A ragged man plays with a blue toy car to amuse the owner's child. An overweight man enthusiastically explains something to a bony woman, looking like a bear and a heron in conversation. The little old widows in their century-old garb stand in stark contrast to their wild-looking granddaughters.

2

IN THE AFTERNOON, WE WANDER about the city until we reach a large waterfront square boasting a massive statue of a king on a horse. A young woman sits hunched on the side of a narrow pier, lost in thought. Seagulls are eating from her hands, and pigeons come to rest next to her. A giant jellyfish washes ashore near her feet. "Viens!" her friends call out to her in French, but the girl stays put, under the shadow of King José I and his horse. She then takes off her clothes and jumps into the cool water.

From their vantage point on the triumphal arch, kings, explorers and horses observe the ocean where the girl is bathing. Streets veer in the same downward direction, and at times it seems as if the whole of Lisbon were an amphitheatre facing the waves.

In the same way, in centuries past, relatives watched from the pier as passengers took off into the unknown. Waving goodbye, they began the long, nerve-wracking wait for the travellers' return. In the past, one could never know if a ship had been wrecked at sea or would come back until it actually reappeared. This place was a point of departure into the green ocean of darkness for everyone who was anyone: warriors, merchants, missionaries, explorers such as Vasco da Gama, slave traders, kings, fishermen and sailors. All were sons, brothers and husbands. The horizon has always symbolized either hope or doom. It meant the difference between cutting a fortune or losing everything. Vessels returned either full of gold or as ghost ships. Today a sizeable Portuguese community forms a diaspora. A great many have deserted the land; a constant letting of blood from land to sea.

"My eyes follow the smoke as if it were my trail," wrote our

Cicerone of this city. He is an animated ghost, better known today than when he was alive. We own an old copy of *Fernando Pessoa: A Quasi Memoir* by José Paulo Cavalcanti Filho. It follows the traces of Pessoa in Lisbon. I search for Praça do Rossio, where the old Café Nicola is located. I interrogate a young man as to its whereabouts, and he passes the question to an older man whose neck is covered in a scarf hiding a throat box. The man spreads his arms as if to say, "no idea", but when I repeat the words "Café Nicola", his eyes light up. He rasps, "Follow me," and leads us to Rossio Square. He is courteous and good-natured as many here are, master of his own time.

And there it is, the famous café where Pessoa used to sit; the man who wrote under many pseudonyms to circumvent reality, who was everyone and no one. The art of being careful, they used to call it. Sometimes there is more authenticity in a pseudonym. Pessoa wrote: "Countless people live in us," and, "I'm also an escapee. As soon as I was born they locked me in." Next door is the restaurant where he ate, but the room where he wrote has already been demolished. Of tobacco, he said, "I smoke life," and of its taste, "the light taste of dust". In the smoke he could bring to life moments from the past. Smoke was the nearest thing to a ghost, a vision, a dream, and Lisbon itself.

All around us buzz the vendors of selfie-sticks and sunglasses, made to conceal the eyes rather than protect them from the glare of the sun. A blind woman whose eyes disappear beneath growths of flesh plays a monotonous tune on a flute by an iron watchtower, a relic from a different century. In Lisbon, I feel like a man happily swimming in a calm sea who suddenly spots a shipwreck in the underlying depths of the clear turquoise water. With a flash, he imagines what always lurks among rocks, reefs and fish.

3

AT THE FLEA MARKET, I sift through a pile of old photographs: cardboard fragments of unnamed lives. Many of the *lisboetas* in these photos do not strike me as native Portuguese; they have different shades of brown skin, slanted eyes or Nubian noses, evidence of the complicated relationship between Portugal and its colonies. Michael Harsegor the historian wrote, "the Portuguese who came to colonize Africa ended up mixing with it." A quick study of Portuguese faces, he claims, reveals that African, Arab and Israelite blood now flows inside the veins of former Lusitania. And yet it has come to form one of the most cohesive nations on the planet: integration through eros.

Harsegor quotes Gilberto Pereira, who said that "after Jesus Christ, Portugal has done more than any other people to establish fraternity among the several constituents of the human race." Roaming the city, I recognize traces of the once-thriving Jewish tribe that lived here and was expelled or forced to convert. Every other Portuguese I meet conjures up a Jewish ancestor or reveals a surname signifying a fruit tree, olive or pear perhaps, typical of converted Jews fleeing the wrath of the Inquisition. History is alive and present. When they claim that Lisbon is frozen in time, a stunted, withered entity comes to mind, but life in Lisbon sizzles from among the unrestored ruins.

At times Lisbon seems like a set design for a period drama: haberdasheries, perfumeries, bakers' shops, stores selling nothing but tinned sardines; small family-owned businesses that have existed for generations, not yet gobbled up by corporations.

Happily chattering old widows slam their espresso cups on granite countertops. A blind lottery vendor passes in the street, tapping his way with his cane and singing a monotonous yet seductive tune of the hidden prospects buried in his tickets. A man approaches to hug him and walks beside him for a while, talking and laughing, the blind man attentive.

Tram 28 passes so close to pedestrians that it ruffles the plastic flowers of a small shop; the driver in turn brakes. Everyone here tries to slow down, taking care not to be in the way. It seems that Lisbon, just like Pessoa, intentionally chooses to abstain, to stand back and observe the world in movement. Portugal is a land exhausted through its past: extensive colonial rule, minor revolutions, military coups and the long sleep during the time of the reticent dictator, Salazar. But the modern world comes a-knocking on its gates trying to rouse it as if saying: "Go on Lusitania, join the money game."

After a while, all this historical baggage has me running back to my room for refuge, but curiosity compels me to venture into the streets again. At the entrance of the café A Brasileira is a small nook hiding a tobacco and newspaper stand. Inside the café, the ample interior is decked out like the inside of an old ocean liner: laden with mirrors, copper pipes, shiny balustrades, crystal bottles and the scent of coffee and baked goods. "First and most significant of all of Pessoa's cafés," says his biographer of the Brasileira. It opened when Pessoa was seventeen, as he returned to the city from Africa on board the German passenger ship *Herzog*. Around this time, he began reading Baudelaire and moved into the first of the sixteen apartments he was to inhabit until his death thirty years later. He would never drink with strangers at the cafés. He was a shy man of few friends and solid routines. Another writer described him as small, melancholy, dark, but possessing a very shrewd gaze, a strong, wicked smile and "a face overflowing with a secret life". What a great description. In the darkness of the ever-smoky café, it felt as if the air around Pessoa was "richer with oxygen". He loved the Lisbon cafés. "They were the most intimate places he had been allowed to know since he lost his true home in his youth."

The newspaper vendor covers her face with paper as I lift my camera to record the scene. The world is as Pessoa believed it would be after his death: suffused with him. The image and figurines of this man, once so overlooked, are to be found everywhere in the third millennium. Eighty years after his death, Lisbon has become "the city of Pessoa", even more so than Paris is the city of Baudelaire. Even on the city's walls, he is an undisputed icon; his only rival being perhaps Kafka in Prague, another shy bachelor of the cafés.

4

When night falls, we realize that despite an ongoing property frenzy, many Lisbon buildings stand vacant. Dark windows appear everywhere, some broken like missing teeth, barricaded doors, shutters turned down, blind homes. The remains of a centuries-old imperial capital that has dropped out of the race are slowly descending into oblivion. The glory of the past resembles the memory of the elderly: entire chapters are absent.

A wild tree sprouts out of an ornamented drainpipe. Cigarettes like fireflies flicker inside stairwells whose doors stand ajar. A mother and daughter are playing dominos. "I am the ghost of a king / Who ceaselessly roams / The halls of an abandoned palace... / I don't know my story," wrote the resident poet of doom. Through the writing of Pessoa, I get to glimpse the soul of the city, which resembled his own. Pessoa took cover behind 127 different pseudonyms, authored several detailed biographies and seldom fell in love. He did, though, have a great love for his mother and longed for his dead father. Like this insomniac city, he slept little and had a restless soul, a sense of lingering absence, a longing for those who will never return, and his writing embraced this chaos.

Even the veranda of our charming rented rooms overlooks the neglected backs of deserted buildings; apparently closed, they can open no more. Lisbon seems to be entirely made up of sealed chambers, a pyramid of hidden tombs. "Now the room is closed forever / My heart is closed forever / The whole room is buried alive," wrote Pessoa lamenting his "dreadfully lost childhood city".

He was both a poet of genius and an impractical individual who tried to make a living from many a failing commercial

11

venture: a printshop, manufacturing paper envelopes and games, a publishing house and magazines. His interest always cooled off at some point. He was left in debt. "A practical life has always seemed to be the least convenient form of suicide," he wrote, speaking for many of his countrymen who felt that the possibility of succeeding or thriving had been lost forever.

5

"AH, PESSOA," SIGHS THE AMBASSADOR, "everyone can find something of themselves in Pessoa." Sometime before our journey to Portugal, I made my way up to the Portuguese embassy set in a black tower in Tel Aviv. Fifty-year-old Ambassador Miguel de Almeida e Sousa is a well-travelled intellectual whose speech is direct and genuine rather than convoluted. A thin beard decorates his handsome, serious face. A soft-spoken man in the Portuguese manner, he grew up in a family of naval officers, yet speaks of Pessoa as he would of an intimate.

"When I am at home in Portugal many things upset me. But when away, I miss it very much. We Portuguese form a love-hate relationship with our country, torn between nostalgia and the desire to break away. We share the intimacy of small, isolated places."

His description hits close to home for an Israeli such as me. Familiar to me are collective manic-depressive spells, nostalgia for a glorious past, forms of messianism, a shared wanderlust and firm views on pretty much anything. Once during a conference, he described to me how he had been warned before coming to Israel that for every four Jews there exist five different opinions. "I listened and thought, no worries. In Portugal, we say: one Portuguese is loneliness, two are life, three are a revolution."

He describes the tumultuous history of Portugal as if he has witnessed it in person. As if he loved, despaired of, rebelled against and sorrowfully relinquished the monarchy, only to end up with the dictatorship. "For many years, we remained untouched by contemporary events, isolated at the brink of Europe, as if frozen in time." He speaks with nostalgia of the "Belle-Epoque" in Portugal, the decadent delights, the artistic

13

elite and ambitious bourgeoisie. At the time, foreigners referred to Portugal as that "lovely land". By the end of that era, kings, anarchists and republicans were already at each other's throats. Coups followed, then the introduction of a democratic regime, which in turn became a dictatorship. Salazar came at a time when the prevailing emotion was one of despair. People had tired of revolutions, blood and anarchy. Initially, he enjoyed the widespread support of all those who yearned for peace and stability; among them was Pessoa.

The young Salazar reformed a country deep in national debt, ruin and chaos. By the end of World War II, Salazar was also applauded for keeping Portugal out of the conflict, unlike the previous war when many Portuguese had been killed. Despite its geographic location, Portugal miraculously managed to remain out of harm's way. "But by the end of the war," says the ambassador, "Salazar had already become a fossilized, stagnant dictator. When Europe rose again out of the ruins, Portugal calcified culturally as well. We became comatose; that was the price for not having taken part in the war. We were not part of the rehabilitation efforts. Foreigners were already calling our country "the sleeping land".

Portugal was trapped in the past without its previous glory and splendour. Many of its sons had emigrated. At the same time, new immigrants from the colonies were coming in large numbers to the metropole: Brazilians, Mozambicans, Angolans and Chinese. Immigration became an accepted form of life and is well-tolerated to this day.

We sit in his office for what seems like a long time. It is as if nothing more substantial has precedence over his day. This is a trait I am to become well-acquainted with in Portugal. Conversation is vital and must never be rushed because it is at the heart of life. "During our years of forced slumber, there was one part of us that never slept: the *conversação*, conversation. It forms an important feature of Portuguese culture." Our own *conversação* continues until coming full circle again to the topic of Pessoa. "In his essence, Pessoa is profoundly Portuguese. He explores feelings of helplessness, passivity, fatalism, the powerlessness of people in times of great changes, life under economic pressure, and loss of individuality, all prevalent during his time. Perhaps this is also the origin of our famous sadness: *saudade.*"

6

THE DAMP SMELL OF CYPRESS trees and resin saturates the air at the final stop of Tram 28. Behind the square where the old streetcar makes a U-turn, we walk down towards the ancient Prazeres cemetery. The city of the dead is quiet and neat. The entrance hall boasts a shiny coffee machine. The cemetery is divided into burial plots and family mausoleums, just like Père Lachaise in Paris. But the set-up is different here: rather than buried in graves, caskets are placed on shelves inside tombs that are open to visitors. Every mausoleum is a display case flaunting its dead. Curtains hang over some of the wrought-iron and glass doors, mimicking the houses of the living. A door left ajar displays small stone cradles placed on bunk beds, suggesting some grotesque boarding school.

Tombstones denote the occupation of the dead: author, poet, actress, general, minister or entrepreneur. No one in this cemetery sheds a tear. Even the offspring of the deceased have long since died or emigrated. Some doors have a sign indicating them *abandonada*, vacant, as if all other graves are humming with life. "Twice a year they think of you," wrote Pessoa, "twice a year they who loved you sigh over you, and now and then sigh if someone happens to mention you." Upon his death, in December 1935, the poet was taken to Prazeres to be put to rest by his grandmother, D. Dionísia Estrela Seabra. The grave was too narrow to contain all the imaginary poets under whose names he wrote, and whose writing styles were so utterly different. Only many years later, after achieving renown, was Pessoa taken out of the family tomb and transferred with due ceremony to the national pantheon on the old grounds of the church of Santa Engrácia.

A House in the Net

"Once, I sold three houses in a single day, but frequently it is a matter of months. Some houses are complex. And as long as their story is unclear, and I do not fully understand it, they remain on the market… a house is a maze. One must find an opening to get in and out."

Marco Lodoli, *Vapore*

7

SEVERAL MONTHS BEFORE LEAVING ON a circular Iberian journey of 2,500 kilometres, at the end of which the die would be cast in favour of Portugal rather than Spain, I began surfing the web. I was looking at houses in both countries, initially as some pastime fantasy game. But the game took over, and I found myself captivated by a virtual wonderland. The Kyero website helped me navigate among thousands of mostly Spanish homes and filter them according to price, size, location and type of residence. Listed under "property", I found such things as a single stone wall or a run-down watermill. Many properties included large plots of land, riverbanks, streams, private woods and natural springs.

And so I sat in a tiny Tel Aviv rental imagining myself the king of expansive properties going for the same annual rate as my dreary two-bedroom apartment. The selection was immense, and everything seemed within touching distance. With a proper internet connection, I told myself, it would be possible to live there, write and create. An ancient thirst for the land and rivers suddenly stirred in me. Then the thought occurred to me that soon all available agricultural land would be filled with useless city-boys like me who want to become one with nature.

I filter houses according to a €50,000 budget and select "country property", having in mind perhaps the Polish rural home near Warsaw where my mother was born a century ago. Every night I tour dozens of such properties until I have a clear grasp of my dream home. I begin with Andalucia and the magical Órgiva in the Alpujarras, working my way up through a digital real-estate *camino* to Galicia. Passing from cave dwellings to stone farmhouses, I peek inside wine cellars, winepresses, storage rooms and attics. My mind grows dizzy with terms such as riverside views, dovecotes, barns and orange and olive groves.

I surf the web like an adolescent discovering porn sites for the first time, lasciviously compiling file upon file of select destinations. Some houses feed my desire for the old and for renovation work; others are ready-to-wear: bright homes, dark homes, dusty homes, fully furnished or bare. I realize with glee that the Iberian real-estate market is slowing down. It seems supply is constantly growing. But a nagging fear warns me that soon the magic might wear off, and I will see myself left behind as before, without an Iberian home to call my own.

8

AFTER LANDING IN MADRID, WE set off straight away in a rental car, eager to begin our real journey. My computer game is transformed into tangible features:, thick forests and hills, authentic villages, dilapidated houses and abandoned mansions. I feel like a man who, having stared for months at dating sites, finally finds himself in the presence of a flesh-and-blood Eve, acutely aware of her body odour and temperature, skin and hair texture, and voice. Leaving the city, we drive along the motorway turning at times into side and country roads. We roam about villages without a set plan, assessing deserted structures, *fincas* and stone cabins. Some of these places are now home to wildlife only; weeds and trees have taken over the deserted interiors.

We stop beside houses displaying signs with telephone numbers of estate agencies. In some places, phone numbers are spray-painted directly on the walls or there is a simple message: FOR SALE. Occasionally Orit and I fall in love with a house and immediately begin redesigning the rooms. The attic as a studio for Orit. A study for me to write in. Changes come to life as we envisage ourselves living in these valleys, mountains and woods, surrounded by the melody of streams and water-canals, birds and insects. Roads disappear into forests, animal trails wind through the grass and out of sight.

Leaving one town, a derelict mansion captures our attention. The American author John Updike once described a similar building as "a silhouette of painful grandness". It is a magnificent structure eaten away by time, sporting a tall chimney, a crumbling tile-roof and a small tower that should belong to a citadel with no sentry. This Spanish mansion is shrouded by a thicket as if protected from invaders. Timidly, we enter the courtyard through

21

gates of ornate metalwork. Its circular windows still display beautifully intricate woodwork despite their degraded state. Then there are galleries and walls where time has redecorated the plasterwork. Erosion is a great and inimitable artist. Neglect pulls at us with a haunting pathos. Sometimes an abandoned house may stir in one a desire to replenish it with life. Such a story is recounted by the Cuban writer Alejo Carpentier in his book *Journey Back to the Source*. As workers are demolishing the remains of a decrepit mansion, the author gradually returns to the past, restoring its previous life. Carpentier resurrects its owners as protagonists, bringing to life the tobacco smoke, bell chimes, the chatter of family conversations and the whispers of lovers once heard within its walls. Thus he recounts the entire life story of Marquis Don Marcial, the previous owner of the house.

The Iberian Peninsula is a wonderland of old mansions and abandoned houses. The best way to discover them is to get lost, let the roads lead you like a blind man to your heart's desire. There they stand as orphans, tenantless and growing wild. It appears that among all the deserted properties, larger ones are more common, or perhaps they simply stand out more.

We push open an iron gate with a broken lock and make our way through a jungle of wild raspberries, with thorns as sharp as the knives that scratch those who enter Sleeping Beauty's wood. We climb a staircase until we reach a partially torn down mural, then enter a damp passageway with light filtering through a crack in the tile-roof and revealing a rotting floor. The cellar has a winepress under giant wooden planks, and next to it a wooden boat which seems to have been swept here by a flood from the nearby river. Stairs creak as we climb up to the attic. Almost everything has been plundered. Only a thick skin of dust remains. "The flesh of time", as an exiled poet once described the dust of a different place.

9

AN OLD PILGRIM WAY STRETCHES away behind the eerie mansion. We spot three non-believers making their way along the path. Overhead, two storks are resting inside an intricate nest of twigs. For centuries, this road has crossed a region that serves as a launch pad for migrating birds. Pilgrims have also been coming here, to where it is believed that the bones of holy James, son of Zebedee, AKA Saint Tiago, have lain buried for over a thousand years. The first of the dozen apostles to have been executed, his head was severed with a sword and buried in Jerusalem. But his body floated inside a seashell until washed up on the coast of the Atlantic, in Galicia. Since then he has become the patron saint of Spaniards, fur makers, veterinarians, pharmacists and some of these pilgrims, many of whom make the journey for reasons other than religion. Orit and I roll the name Santiago de Compostela on our tongues, relishing the sound. It signifies "Holy Jacob of the field of the star". This title given to a city is a beautiful image, which sounds lovely in other languages too.

The pilgrimage draws the afflicted, the broken-hearted, salvation seekers and many young people and adults who have read the bestselling novel by Paulo Coelho describing this same journey. They are equipped with comfortable backpacks, good walking shoes and blister creams, rather than the traditional sandals and healing herbs.

We stop to rest by a narrow stream flowing through a tall poplar wood. The trees' white trunks stretch upwards to a green canopy that filters the light, and I take off my clothes and go down to the water, tripping over two hidden tree stumps. I sink into the stream's muddy bottom, and when I stand up again, thrilled with the cool sensation, the weight of many worries seems to lift. I purge myself in the last Spanish river before the bridge to Portugal. Over there, a friend is already waiting for us by a church, past the Minho River.

What was once was the border has since disappeared and with it all signs of the divided past. No more fences, barriers or the guards who once separated two hostile dictatorships. Gone too are the smugglers, border-policemen, night boat patrols and the sounds of gunfire. The new bridge crosses a gushing river on its way to the nearby Atlantic Ocean. Slate-roofs change into tile-roofs. The faces of people are softened, with less arrogance and anger, more subdued. Historian Ron Barkai referred to Portugal as "a gentle nation". And here is the small town and its lovely fountain installation whose water gushes upwards against a huge suspended rock. Our good friend awaits us, as does our home, of whose existence we are as yet ignorant.

Hereinafter "the Estate": Candemil, Vila Nova de Cerveira

10

T<small>IME IS MARCHING ON AND</small> still no sign of our friend, Zadok Ben David, whom we were supposed to meet by the church at Vila Nova de Cerveira. Sending out a smoke signal via my smartphone, I realize our blunder is due to the time difference on either side of the Minho River. Moments later, Zadok, an energetic man of average height, tanned and youthful looking, finally appears. A celebrated international sculptor, Zadok frequently travels between time zones: Tel Aviv-Shanghai-London-Siberia-Gondar. He is full of salacious anecdotes and forever engrossed in his artwork, creating figurative metal sculptures.

We follow him in our car through villages, across hills and forests to his home in Gondar. The house is airy and spacious, its bright rooms looking onto the forest. Exhausted from our long Iberian journey, we throw ourselves onto the plush bed drifting into a gorgeous dream sleep. A few hours later, we wake to discover a vast cork oak spying on us through the window.

The evening has us strolling down a paved-stone path among shadowy houses to a cheerfully lit terrace where several garrulous youths are drinking. Inside, a few strategically placed armchairs form the café's interior, where an old woman is dozing off on a sofa while watching a noisy daytime TV drama A lovely young woman is boiling lemon peel for a tea-like beverage at the back of the small bar. As the soap opera on the screen picks up, the older woman is suddenly roused, darting off to return with her grandson. A man rattles his coffee cup on the bar as his friend drinks red wine from a terracotta beaker. From outside come the delicious smells of spice, grass, wet earth and smoke. Leaving the café, Zadok's companion brushes her long hair against a lavender shrub, capturing its perfume. At a nearby house a dog is barking. The sound of trickling water is everywhere. Water in this area is an ever-present entity. It flows through irrigation canals, cascades from mountainsides and is even audible as we round the corner back to the house.

Sometime around two in the morning, I am roused from a deep sleep by a tremendous noise. From somewhere in the dark skies up above come the cries of a flock of migratory birds. The piercing sounds drop in and out of hearing range in the impenetrable darkness. Perhaps they are passing over Gondar now, driven by the changing seasons. The air fills with the calls of birds beckoning each other. I find myself hypnotized by the sounds. Only as they fade into the distance do I return to cuddle up with Orit in a room which the wind envelops as if it were its own.

11

Two days later, Gilberto Duarte Carlos, architect, sets up a meeting for us at a vacant property. It is an old two-bedroom house with additional stone outbuildings. Set on a wooded hill in the village of Candemil, it is within walking distance of Zadok's home. Around this area, vacant houses can remain unoccupied for years waiting to be salvaged, the "for sale" signs becoming as faded and decrepit as the houses themselves. But the transaction that is to take place this morning is anything but sluggish.

The architect waits for us at the crossroads, where the N302 divides into roads leading to the villages of Gondar and Covas. He is accompanied by the estate agent, Emanuel: son and faithful aide to Laura, also in the business of selling houses. Emanuel, tall, lanky and unusually silent for an estate agent, does not lavish praise on the property. Above us towers a dark wall bulging like the belly of a beast. It is made of large stones shaped like pyramid blocks, dark with time and hyssop. Above the wall can be glimpsed a cluster of stone structures and a house with a tiled roof, hereinafter "the Estate".

Next to a gurgling fountain sits an older man wearing a black cap. He is as indifferent to us as might be a random passerby stopping to rest on a bench. Only when we climb up to the property does the cap-owner rise to his feet to join us in silence. He unhooks a large key from a keychain to unlock a metal grate beneath a stone arch. The gate hinges creak. He presents himself: Manoel Joaquim de Barros. "The seller, heir to this property," remarks the agent. He lives about 200 metres up the hill with his wife, Maria da Conceição Senra de Sousa. Hereinafter "the Vendors".

"This is the only property for sale in the area that is within your price range," says Emanuel. The courtyard is as wild as a small jungle, weeds shooting up from between the paving stones. Outside is a stone building: two decaying wooden doors open to reveal a dark space. It served as the animal pen, housing pigs, cows and chickens for a hundred years. Now it is divided up by crumbling stone walls. Glancing into the darkness, I smell old hay, decay and dust. A dozen concrete stairs lead up to a metal door which Manoel Joaquim opens after fumbling with his key. The house has been locked up for years. The dust of empty times hovers over the space while a grandfather clock on batteries still ticks the precise hour. Under a low plywood ceiling, we note the belongings of the previous owner, Marília, a relative of the vendor. She died here a year and a half ago. He explains, Gilberto translates. Chandeliers hang from the ceiling. The tall estate agent bashes his head against one of them.

"She was a tiny woman," he explains.

Most of the furniture and belongings have been removed. What remains is a two-door wardrobe, an old kitchen countertop with candles, matches and some sewing items, a few towels, brooms and a plastic dustpan. Next to the chimney from the stove, which vanishes into the ceiling, a door is ajar displaying a small laundry room. The kitchen ceiling has an open gap through which Gilberto examines the condition of the roof support beams with an experienced eye, a routine check. A tiny bedroom, the size of the laundry room, has a window overlooking the village square. The wall reveals deep markings in its plaster as if the bed slats have rammed it. Marília lay here during her bed-ridden years, explains the man with the cap, his hand caressing the scars. An enclosed terrace looks out onto the courtyard. Next to images of the virgin, her son and the cross, four wooden chairs stand in a circle, as if expecting mourners.

We glance over the crude stone buildings in the yard: a small winery containing a winepress, a cool cellar filled with water bottles, another stone shed and the ruins of an old house whose insides have rotted away, leaving only its shell: a roof and stone walls. At the front of the courtyard and facing the square, I enter a stone shed where a loom and other weaving tools have been left. Also left there are an old sewing machine and wooden scales. There is something about this place, a precise and efficient honesty, which captures my heart at once.

The untold history of the house is in evidence everywhere: an empty chicken coop, a harrow, some firewood, a plough and empty barrels. In the small garden grown wild are trees whose fruit - pears, apples, figs and oranges - lies rotting on the ground. Everywhere there is the intoxicating smell of fermentation. I see rose bushes and vines clinging to the courtyard fence.

12

A **COMPLETE ESTATE IN MINIATURE, THE** house and courtyard are imbued with history. Neither of us wants to continue the property hunt. We believe that the home of Marília is meant for us.

"Don't be so eager," whispers Zadok, but in any case both owner and agent appear deaf to our cries of enthusiasm. Standing in the courtyard as the horizon glows a deep reddish hue over the Minho River, we begin quizzing Gilberto as to the cost of it all: the tearing down and putting up, repairs, adjustments and modest renovations. Excited, we discuss keeping the old roof which appears intact, installing insulation and a new kitchen, and eventually moving in, perhaps within a few months. A bemused Gilberto remains courteous. "We will have to examine the wooden skeleton of the roof more closely," he observes while opening his lovely *diario grafico* to take down notes in a thin, precise script using a sharp pencil. He uses it to sketch an outline of a new house to merge into the old.

As we pressure him for a quote, he gives us a rough estimate for basic renovation work: insulation, roof repairs, new windows, a new kitchen and a toilet. Cautious as ever and not wishing to be the bearer of bad news, he presents an immediate estimate that will turn out to cover about a third of the eventual costs. But all this still lies in the future, a year and a half from now. Just as with a human being, falling in love with a place blinds us to apparent defects and hardships yet to come. Therein, however, lies precisely the strength of the bond, propelling this old house into a new and unlikely journey.

Standing in the courtyard of a semi-ruined building relying only on the imagination and foresight of our architect, we are already contrasting new against old. In buying the house we seem to be securing both its past and future. Imagination, we know, is the quickest of all builders. We make our own list of priorities: first, clean up the large, older outbuilding, hereinafter referred to as the *ruina*, or dump.

The house itself will require the uprooting of rotting and bug-ridden floorboards and the demolition of wooden ceilings. We will have to take down the smaller sheds while saving the stones for a future wall, restore floors where we can, construct a new kitchen, locate *azulejos*, traditional tiles, acquire an old sink, expand the kitchen into a central living area that will include a dining room, transform one of the sheds into a studio or a guest room, exposing the original stones behind the old plaster, and finally plant a sizeable garden. The list goes on and on. Also, we wish to purchase the adjacent field to expand the estate to include its narrow waterway and small reservoir. We decide to leave in the old stove and other valuable furniture, such as the wardrobe and kitchen counter. Our imagination roams about undisturbed.

"Asking price is very fair," declares Gilberto. The eye of this young planner, so knowledgeable about traditional homes, appreciates the actual value of the old house. We tell Gilberto and the estate agent that we do indeed wish to lay claim to this property. True to the way of his people, Emanuel gently cools down our enthusiasm. The whole deal will require time to be arranged, perhaps several weeks. We have heard of cases where purchasers waited for years on account of disputes between heirs. "In this case, however, everything should run relatively smoothly," Gilberto assures us, "but it will require time." A Portuguese never rushes you. He marches slowly to the beat of his own drum. In our rash minds, our new home is already standing before us. Yet we have still to see or sign any paperwork or even learn a single line of the language spoken by the agent, vendor and architect.

13

"THERE ARE STILL A FEW details to thrash out, but seeing your enthusiasm for the old wooden floors made me realize you were the right buyers for this house," Gilberto tells us in his quiet, fluent English following our visit to the property. Gilberto is a young man of forty who sports an elegant thin beard. Born in post-revolution Lisbon, he lives in an apartment in Cerveira with his wife and two small children. While overseeing renovation work for our house, he plans to build a house for his own family in a nearby village on half an acre of woodland purchased two years before.

His daily routine is typical of neither a quiet country life nor a busy urban existence. He teaches in an architecture school in town and designs and oversees projects in far-off Lisbon. A sought-after architect, he works under constant pressure, juggling several different projects at any time. He is content whenever he manages to salvage an old building from demolition. From that day on, and throughout our collaboration - planning, designing and chasing after workers who seem to disappear and reappear without warning - we meet frequently and establish a friendship. I come to know a man who, despite being modest, is bursting with ambition. As someone in a position of power over his clients, he struggles with feelings of omnipotence. He is a curious mix of authority verging on hubris with Portuguese caution and thoughtfulness. To watch him is to witness a fight between two conflicting urges symbolic of the past and present, thus typifying the modern Portuguese. He is a man of his time.

From Lisbon, Gilberto went on to study architecture at the University of La Coruña in northern Spain. He continued his studies in Tokyo. Upon graduation, he decided to move to the quiet north rather than return to chaotic Lisbon, where a fierce and almost violent property boom had begun. Gilberto has a passion for old traditions and combining them with the new. For a time, he worked in East Timor constructing a hospital and saw "the ugliest capital in the world, where new money and oil corruption are wiping out the more beautiful traditions". Like many Alto Minho residents, he is concerned with the effects of new money over his well-preserved and beautiful region yet tempted by the affluence it suggests.

He knows the area well through searching for land to buy for himself, his clients and his father-in-law, who wanted to move closer to his grandchildren.

"There was something almost magical in the way this place was handed to the agency just as I came to look for a house for my father-in-law and yourself. As if it had been lying in wait. Many houses remain on the market for years due to inheritance disputes. But for this house, the will was clear-cut, the paperwork in order, and there are water and electricity connections. That is rare."

He suggests fixing it up rather than tearing it down. There is an instant connection between us. Although strangers, we see eye to eye on many issues. From that initial meeting, Gilberto acts as our architect and project manager and as a companion and translator of language and culture for my personal research into the region. I begin by asking him about *saudade*, that term which many young Portuguese find distasteful, antiquated, diseased, an irremovable stain. But when Gilberto hears the word, he seems to wear the emotion and the longing it suggests like a warm coat to protect him from the evening chill descending on our conversation.

"Some believe that *saudade* has its roots in the constant bleeding of the Portuguese population; a third of us live in the diaspora." The migration, which began during the time of the

Renaissance, continues to this day. Fathers, mothers and children leave in search of a livelihood. The most recent departures have inspired a sense of defeat as if only the feeble remain behind. He has worked abroad, is well-travelled, has attended architecture conferences the world over, yet opted to return home.

"It is a great country with brilliant people in every field. Mine as well. I know a building in Porto that houses two Pritzker award winners, the most valued of architecture prizes," he says with evident pride. "But many left because the country was languishing. The old hierarchies still stand strong. A considerable part of local resources remain in the hands of a few influential families, who would prefer an inept family member over a competent manager."

"Even in the times of the empire," says Gilberto, "abundance became a hindrance. The empire ruled over vast territories, and there were too few of us to govern them. It consumed us, and while the Dutch accumulated a fortune, we grew poor." As if to console himself, he reminds me that Portugal enjoys an enviable location. "We have the advantage of the ocean commanding the Americas, Africa and the Mediterranean Sea." He speaks as if the place is still a starting point for maritime adventure, as though a new Vasco da Gama will soon bid for a billion euros from the EU to discover a new continent.

Poland, Palestine, Portugal

"The further inside you the place moves, the more your identity is intertwined with it. Never casual, the choice of place is the choice of something you crave."

Frances Mayes, *Under the Tuscan Sun*

14

"THERE IS A REASON WHY we met," strangers, soon to become friends, often say as if a mystical sensation permeates the cool air of the Alto Minho. A fertile mist. I sense something similar, despite my rational mind. "There is a spirituality about the place," says one villager when explaining its uniqueness: frequent coincidences and chance meetings with long-lost friends; people open the door instantly resuming a conversation as if it had never been interrupted. Other friends suggest that we climb a certain mountain nearby where we will "feel a connection to something greater".

This feeling is not just an expression of recently purchased New-Ageism, shamanism or ashram-related fashion. Rather, it stems from multi-layered and ancient local creeds. Clans and peoples, conquerors and defeated pagan and monotheist religions have all passed through here. In times of both peace and war, Neanderthals, Vikings, Visigoths and Romans have all left a mark, a belief, a ghostly remnant.

Abundant expressions of nature complement these rustic pagan beliefs: the constant presence of water with its miraculous appearance from rocks or hills and the intoxicating smell of flowers in bloom. Mysterious relics further amplify the sensation: empty dwellings, a twinkling of light reflected on the wall of an ancient building, dead objects left behind in plundered homes and deserted orchards with exquisite fruit. A plethora of chestnut trees, peaches, apples, pears, figs, olives and vines are heavy with fruit according to the seasons, but in the absence of fruit-pickers they drop to the ground to return to the roots and be reborn the following spring.

And so one gets the feeling that an invisible process is taking place. A silent yet powerful force inhabits the area. Walls seem to crumble of their own accord, water strays from its natural path to visit a locked palace and a tiled roof collapses noisily. On a small beach in Seixas, the river mouth spits forth ancient fragments of broken china weirdly standing erect, their pigments facing the skies.

A group of wild horses feeds close to the edge of a cliff of black rock. At the bottom, a herd of goats grazes on the soft grass while their shepherd gathers small sticks in a basket carried on her bent back. She lifts her head to smile at me, and the smile lights up her wrinkle-worn face touching my heart and filling it with love.

15

I HAVE ARRIVED AT ALTO MINHO after two years of desperate struggle over my home in the country where I was born. As a young man, I fought two wars as a tank commander. I studied, raised a small family and buried my parents, who were among the early Zionists.

For over thirty years, I was an investigative journalist in love with my work, writing hundreds of stories for a weekend supplement. I was attracted to the drama of crime. I was present at hundreds of crime scenes, following murders, kidnappings and disappeared children. I joined politicians on their election campaigns but preferred a thousand times over to interview poets, murderers, prisoners, scientists, authors or victims.

I often returned with interviewees to their childhood haunts. I believed that the root of every drama, from murder, serious crime and suicide to creative endeavour, failure, defeat or victory, lies in the early life of its protagonist. In his home, family, childhood. In his country and its story.

After all I have seen, I still believe that every drama has a critical moment ticking away in the past like a time bomb. I wrote ten books, primarily documentary, and covered every inch of Israel - founded only about three years after my birth - from coast to coast.

It is a tiny land, about one-fifth the size of Portugal, and ever since its creation, it has known armed conflict. I call it "the sad dream" or "the cracked refuge". It seems tragic that the people who sought shelter from war and destruction found themselves at war with the natives of the land they had come to occupy.

I love the horizontal and vertical journey. The conversations with people, entering their homes and lives. I am naturally curious. With my writing I have often fought a politician or an individual whose deeds I felt threatened my country. My father taught me to be a highly critical patriot. In Prime Minister Netanyahu, from the moment he took office about twenty years ago, I saw a grave menace to the land where I raised my children.

I often attacked him with my pen. A few years ago, my name came up in a harsh exchange of words between the Prime Minister and my publisher. It was a criminal conversation with overtones of bribery, and its contents reached the press and the court. In this conversation, my head was laid on the block. The ruler detested my writing, and the publisher, who was tired of the pressure and my insistence on writing what I felt was the truth, told him in violent terms: "Do whatever you like. Kill him." He meant only the former.

About three years went by, and the Prime Minister found a pretext to sue me for slander. On Facebook, not in the newspaper, I had written that an incident that took place in the PM's heavy security convoy ended with his wife throwing him out of the car.

She is infamous for her tantrums.

All witnesses to this incident were secret service personnel, Security Unit 730, bound by official confidentiality. My source, too, kept silent, and I respected this. I was duly tried in a libel case and defeated in three courts. The strong man who rules over us all, so I felt, dictates the opinions of judges as well. After the trial I was fired by the newspaper that had employed me for thirty years. I was free, very vulnerable and almost ostracized in my homeland, vanquished by its ruler and his wife. I felt like someone who had lost his case but won his freedom to do whatever he likes.

"The house protects the dreamer," wrote the architect Gaston Bachelard.

In 2017, more than at any other time in my life, I needed a new home to protect my dream. "The houses that are important to us are the ones that allow us to dream in peace," observes Frances Mayes. "Where you are is who you are… Never casual, the choice of place is the choice of something you crave."

Such is the Candemil house we have chosen. "The further inside you the place moves, the more your identity is intertwined with it."

For many years, I felt this way in a small, expensive apartment I rented in Tel Aviv, a flat that had been my cave for years - where I was protected and calm in the heart of a volatile land. There I sat and wrote, lived and loved. Thus, in Candemil I plan to sit and write in the studio or bedroom, in the attic or in rooms on the ground floor, where the animals once lived. A house with a window overlooking a lush green European landscape, a sight I had long and unknowingly yearned for.

16

Orit flies back to Tel Aviv while I stay behind in the large room in the house in Gondar. Zadok and I grew up around the same time in the same newly founded country. But while Ben David's parents are from a small village in Yemen, mine came from Poland. Zadok grew up in a farming community established by the original Zionists in the nineteenth century, where his elderly parents still live today. He studied sculpture at St Martin's School of Art and became a well-known and wide-ranging sculptor. In London, he has his apartment, workshop and fifteen assistants, but he keeps a large country residence at the edge of Vila Nova de Cerveira and another studio on the outskirts of the town of Viana do Castelo.

In the early 1980s, he was invited to participate in one of the first Cerveira biennales. At the time, he was already a promising young Riverside Studio artist. On reaching Portugal, he immediately fell in love with the villages on the banks of the Minho and quickly grew attached to the wooded hills, riverside views, local people and a growing community of artists. He has been returning ever since. While in Cerveira he works in a studio allotted to him by the regional administration. He holds occasional local exhibitions and contributes artworks to the town; the metal sculpture of a deer, Cerveira's emblem, which stands on a pedestal in a central square, is his creation.

Over the years, Ben David has become an intrinsic part of the local art scene, made up mostly of Portuguese and North American artists who have formed a pearl around the grain of the biennale. Initially, the biennale represented the first deep breaths the country took after forty years of harsh dictatorship. It turned the sleepy village of Vila Nova de Cerveira into a vibrant art town whose reputation belies its actual size.

In the evenings, I walk up from the house to Carla's café, where I have already become the *Israelita*, the white-haired foreigner. I place my laptop on the table, order an americano and begin typing in front of a large plasma screen, typically showing yet another soap opera. Thus my initiation into the lively and gregarious family of the café. As locals lean on the bar, Carla, petite and skinny like a pretty bird, pours the blood-red *ginja*, an alcoholic berry drink, into small goblets or prepares the *cariocas de limão*, an infused lemon-peel drink, in ceramic cups.

Two vivid oil paintings hang on the wall, the work of a couple of biennale old-timers who frequent the café: painters Henrique Silva and Henrique do Vale. Next to them is an electronic dartboard and, in the corner, a cigarette vending machine. A loveseat and several chairs placed around a lit fireplace are occupied by Carla's sometimes snoozing mother, a young woman with a baby, several card players and other visitors. Teenagers who smoke as they play table football gather on the balcony. Café Da Carla is the heart of the village nightlife. The surrounding houses are so quiet and dark that a stranger would think them deserted.

Amid this gentle commotion, I lean towards my screen, typing in Hebrew, and the place cradles me as damp earth around a new seedling. No one stares, and conversations do not stop every time I show up at the door. Instead, they welcome me quietly and courteously and do not seem to gossip much about a stranger. Still, Margarida tells me that the villagers are in fact interested and discuss everything and everyone amongst themselves, including herself and her husband.

Margarida and Henrique are Portuguese artists who have lived in Gondar for over thirty years. The locals still talk about them. "For them, we will always be the city artists, foreigners.

Our lifestyle still perplexes them." Their large, crowded house lit late at night, the cheerful yellow Mini Minor parked in the garage and the dogs that run and bark after passing cars are all matters of interest to the locals.

I discover that even when it comes to cafés, which I love, the area suits me. In tiny Cerveira, at the foot of the hill, a mere seven-minute drive away, someone can sit in a different café or restaurant every day for a month and never go to the same place twice. "It is easier to change religion than a coffee shop," said a friend to Pessoa once as they sat at their regular table.

17

BETWEEN FLIGHTS AND CAFÉS, TIME passes slowly, Portuguese-style. I pay regular visits to the house, not yet mine, acquainting myself with the strange layout: storage rooms full of old work tools, the cool basement on whose floor I find dusty sealed wine bottles, and the animal quarters. I am growing accustomed to my new shell of a house. Finally, I meet with Gilberto to discuss details of the renovations and inquire whether the electricity line running over the house presents any danger. Gilberto replies that everything has been checked and found to be in good order. Ownership papers are legit, the electricity line is not high-tension, and the house owner died at the respectable age of ninety-one.

Weeks pass until at last the estate agent calls Gilberto asking that we visit the office to sign the contract, transfer the money and receive the keys to the house.

I sit on a narrow sofa at the agent's office with Manoel and Maria, the bashful heirs. Manoel is wearing an old jacket over an ironed shirt; next to him is the sturdy Maria. I observe his large hands that, even at his age, seem ready to take on any strenuous work. Conversely, Maria looks as if she has taken upon herself all the burdens of existence. They seem out of place in the office, as if someone has dragged them against their will from their village to the big city.

I pass the cashier's cheque to Julia; she hands it to Laura, who glances at it before giving it to Manoel and Maria, and the four of them have a quick discussion in what for me is still a secret language. I note that it instinctively raises my suspicions when people around me speak in a foreign language. I trust them, and yet am afraid that something will go wrong. It is hard to grasp that I am to become the owner of that God's Little Acre on a hill for the average price of a four-wheel drive in my own country. Everything seems unreal. Perhaps, candid camera-style, someone will soon pop out from behind a screen with a crazed laugh. Gilberto, who joins in the conversation as translator and interpreter, explains some of the practical details.

Manoel and Maria worked in France for years. They have two children and grandchildren. Their French is flawed, as is mine, so we converse like three people with the same speech impediment. I greedily enquire about the field adjacent to my plot and the ancient stone waterhole that fills with water lilies every spring. They say that the land with the reservoir belongs to Albano Dantas, a hundred-year-old childless neighbour who lives in a retirement home in Caminha. Yes, he is still lucid.

18

AT THE LAND REGISTRY OFFICE across the street, I sign some forms and pay a fee. Then, in broken French, Manoel explains that he has used stones to mark the edges of an old cesspit on the property so that the workers who will do the renovation work do not drive over it with a tractor causing a landslide. He has also trimmed the grass in the yard, as was his habit every summer while Marília was still alive.

"Guinea-Bissau," explains Manoel when he sees me staring at his slight limp as we pass from office to office. Like many others, he was just a young country boy when drafted into the army. They sailed in 1966 from the port of Lisbon aboard a military vessel for five days and afterwards continued in riverboats into the colony of Guinea-Bissau, where they fought with bazookas in the bush. Once he even stumbled into a lethal ambush laid by African rebels.

For two and a half years, Manoel Joaquim served in a company called "Tigra", fighting rebel guerrilla forces supported by Fidel Castro. The bloody "Portuguese Vietnam" was where many boys from Candemil, Gondar and the surrounding villages lost their lives. "We suffered from the terrible tropical weather. There were so many mosquitoes; even the donkeys refused to march. We were just sitting ducks." He recalls meeting an African prisoner-of-war who told him: "you call yourself white and think me black but cut your finger and see it is the same colour inside." The traces of those times are still visible on his skin. His wife Maria traces her fingers across the scar from his wounded heart surgery as if to console him.

I interview them while we wait in between offices. It is a lifelong habit that stems from curiosity, passion and a need to uncover narratives. They live up the hill from the house I have now purchased, in the same home where Manoel was born seventy-two years ago. He grew up in Candemil, was drafted in Cerveira, and upon his return from the war travelled to France to make money and get away from the country that had sent him to the killing fields. Later he married Maria, who comes from a village one and a half kilometres from Candemil. They had three children: one lives in Porto and two in Paris.

We converse while the office staff scurry from side to side. Finally, after a while, they fall silent and it seems as if Manoel and Maria have fallen asleep amidst the bureaucratic hubbub. We are then requested to approach the desk to make the sacred transfer of the water meter over to my name. I ask for the name of the previous house owner, and Manoel says that he knew him from his childhood. Even then, Senhor Franco, Marília's father, was an old man. He was a sturdy livestock dealer and landowner, and when he died he left his daughter two cows that lived in the dark, humid cellars of the house.

"Each downstairs room had one cow," says Manoel. "The first was named Galiga because she was from a light and strong Galician stock, and the second was named Bonita because she was beautiful." He remembers that the cows got to keep their horns and were suitable for work in the field. Marília would bring their milk in jars to sell in the market. Sometimes she would lead the younger cow to a stud. Later, when a calf was born, she would wait for it to grow before selling it. Besides the cows, she raised chickens, rabbits in mesh cages and a black pig which lived in very cramped quarters and whose meat tasted good.

Senhor Franco and his Sad Daughter Marília

19

MANOEL INVITES US ALL FOR coffee at the café above the Registry during a break between visits to offices. There is a festive air about him as he waves his hand in a generous gesture. As if on cue, three fellow villagers from Candemil enter the café: a married couple who are neighbours and a sixty-year-old man summoned to expand on the narrative of the last tenant of the house. I feel intensely curious about its genealogical history, a desire to bring the stone walls to life.

They whisper among themselves, distrustful of the inquisitive stranger. Why is he asking all these questions about the past? "*Escritor,*" clarifies Gilberto. "Ahh," they sigh in relief. Everything is clear to them now: the stranger is a writer. They relax visibly. The discussion resumes. "The real story is the father," says the neighbour who joins in. "His name was Senhor Franco," adds his wife. "Marília lived with him and later with her mother in this house. He owned land in Candemil and was never married."

An unmarried father in a traditional Catholic village, I am intrigued.

"Yes, Franco never married," affirms the lone neighbour.

"And he had four children." They recite their names using their fingers. They then get confused and enter into an argument about whether he had them by three or four different women. They are well versed in the details, equipped as they are with a small-town appetite for drama. Gilberto is so intrigued he forgets to translate. I pull on his sleeve: "Translation. Now. Please."

"For every woman he had children by, Franco left a house and a plot of land." "Yes," they nod, "one of them was Deolinda Barbosa Franco, the mother of Marília."

"The three women never remarried," says the neighbour, and his wife nods in agreement. After fifty years together, they speak with one voice. Manoel and Maria are more cautious with their words than the others. When Manoel wants to add something, Maria digs her elbow in his side, silencing him. He is a talkative, sociable man, while she is a worrier. "This is a small place, let the others do the talking," she mutters.

"Today we have Facebook," says Manoel attempting to quell her fears, "there are television shows about everything. Information spreads either way." But from these half-sentences I piece together the whole picture: the house I am purchasing belonged to Senhor Franco. His daughter Marília, born in 1925, never married or had children and lived there with her mother. When Marília died in January 2016, the house passed to Manoel and Maria, close neighbours and friends who nursed her in her old age. Manoel is a distant cousin of hers. The mother of the late Marília was Deolinda Barbosa. The people of Candemil speak of Marília with an approving nod of the head; she who had never known the joy of a child or a man; she who only cared for the son of God.

"And Senhor Franco?" I ask.

"Oh, he was the Casanova of Candemil," laughs Gilberto. "We seem to have a complicated drama on our hands," he adds, as I begin to grasp that this is a plot worthy of Gabriel García Marquez with more twists to come.

"This Franco character had several women because he owned land, property and livestock." Back then, these were the most valuable possessions to be had. The three women were poor fieldhands with no land or property to their names. He courted them, had children by them and left them some property. Eventually, all the protagonists were gathered together in the cemetery near the house.

The villagers add another fact: "a blind woman lived with Franco."

"Blind?" The plot thickens further.

Someone remembers that Marília's grandmother was also blind.

20

As the narrative comes to a dead-end, we are summoned to the notary's office to sign the purchase agreement. We take leave of the neighbours and go inside another office next to a veterinary practice and a Chinese minimarket smelling strongly of plastic. A single man in a dark suit sits at the centre of the office, surrounded by women typing at top speed. We are called to the adjacent room, where at the head of the table sits a young female notary who goes over the details with us: two separate plots of land, one comprising a small field with ruins and two storage rooms, and the other including the stone house with its outbuildings, yard and orchard. Other heirs have made no claims. Everything is read in Portuguese and translated into English for the benefit of the buyer. Both parties sign the agreement.

Across the street, at the Registry Office, we discover some previously unpaid bills for the house, now under my name. I make some anxious enquiries across the road until it turns out to be a mistake, and the Registry staff who feel they are in the wrong, apologize profusely and correct their error. In small towns, officials and residents live side by side, so there is no tolerance of condescending behaviour. I ask Gilberto to translate for me: "you are the nicest bureaucrats I have ever met."

"*De nada, de nada*," they say, you're welcome, and we cross the road again to the Registry Office for the ceremony to seal the transfer. At the head of the table sits a slight woman with a sharp nose and flaming red hair. She reads from the contract, and Gilberto translates. She goes over the details once more. "Are both parties acting in good faith?"

Manoel and Maria say yes.

As do I.

55

It is an age-old ceremony that bestows familiarity on the room where a dysfunctional air conditioner is allowing warm air to build. We are all there: Laura the estate agent, the vendors, translator cum witness Gilberto and me. Julia, the notary, is tall, absent-minded and kind. In the twenty-first century, women administer land transfers in a country where before only men could own land. Now, under the eagle eye of the red-haired registrar, the property of Senhor Franco, dead for fifty years, passes into our hands. The new owners are the son of Polish immigrants who fled from Europe eighty-three years earlier and the daughter of escaped Iraqi Jews. Maria puts two sets of keys in my hands. A big metal key for the gate and two smaller keys for the door of the house.

21

At night I pass Candemil's cemetery, the set of keys in my pocket. Four street lamps cast their bright beams, while other village streets are submerged in darkness, houses barely lit. Only the polished tombstones return the shimmering light. Shutters help to cover the façades of the houses. "It's not just the Alto Minho where people like to hide," a local explains. "Most Portuguese are private people; though curious, they don't easily open up to strangers. They are courteous but lack social skills, dislike surprises and react slowly to change."

It seems that the dead, such as Marília, her parents and others long gone and buried, possess a special elevated status. They remain a part of everyday village life even years after turning to dust. From their underground chamber they listen in on the prayers in the nearby church, the gossip of neighbours and negotiations over the sale of their property.

I have visited dismal burial grounds in my own country and in other countries in Europe where tombs are placed on the fringes of towns far from the heart. Here, the dead reside alongside the living.

"Up until fifteen years ago," says Gilberto, "the cemetery consisted of a simple collection of earth mounds with wooden crosses and a handful of tombstones belonging to departed property-owners." The struggle for survival left no extra money for indulging the living or the dead. The young had sailed away; the old died and were buried with a modest ceremony. Only other seniors, left behind, visited their graves. With the post-Salazar economic growth, some exiles returned to their village and neglected family estates and began setting up their extravagant and often tasteless *casas de emigrantes*. Feelings of guilt and remorse arose at the thought of the old relatives left behind. One returning migrant put up a polished granite tombstone over the simple grave of his dead parents and carved his name as the mourner.

"From that moment on," says Gilberto, "it started raining granite slabs over modest graveyard plots" as a ravenous hunger for white stones took over the villages. The coveted tombstones depicted images of the deceased as if they had posed post-mortem at the local photography studio. The thought reminded me of Virxilio Vieitez, who would ride his Lambretta from village to village in Galicia, cutting hair, trimming beards and photographing villagers at forlorn county fairs. The new tombstones multiplied and grew in ornamentation due to competition between the returnees. They felt the need to declare their devotion and affluence by setting up a monument to honour their parents.

Every day, I notice the village women carrying bouquets from gardens and forests to place on the graves. They even put them on the mounds of soil that remain unclaimed.

22

JORGE IS A SKINNY GUY whose sagging trousers cling to colourful braces. A tassel of dishevelled hair bursts from under his hat like a visor, and a wild beard covers unexpected wrinkles. He joins me as an expert witness to decipher how the house operated during the time of its previous owners, Franco and Marília.

Jorge Filipe Correia Maciel is a talented artist who works as an assistant to Zadok. He shows up to our appointment at Casa Marília looking like a sylvan elf, carrying his dramatic life story upon his slender shoulders. As a child, his parents emigrated to France to earn a living. He was handed over to his grandmother in the village, as was the custom during those hard years.

Jorge learned about life through the experienced eyes of his late grandmother, and everything reminds him of that childhood home in the village. Even now, he can work an entire day in the yard in the intense heat, uprooting weeds without stopping to rest. When he tires, his moustache droops, and only when he steps out of a refreshing shower does it rise again, its waxed tips curling up like those of the Belgian detective Hercule Poirot. He speaks reverently of the sturdy, resourceful matriarch who raised eleven children, followed by grandchildren such as himself; a Portuguese villager who raised animals and had a vegetable garden, who slaughtered, salted and ate, planted, dressed and bathed.

We enter the courtyard, and Jorge starts to explore every item, thrilling at the familiar sights as if returning to the childhood home forever etched on his soul. He places his hands on an iron mesh enclosure covered in snails. "This is a cage for rabbits, *coelhos*, and here, next to the animal pen, is where the chicken coop was." He points out the stone winepress with cavities for the wine to run through and the cool wine cellar next to it, where they would lie down to rest on hot summer afternoons.

Jorge shoots from place to place, pulling up his trousers to keep them from falling down. He holds up a shearing comb with knots of wool still clinging to its ragged teeth to explain its function. Here are a wooden loom and spinning wheel used for weaving fabrics. The kitchen has an old wood-burning stove and pipe where he imagines his grandmother preparing a warm meal for him. Here they would hang the meat to smoke, here they would light the logs on the grate, and here were the air vent and ash pan. Families used the stove to heat food, water and the entire house, connecting pipes to the radiators on top of which they would also dry their muddy boots. Finally, he finds the name Marília inscribed on an old spinning wheel. "Here is a woodworking tool that is still repairable," he says. His grandfather was a cooper, a barrel-maker. Here are some iron hoops from an old barrel and a bundle of twigs that served as a broom.

Casa Marília is full of memories from Jorge's old life. First is the device for crushing leftover grape seed and skin pomace to make *aguardente*. Then he stops near a small chamber, our designated electricity and fuel tank room, "The pigpen," he laughs as if he has reached the core of the house.

"Grandma always said that only a tight space would do for pigs." It is certainly a dark, dirty and very narrow hole with a stone trough. "The pig ate all our rotten leftovers and made for great meat. He ate everything my grandmother kept for him in a special bucket, the smelliest waste. He was put in a small, cramped cell where he couldn't move, so producing fat rather than muscle. While the other animals ran around the yard, he just stood, ate and got fatter." According to Jorge, the pig was a wondrous organic machine that turned unwanted scraps into the most delicious meat.

When his grandmother eventually slaughtered the pig, who was like a family member, she threw away nothing. "When she had finished cooking the pig, not even an ear remained." Instead, she used everything: flesh, blood, bones, legs and the salted ears, still on offer in butcher shops today. In a concrete trough she put all the leftover meat with twenty kilos of salt for preservation. It was then smoked to keep it from rotting. On a soot-blackened wall in the ruins behind the house, he shows me some long iron hooks. "They lit a fire downstairs and hung chunks of pork over it, and the smoke came out through this opening in the tiles. No chimney. Pig blood was used as a sauce for the rice. The rich had blood sausages with meat. The poor had blood sausages with onions, called green chorizo, *chorizo verde*."

He kneels next to a storage room destined to be my studio, enclosed by a dry-stone wall. He clears the dirt from the large dark flagstones. "This was used for drying corn, kernels and legumes in the sun. And these are granite pillars stuck in the ground for building vine pergolas or fences." He reveals crude semi-carved columns buried here and there in the yard. I would find old sinks, work tools, metal utensils, vintage soda and wine bottles were I to dig more. He gives me a tour of the Marília estate as if he were the son or grandson she never had.

His decrepit Mercedes, which he repaired himself, is parked outside. He worked in Norway for several years, then England. He travels wherever he can make a living, just like the generation that preceded him. "If you want, I will help you out. I know how to do carpentry work. I can dig a garden. I learned everything I know from my grandmother."

His eyes are moist now, not from the smoke.

23

Twice a day, I make the journey between Zadok's home and Vila Nova de Cerveira at the foot of the hill. I go for morning coffee at Café Velha Rosa and for evening coffee at the Lenta Café by the river or at Curt'isso, with its lovely cork walls. The road never disappoints. Fourteen times a week, hundreds of times a year, the magic persists. I drive on a narrow winding road of changing colours through beautiful scenery which shifts hourly, daily and seasonally, from heavy fog to bright sunlight and the pale hue of rain.

I watch the bakery van driver hang bags of fresh rolls on house gates each morning. On weekdays, schoolchildren wait by whitewashed shelters for the shuttle bus. The fishmonger's car, merrily honking between villages, unloads crates of ocean and river plunder kept fresh on crushed ice. Armed with strimmers, weed control teams wear their protective gear like knights once wore armour while the delicious scent of freshly cut grass lingers in the air. The fertile land, quickly covered by thick grass, requires workers to strim the roadsides once a month, or vegetation would overwhelm them. Yards, fields and doorways require the same tending. Local hardware stores display a vast selection of strimmers, scythes and pruning shears. Sometimes these roadside knights get down on padded knees to fix a hole where vegetation has pushed through the paving stones.

The rural landscape is abuzz with maintenance workers, tile cleaners spraying high-pressure water to remove moss, collectors of pruned branches, loggers and wood delivery trucks. The smell from the sawmill pervades, complementing the plumes of chimney smoke during winter. Haymakers push bursting wheelbarrows, men on tractors plough the side of the road, women hoe their small gardens. They sow cabbage, plant trees. The old kindling ladies collect eucalyptus bark. Roaming about are sheep, goats and lambs. Baas and bleats. Donkeys braying. Forever curious, they will raise their heads in the middle of their work to peek at a traveller, a stranger, a passing vehicle.

Even at night, the road is a spectacle. At times the forest is lit by traffic lights at the bend: there goes a hedgehog, hurrying across the street. Dogs bark at the moon from the distant yards. By the roadside are illuminated effigies of Jesus, crimson blood flowing from his wounds, mouth agape, flowers at his feet. Forever iridescent, like an all-night store, Jesus is awake and ready to plead for salvation 24/7.

24

Gilberto fills his notebook with records of the house. He is the first person to document its history since its construction in the late nineteenth century. No details exist of its deeds or early plans as poor rural homes were never documented during their building or expansion. He takes time off from his other pursuits to come to measure the size of rooms, wall thickness, ceiling height, roof area and the length of the main girder.

"Over a hundred years ago," he says, "Franco's father or maybe his grandfather built this room on the south side of the house. This was the original front door." He points to a sturdy wooden double door with an impressive lock. Back then, every house was constructed on top of a stone chamber above which the family lived. The ground floor was not intended for human habitation but served essential economic functions: livestock quarters, wine production, fishing boat, work tools and plough storage.

The original ground-floor room was half-buried in the ground, so it was always damp. Above it, the owners erected their living room and a kitchen area of about twenty-five square metres with thick stone walls. Floors were made of wood, except in the kitchen, which had a stone floor for fire protection. All houses had a chimney or a simple opening in the tiles for smoke to escape. The hearth is where the family would live, eat, sleep and keep warm.

When a child was born, they would set up a wooden partition to create an *alcova*: a nook or niche. It was a wooden cubicle the size of a bed, where a child would sleep or future children would be created in relative privacy, "without traumatizing the existing children," he laughs. "Behind your house, in the ruins, you can see it exactly as it was, unchanged."

During that century, Portugal passed from monarchy to republic, from chaos to dictatorship, and Pessoa created all 127 of his heteronyms, filling thousands of pages with poems. At the same time, in Casa Marília, children multiplied, crowding the alcoves, so they added a hall to connect the two rooms and serve as a balcony. They cut an opening for a chimney, sealed a door, repartitioned a large room into concrete and wooden cubicles and installed a toilet. Finally, they added plumbing and inserted simple electrical wiring. None of this was on record until the 1980s when a request appears in the Cerveira Archives to repair a crumbling wall.

"Fortunately for you," explains Gilberto, "your house is connected to electricity and running water. These are procedures that can take up to a year and require a lot of paperwork." To our relief, he has already received the relevant documents from the estate agency, and everything seems to be in order.

We have not yet begun renovations of the house, and it remains as it was in the days of Marília, full of old furniture and woodworm that continue to gnaw on floors, cabinets and rafters. But Gilberto, with his pen, has already drawn a new home for us, made of paper and imagination. He understands that our only wish is to get on with the renovations quickly. All we require is a two-bedroom house complete with roof.

First to arrive is Jaime, an octogenarian roofer. He climbs up to check the rafters, pushing a pencil into what looks like a slightly chewed beam. His pencil goes straight through, and so we discover that there is indeed a problem with the roof. Some rafters are missing, and others are made of eucalyptus, a tree which carpenters despise because it is prone to unwanted movement. The master determines that the old roof be taken down and a new one built in its place. He sends Gilberto a quote. "The roof is the house, Jaime has a good reputation, and his offer is reasonable," confirms our architect. We consent. The removal of the existing roof is to begin immediately.

Initial estimates silently start to crumble and disintegrate. Then, a small and humble parade of experts make their appearance, headed by Senhor Franklin, whose job is to remove the old roof and install a foundation for the replacement. They come to glance at the property, talk with Gilberto the foreman, get an idea and estimate of the work and materials, and work out the costs. Then they disappear for a week or a month before returning with a detailed offer. Everyone seems to take time out from their real jobs on more important construction sites where honest work is executed. And then there is absolute silence and quiet returns to Casa Marília.

The sweet melody of hammers and drills is yet to be heard anywhere. *Nada.* Quotes begin to pour in. New costs arise, and old prices inflate. Estimates are jotted quickly on paper, with no contracts. All agreements over demolition, evacuation, reconstruction, roof, floor, insulation, paint, electricity and water are verbally sealed. Gilberto charges a commission for the entire renovation. There is no written agreement between us and anyone. Deals are clinched with a firm handshake or written in the notebook. There is no set schedule. Workers inform us of future delays half-jokingly.

Some day we will have a great home.

The Business Class
Carpenters

25

OUR INITIAL ENTHUSIASM RUNS INTO a brick wall. Throughout September the house remains deserted, and I am its sole visitor; no builders or masons, just me. Senhor Franklin is delayed at another construction site and Jaime and the carpenters wait for Franklin before beginning. When Franklin fails to show, they move on to another job and a dance of tardiness begins. Every morning when I open the gate, a lonely house welcomes me. Fruit collects under the trees, yellow mounds of apples and pears, and small figs from two crooked trees in the corner of the courtyard. Grapes dangling in dark clusters on the fence, small, pitted and very sweet, wait for the winepress, clinging to the vine without dropping, merely shrivelling. The fallen nourish the earth. In late autumn, the fruit of the lemon tree is still unripe. Pink flowers like lilies shoot forth from the crocus bulbs, and their fragrance combines with the fermentation of rotting fruit.

Deprived of irrigation, the ruins still burst with life: blossoms, foliage, decomposition - but no fruit picking, no harvest, no electricity in the rooms, no light, and barely a trickle of water in the tap. When Orit returns for a visit, we wander between rooms excitedly. "Here, next to the winepress, I would like to have my studio," she says, "and there you can have your study." It will be her first real home since tragedy struck her childhood when she was still an infant. Her mother, Daisy, died following a serious illness, and a devoted sister, only five years her senior, took care of her. She then had to bring herself up in her father's house; she moved to a boarding school, university dorms, rented apartments. As a child, a teenager, a woman, she has always been a nomad. There remains something of the orphaned child about her.

Together we tour our desolate estate, forcibly pushing through the massive, time-eaten doors of the animal pens. The dark spaces are enveloped in the smell of dung and the remains of the lives of cows and calves. We wander from the storage room to the ruins and to another storage room. An accumulated abundance of over a hundred years of life, now belonging exclusively to us: rooms, trees, a field, fruit, fences, attics, basements and rafters. It feels like a time capsule from before the distant deportation of our ancestors from Portugal.

26

In the morning, a blanket of fog covers Gondar. From the vantage point of our wide bed in Zadok's home, and well protected from the cold, it seems that the whole forest is nestling in a cloud. "I have always wanted to hold on to the fog," says Orit as she reaches out to touch the water beads on the window.

Our house is just a one-minute drive from where we are staying. I begin clearing the warehouse that is to be my study. I shake off decades of dust which swirls and floats in the air, light yet slightly suffocating. I bury bulbs in the ground, plant a rosemary bush and a climber. Finally, I pull out the remaining tools: weights, spinning wheels, an iron shearing comb. The work kindles in me a desire to build my nest alone, independent of unreliable workers.

I love everything about my future study, its dimensions, the exposed wooden roof, the way beams support each other, clinging to or hovering over each other. The storage space has stood empty for many years. The floor is coarse and doubles as a ceiling to the basement sheep pen. The thick walls stand right by the road, and there are two window niches with stone benches, typical of traditional construction. They are called window loveseats. When I remove the dust and sand from the window niche, rusty nails, pieces of wood, leather and metal are exposed, as if in an archaeological excavation of the interior of a house. I collect everything, from an old lock and the remains of a lady's shoe to small broken tools. I wonder what I will find when I start digging in the yard.

I remove dust and flour residue from the rough planks of the corn cob storage space. If dust is the flesh of time, I must have reached its bones. The dust lies so deep that it penetrates everywhere. It also collects from the reddish earth mortar that once held the stones together. I spray the concrete and wood with water, and they regain their deep hues as if returning to life. The dust becomes a solid, moist mass. I find a small axe in the corner of the room, two artisan's hammers and an old yellow rubber suit.

An architect friend who comes to offer advice suggests using the restored roof as a high ceiling running through the length of the house. In addition, he proposes we build an attic above the kitchen space as an open study with a large round window. The window would illuminate the house and overlook the square, village café, grocery store and the road to Gondar. Through the windows we will also be visible, Orit and I, residents 256 and 257 of the village of Candmil.

From demographic graphs I find that while the population of Portugal has been gradually on the rise despite emigration, the numerical chart of Candemil's inhabitants undulates like its craggy landscape. In the 1930s, the number of residents doubled from five hundred to a thousand but has since declined, risen slightly, then slowly faded. I live in a village populated mainly by adults my age, rather than young people and children. At the beginning of the Salazar dictatorship, the village population grew due to the global crisis. Across the river in Spain, chaos prevailed, rulers were replaced and reforms carried out, while Portugal remained stable under the rule of the young Salazar. Gilberto believes that owing to medical advances, there were fewer infant deaths. It is also possible that the growth in population was due to domestic migration to areas where food was plentiful. Households were filling with children who constituted a natural resource for farming.

I wonder if twenty-first-century graphs will reveal a rise in the population curve. It may be that exiles, refugees or migrants such as Orit and me, or young folk who cannot afford to buy in the cities because of the real property boom, will eventually take over the villages of the Alto Minho.

27

ORIT GOES TO THE GROCERY in the square to get fresh rolls. She calls me from the shop, asking me to come over. The proprietor is an excellent source of information and speaks English.

"You live in Casa Marília," Natalia says. She is well acquainted with the story of Senhor Franco, who fathered several children. Her sister was Franco and Marília's godmother. In her shop she hears all the latest gossip about everyone. She remembers all the local grievances, ancient hostilities, recent feuds and love stories.

Twenty-five years ago, she lived for a time in Toronto, where her father-in-law owned a Portuguese restaurant. Then, after five years, she was called back to Candemil to take care of her ailing mother and has stayed here ever since. Her father was the cultural heart of the community, and his reputation as an accordion player preceded him in the surrounding villages. "Here, my father," she proudly points to a yellowing poster at the centre of which is a thickset villager with an accordion draped over his chest. Behind the store is a fishpond home to a single fish and the door to a café called Fontela, the fountain. Natalia makes a hand gesture implying no affection between the only two meeting places in the village.

When I return to the courtyard and begin taking apart the empty rabbit hutches, two women who are leaving the grocery pause to watch. Shielding their eyes from the light, they squint in the direction of the yard above where the elderly stranger is going at a brick wall with a hammer. Little do they know that their new neighbour uses the hammer to vent his anger at his absent workers. I smash through a wall, drag rusty steel meshes, plant bougainvillaea, enrich the soil with horse manure and excavate potsherds, slates and iron tools.

73

Only then does my soul rest at ease, and memories flood into my mind of my late mother, who eighty-four years ago arrived a beautiful young girl at the port of Haifa, Palestine. She began working as a fieldhand the very next day, picking oranges. Born in Poland, she grew up working as a farmhand in a poor smallholding near Warsaw. She could easily have been one of those villagers gathering cabbage in the adjacent *horta*. My father would faint at the sight of a galloping horse, while my mother knew how to hold on to the harness and restrain the unruly animal.

I begin dismantling the chicken coop at the entrance to the cow shed. Its materials come apart easily: steel wire mesh, rotting wood, bricks and clay. I pull out some planks hammered to the wall and uncover a snail cemetery; I find a stone trough and remove a large plough from a rotting haystack. The heavy plough drops from my hand, pulling on my other arm so hard that I scream in pain.

Something in my arm seems to have torn.

When Gilberto arrives, my arm dangles at my side as if after a stroke, and every movement is excruciating. I hold the arm in my other hand to keep it from moving as we discuss details such as tile size, the shape of the toilet and the width of the concrete foundations. I am impatient with the details; all I want is a simple house. Also, I am in urgent need of my hand. I have no time for even a partial disability. According to Gilberto, Franklin will not, after all, be available until the wet season. So naturally, the carpenters cannot begin until then. "Around these parts, carpenters are as rare as astronauts," Gilberto tells me. Many of them left during the troubled years when there was no work to be found. Some migrated to France. Now that demand is on the rise, it is difficult to locate master artisans who can manipulate the giant beams used to construct these durable wood and tile roofs.

"Some of them work half the month in France. They fly back and forth so often that business class is always full of upgraded Portuguese carpenters."

He calls another recommended contractor, and everything starts anew. The contractor/stonemason, Manoel, shows up at the house. He is about forty, short, stocky and efficient-looking, like the good cop in a French detective film. He surveys the battlefield, and Gilberto informs him that we need to dismantle the old roof urgently before the rains arrive and lay the concrete strip foundation. It should dry for a month before the wood is put in place. But Manoel explains that he is unavailable for work this week.

Standing in the yard next to my growing pile of junk, I tell Gilberto that if left alone any longer, I may have to take down the roof myself; my resourceful mother taught me that dire times make the impossible possible. He smiles gently and drives me to the clinic.

The physiotherapist touches my aching arm with a skilled hand. Gently exploring, she determines that I have strained a tendon. It is only a matter of time and rest, she reassures me. Then, carefully massaging the area, she instructs me on how to exercise my arm. From that time on, the one and only worker on site to demolish structures and drag planks is disabled.

Visiting hardware stores, as popular in Alto Minho as beauty salons in tourist resorts, I point to different tools learning Portuguese names for nails, paint, varnish, wood, stone, iron and concrete. I encounter the famous *Bicho de Madeira*, or woodworm, local wood terrorists whom I come to know intimately. The local carpenters help explain which types of African wood are worm resistant and which local wood is durable or vulnerable. I listen to horror stories about houses eaten from within and look for the signs: small honey-coloured sawdust mounds. I learn which is the most effective substance to use against worms and how to treat wood with it. But I do not fear them; they have lived here long before me and will endure after, and anyway they take a long time to eat through an entire house; I will be long gone by then. The *Bicho de Madeira* works on Portuguese time to make progress, and that is measured in centuries.

28

EVERY SATURDAY MORNING, I STROLL to the foot of the old fortress for the weekly market. There, under white awnings set up across a Cerveira carpark, a dizzying array of fabrics, sheets, blankets, shirts, coats, towels and winemaking equipment is on display. In the background, by the river, freight and commuter trains pass on an elevated track with a cheerful roar. There are stalls for household goods, power tools, flowers, fruit tree saplings, hoses, axes and Buddha figurines. Fine Portuguese and cheap Chinese textiles lie side by side.

Thousands of Spaniards cross the river and crowd into the small town that seems to inflate like a balloon for a single day. By evening all have disappeared without trace, as nimble maintenance workers efficiently clear everything away.

In the centre of this large market, under a wooden pergola, a group of elderly villagers sell their traditional small-farm wares. They offer fruit, rabbits in wicker baskets, chickens and chicks in crates, garlic and onion braids, flower bulbs, vegetable seedlings arranged like soldiers and bundles of strawberry seedlings covered in dry leaves, with damp newspaper protecting their roots. Under bunches of garlic and a pot full of orange lentils, two bunnies peek from inside a basket like a heartbreaking portent of a future rabbit stew. There are egg baskets, home-made sausages, cakes and a special delicacy of fried white bread floating in sweet wine garnished with pine nuts. Fragrant smoke rises from the roasted chestnut stall. Next to it sits a young guitar player with his dog, providing the soundtrack for the entire marketplace.

I buy a woollen scarf, a flowerpot, several soon to bloom flower bulbs, two clay pots and a plaster angel with wings spread and a tormented expression, the size of a baby. Every object, whether cheap or costly, is carefully wrapped by its vendor. When I return, I place the angel on the steps to the house and immediately feel its spiritual patronage loom over the entire property. I plant fragrant jasmine in the desolate backyard. Then, kneeling, I dig my hand into the soil, making a hole and burying the bulbs; I feel closer to the earth and fresh grass than I have ever been. In a book by a well-known British gardener, I read that my only concern should be to prepare the soil since every plant, weed, worm, butterfly and bee then has its role to play. One should avoid any external interference and let them be. Garden and nature are one and the same.

My debilitated left arm assists the right like a child helping a parent. I dig holes and cover them up. I tear out stubborn worm-eaten planks clinging to the stone slabs into which they were inserted a century ago, using my one good hand. Each nail is crooked as if struggling for survival. When I manage to uproot a board, the grey flakes of time rain down on me: dust, wood chips, dried seeds, insects and a shower of old corn kernels. I am careful not to step barefoot on a hidden nail awaiting its victim.

I uproot the door to the pigpen where Gilberto is planning to place the gas tanks, heating boiler and electrical system. A mournful yelp, and the old wood parts with the stone forever.

Franklin, the general contractor, has vanished for good and his successor, Manoel, fails to appear. Meanwhile, Gilberto has been invited to a conference on architecture in Yazd, Iran, a city famous for incredible ancient architecture and waterways. He is debating whether to leave his projects unsupervised and accept the Iranian invitation. When I was his age and like him the father of two young children, I received a Fulbright scholarship and an invitation to participate in a two-month writers' workshop in the Midwest. Despite hesitations, I decided to go ahead. I was happier there than I had been for years.

I encourage my architect to travel. However, Gilberto has a hard time deciding; his children are young, and he likes to visit sites in person to oversee the work.

"What work?" I ask bitterly. "Go to Iran. Nothing is happening here. *Nada.*"

He hesitates. His speech is so soft and gentle that his clients sometimes believe that if he were only to raise his voice, shout and get angry, the workers would come running. It is a reproach he finds hurtful, an accusation hurled at his quiet manner. Gilberto believes in calm management. According to him, clients who complain do not understand the spirit and tempo of the place. Despite our frustration, we develop a strong affection for our architect, who is just as distressed as we are at the slow progress. But he knows well from experience that all houses will eventually reach the finishing line and stand on their own two feet despite setbacks.

He remains relaxed in the face of an impossible workload. Even when he is late for a project or class, his leisurely manner persists. In the Portuguese custom, he becomes so engrossed in a conversation that I find myself interrupting to remind him that he is in a hurry to get somewhere.

I make sure he knows that we want a modest house; we do not care if there are last-minute changes or alterations to the original plans because a home, like life, is never perfect, with its chipped corners and cracked tiles.

I quote an Indian sage who said that most people have such an intense fear of death that they see it everywhere. Every crack or stain reminds them of the end. Thus they continuously and meticulously renovate and improve, as if they can *will* death away. "This is not a Frank Lloyd Wright house," I tell him and immediately realize that it might be a mistake to instruct one's architect to be less fastidious.

But Gilberto Carlos is the product of generations of hardworking people. His parents were born in the time of

Salazar; his father is a car mechanic who repairs British cars for a living, and his mother comes from a poor rural family of nine children. His grandmother grew up in a well-to-do family until her father ran away with his mistress leaving his wife to care for the children. Gilberto recalls the hard-knock stories of his grandmother, who, when her husband fell ill, decided to sell the last heirloom from better days: a pair of gold earrings. She walked thirty kilometres to the nearest town, sold her jewellery, bought a sack of flour and, rather than a bus fare, some additional meat. She walked all the way home, carrying the load on her back. This was in the 1950s during the economic crisis in Salazar's time.

His mother, who grew up as industrious and ambitious as her mother, possessed a well-developed business sense. Gilberto is the youngest of four siblings, an easygoing and affectionate lastborn. As a boy, he dreamed of becoming a fox hunter, shipbuilder, or architect. He chose architecture because of his childhood passion for drawing. He does not follow a specific tradition but has a human-based approach to his profession. He does not perceive a house as a lifeless sculpture to be forced upon the landscape but adopts the point of view of its inhabitants. He is respectful of the original purpose of all materials - stone will serve as stone, glass as glass, and wood as wood. He speaks of the three Roman principles still in use today: the functionality of a structure, the quality of the construction and its aesthetics; he aims to balance the three. I enjoy our talks, even though they take place against the backdrop of my neglected property. I know that as the last worker takes his leave on some future day, a newly restored house will stand proudly in place.

"Go to Iran," I tell him, fearing the moment I will be left alone, far from proficient in the language and faced with empty promises and vanishing acts.

The Marco Silva
Universe of Old
Objects

29

Come October I drive to the river every evening until it becomes something of a ritual. The Minho is as smooth as a mirror. The Lenta Café, on the riverbank, is shut for business due to the cold weather. I take off my clothes and jump into the water. My eyes open to peer into the green abyss, I swim up to the buoys that warn of dangerous currents. Sometimes a plant clings to my foot like a fine chain and with it comes a momentary fear of drowning. But my worries wash away with the water: the setbacks, the long wait and the interminable dust pollution, all of it. In the water I become a carefree tadpole.

At times, life in the Alto Minho bestows on one a vague sensation, like sleepwalking or floating in quiet waters. The people around me speak a whistling, soft language resembling a lullaby, of which I understand not a word. The landscape reminds me of the utopic scenery that used to inhabit my dreams. Here, I am an elderly villager but at the same time a tourist, a foreigner, a refugee and an immigrant. My essence blurs. My anchors are loose. I still know almost no one here except Gilberto, a few waiters and neighbours. They smile and wave when they see me. My rented car is plush and comfortable, but my hand still hurts, even in my sleep. In this dreamlife that I have built, I am nesting, collecting strange and valuable objects, holding conversations with an architect over non-existent renovation works and visiting the house, foggy and enchanted in the mornings. Then, one day, during one of my aimless meanderings, I stop on the side of the road to Valença to enter a small shop whose door is ajar, bursting with tools, lamps and mirrors. I immediately feel as if I have stumbled upon a treasure chest.

The shopowner, Marco, does not speak a word of English, but through hand gestures and bits of names, I gather that he is from Gondar, brother to Carla Silva, the young proprietor of the café. The woman who often naps on the sofa is his mother. That practically makes me a member of his household. I move now from one crammed room to the next and never want to leave. "*A quantos?*" I inquire of an old, decorated mirror. How much? Marco draws a sign of fifteen on the back of his hand. I purchase a large painted-clay statue of a child reading a book. I note that there is a whole series of them, perhaps from the time of Salazar when illiteracy was prevalent. I set my sights on an old tin toy car with pedals. It is expensive. "Antique," apologizes Marco. Three hundred euros.

From that day on, I return to the shop to purchase items for a not-yet built house. I furnish not-yet constructed rooms. I accumulate loveliness in my cleared storage room. Marco Silva is a robust young man with a babyface, yet he easily distinguishes between what is valuable and what is worthless. Many of the items date to before the economic crisis. They are the former belongings of people who have passed away and, briefly, their heirs, who sold them with a mix of glee and repulsion. Some they sold for pennies to merchants like Marco, who swallow the contents of entire houses like hungry whales. *Saudade* does not imply a longing for old objects, at least not for the objects of poor people.

Every time I step into Marco's shop, I enter a Portuguese time machine. From frequent visits there and occasional glances into country homes, I find that the elderly rarely get rid of things. As a result, their homes and yards, storage rooms and basements are full to the brim with repaired or broken household items. One can find cracked pottery, welded metal containers, buckets whose handles have been replaced with rope, old saws, wood barrels, cracked mirrors, perforated cabinets and blackened pans.

30

Passing stone terraces and cultivated fields, I observe the villagers as they work. Scenes are domestic and intimate: husband and wife toiling together while other family members shovel, plough, harvest and push wheelbarrows. Women with pitchforks. Men on old tractors. A boy cuts ridges and furrows in the dark earth. Small plots of shifting colours are separated by fences, low drystone walls or border stones. According to a local proverb, "Small plots, tall fences".

There are no large-scale farms here with fieldhands, no vast plains of wheat and orchards; rather *hortas*: vegetable plots, small orchards and fields. The *hortas* are single-person or family-size smallholdings. The landscape is hilly, made up of slopes, valleys, canals, streams and fertile earth. This topography shaped methods of cultivating the land. The plots are small because of geology, agrarian reforms and birthrights that divided and redivided the land.

"The natural abundance shapes the people here," say the locals. Each has a small farm of vegetables and livestock: a few chickens, cows, sheep, goats, rabbits and pigeons, fruit trees and a small area of woodland to provide for heating and cooking. They do not need or depend on outsiders for their livelihood. In the past, large families with children had no trouble tending their fields on their own. When children emigrated, only the water resources remained, both visible and hidden: wells, collection ponds, bifurcating waterways, streams, rivers, lakes, natural pools, and the nearby sea.

Due to its lush scenery and heavenly beauty, the Alto Minho has always been a holiday destination for the people of Porto, whether for its second homes, shut during winter, or for visiting retired relatives. Children who have spent their summer vacations here later recall a childhood wonderland, full of flowers and vegetables, a place where they felt happy and complete. It is something they take comfort in during harsh times. They retain the memories as they grow, returning to the region.

When I pick the brains of village residents, it turns out that even during the troubled times of Salazar, people lived in relative peace on their small farms. They were never organized or unionized like industrial workers in cities or the farmers in the south, who cultivated large land areas together and were therefore more militant. That is why some of the older villagers remember that period without anger as a time of stability. None suffered the disgrace of hunger. Then there were also the river smugglers who kept the economy alive. They risked their lives and liberty to make money from trading across closed borders and they created a black market that fed many around them.

Without urban development and industrialization, natural resources remained unchanged, and some small towns kept their original character.

Today, with the growing economy, it is often said of the people of the Alto Minho that they possess a taste for aesthetics rather than business. That is because they have lived on their produce and not on trade. "What you the foreigner perceive as decency and a lack of greed is the absence of a business sense," I have been told. "This constitutes a problem for a modern competitive economy. Many of the young people left because there were no jobs." But I sense that the ancient, constant and delightful trickle of water prevails nonetheless.

With water, it is possible to sustain life in any situation. The cabbage will always grow on time, the peach and fig ripen, and the olives and vines that grow untended will continue to produce. The damp humus soil is so fertile that you will have a thriving blue shrub by summer if you plant a wisteria cutting in the spring. "Spit on the bottom of the cutting before you plant it," a neighbour advises me. The branches I have pruned lie in a pile and still send out roots. The compost heap sprouts a furry surface of grass.

31

FROM MY VANTAGE POINT AMONG the gravestones next to the church, I observe women carrying fresh flowers, sweeping the paths or weeding the burial plots. Cemeteries are the rural archives, and headstones with their photographs are like pages from the Yearbook of the Dead. The old stone slabs inform us of the dates of birth and death, names of grieving relatives, professional occupation, life companion, hobbies and family ties. Until the 1950s, there was no civil registry or records, only tombstones and parish registers of births, deaths and marriages - no divorces, no illegitimate children, no adultery. Such matters were reserved for the confessional or buried underground.

If you keep your ears open, the tombstones speak. One headstone is blank, and another commemorates a large family. Details can be read in the hyphen between the year of birth and death - parents of advanced ages, widows who outlast their spouse, childless women.

Next to the church I spot an elderly couple. Approaching them, I gather that they speak English. Once the owners of a family restaurant in Toronto, the woman is sister to Natalia, who runs the village grocery. Yes, she is the daughter of the same Carlos Nejo, renowned regional accordionist. "Every September 24, a celebration is held in his memory with accordion players from all over Portugal. My father's name has spread far and wide," says Marília. Her husband, David Leal, is a handsome and slender man who seems level-headed. He is among the former residents who have returned to the village in their retirement.

Born in Candemil, Leal lived here until 1966, the onset of a turbulent era that would begin with the fall of Salazar. As a young boy, he travelled to Lisbon to support his family but somehow ended up in freezing Toronto, where he worked in Portuguese restaurants until he opened his own. He assures me that he will give me a complete account of his adventures at our next meeting. When they managed to save enough money in Canada, they returned to Viana do Castelo, where they bought a house. Although they have lived half their lives in Canada, their English is far from perfect; they lived within Toronto's Portuguese community, mainly using their mother tongue.

When I inquire of Senhor Franco, they point to an old grave where we stop to talk further. It features a massive granite tombstone, one of a handful belonging to landowners that are different to the newer marble slabs. The headstone reads, "João Franco", and his dates are engraved: born in 1881, he died on 13 May 1967 aged eighty-six.

"And strong as an ox he was," says David, "at eighty years old, he was still a big character at the county fairs." He flexes his arms to illustrate the muscular biceps of the deceased. "He had a reputation for settling disputes with a stick."

"Why a stick?"

"Because young men from other villages would join the festivities to flirt with the local girls. They would come in drunk or looking for a fight." Franco the livestock trader, a man of his times, was a Hercules who defended helpless beauties. Perhaps he used a cattle prod.

"The festivities centred around the accordion players, father included," says the wife, Marília. "What else was there to do around here? Father played, the girls danced and Franco beat up the rowdy boys."

The names of Franco's parents, buried with him, are also inscribed on the tombstone. When people die here, they are buried above their progenitors. Caetano Luís Franco, father to Franco, born in 1830, was the first to die. His mother, Amélia Rosa Pires, was born in 1837. Franco was born when his father was fifty-one years old. The father died in 1905, while the mother lasted until World War II. They recall that she was blind and died at the age of a hundred and three. According to the tombstone, Franco was their only son, or perhaps the only one left in Candemil to mourn them.

They owned the house we have bought. When Amélia passed away, Franco was about sixty, wealthy by local standards, and the father of four out-of-wedlock children. His daughter Marília was about fifteen years old. I wonder if she moved into his house to take care of him as a daughter or more as a maid.

Marília Leal leads me down several tombstones to the resting place of Marília and her mother. It is a joint grave under a fine marble stone. Heavy slabs cover it, and the tombstone bears the image of the son of God and Marília. An older woman with a square-set face and a short neck, she is smiling at the photographer. "She resembled her father quite a bit," remarks Marília. Born in 1925, she died in 2016.

There is no image of the mother nor a date of birth. Landowners kept many photographs of themselves for posterity, but village folk rarely documented their lives. The same applies to all born in the nineteenth century who lived into the second half of the twentieth.

The third digit is missing from the year of death of the mother. 19-9. Was it seven or eight?

"1979," states David after thinking about it for a moment.

The mother outlived Senhor Franco by a dozen years and died about forty years before her daughter. My new acquaintance Marília attempts to keep up with my quick questions. I note that village women are livelier than the men, more alert, their eyes brighter. They are usually the ones who keep track of things and discuss local affairs. The men sit in cafés; the women meet in the fields, on the road, in their homes or in church. Occasionally I see a group of women walking alongside the road. Facing the traffic, they are usually heading to someone's house to have lunch together.

32

I TAKE LEAVE OF MY SMALL garden by the stone studio room. I leave a small *azulejo* next to each plant to gather the morning dew and water the roots. In my absence, there will be no one to care for them. The house is just as it was, old, abandoned and waiting for its roof removal surgery.

Franklin has finally sent a quote for removing the roof and laying the concrete foundation. "The first step is always the hardest," says Gilberto, "but once work begins, you will see how quickly and efficiently everything moves."

"How are we going to get started when the wet season is coming and the house unprotected?"

"Don't worry," he says, "we will use plastic sheets for cover."

It is a long journey from Porto to Tel Aviv. Every flight there and back has a different stopover, depending on the airline: Prague, Istanbul, Zurich, Madrid, Athens. A short wait, scurrying through the endless aisles of huge airports, opening bags, security checks, metal detectors, sniffer dogs, queuing for passports, and then the departure to Tel Aviv or back to Porto, back and forth, again and again. An entire day on the road. Only birds and the imagination cross borders uninterrupted. My thoughts soar through the air at take-off: swift movement, estrangement and the heights set the mind free. Do we think differently at a speed of a thousand kilometres an hour and at an altitude of ten thousand metres from when we are crawling along on the ground?

It seems so to me.

This autumn, seven years after writing a desperate dystopian novel about an elderly father attempting to rescue his youngest daughter from a soon to be deserted land, I shall leave my birthplace and move to Portugal. Friends regard me as someone waging a quixotic war while preparing to take cover and fall back. The energy needed for battle and migration may seem contradictory, but both stem from the same passion or fearlessness in the face of change. When you are not too old to change, you are not too old. When you lose your fears, difficulties dissolve of their own volition. The ease with which almost everything is conducted in Cerveira is refreshing. And then there is the house that came out of nowhere after quietly lying in wait for so long. In clear-headed moments such as these, I believe that both builders and carpenters will eventually make an appearance.

33

ONCE BACK IN PORTUGAL, I search for the oldest man in Candemil: ninety-six-year-old Albano Dantas, landowner. At the grocery, Natalia says that Dantas is her landlord. Her husband, Luis, has tired of shying away from customers for the moment and is happy to chat. Of their landlord, he says he is "an educated man who has written about Candemil". According to Luis, at almost a hundred years old, Dantas is lucid, but his memory plays tricks on him and his body is fragile.

Luis takes me to see the Dantas estate, where Albano lived. A stone plaque records the date of its establishment: 4 December 1878. The grandfather of Dantas built the house during the reign of Luis I, also known as "The Popular". He was a king ignorant of politics, an amateur poet and a patron of the sciences. In the living room of the now locked house, Luis notices a ceiling relief depicting the four seasons. "Dantas was also an expert on water canals," he recalls and goes on to describe the old irrigation system that ran through villages for centuries. The system consisted of stone reservoirs and waterways which branched into smaller canals, where wooden stoppers were strategically placed to divert the water or fill smaller pools. This was the only water system Dantas had known for most of his life.

Luis explains to the student Pedro, my interpreter, how to find the nursing home. It is in Caminha, in the old town at the end of the pedestrian area where the fishermen live, by the fire station. "That is where we send our rent every month."

We exit Candemil driving through hills shrouded in smoke from burnt vegetation. Pedro says that burning grass is permitted during the wet season.

"Wet? They haven't even begun to work on the roof of my house yet." I feel like time is running out.

"A roof in Portuguese is *telhado*," says Pedro.

"And a house without a roof?"

"It is a *Sem Teto*, meaning decapitated and also homeless," he tells me.

Well, I, for one, own a roofless home and am therefore homeless.

As usual, only the glorious autumn makes me forget my troubles. End-of-season rays of light fall on the rusty dead leaves of October. Dark gold is cast on black mossy fences, and yellow summer ferns burn under the veil of green and fresh vegetation.

"What a lot of flowers there are," I say to Pedro, and quote Albert Camus, "Autumn is a second spring when every leaf is a flower."

"But the tourists have already left," says Pedro, "the hot season is over, and they don't realize how wonderful the Alto Minho is in October. They come here for their summer vacations or to visit relatives, parents or grandparents. This time of the year, it is deserted."

He is an attentive, opinionated young man, the son of the notary. We cross the bridge over the estuary, park the car by the Caminha fire station and knock on the glass door of the nursing home. No one pays us any attention. Behind the glass we note slowly moving figures like spectres. Only after a long wait does the door finally open.

In a room smelling of polish, elderly men and women rest in wide armchairs. They look like villagers torn away from their fields after eighty years and left here to die. I ask about Senhor Albano Dantas, and the nurse leads us to another large room where a dozen or so old people are staring at a TV screen showing a church ceremony.

"He is the one lying by the door," says the nurse.

The oldest man in Candemil is skinny, shrunken and wears a beret. Currently he is napping, curled up in a heavy coat under a blanket, despite the heat in the room.

Pedro kneels down to whisper in his ear: "This man is an *escritor*, an author who is writing about Candemil. He has come to talk with you." Albano has a delicate, almost wrinkle-free face; his slightly open eyes are scanning me. Yes, he is ready to be interviewed.

"I was born on 13 October 1921," he says. His mouth is crooked, but his voice is strong and clear. "My father was Alfredo Jorge Dantas, and my mother Ana Áurea Pereira Virgínea. My father had two brothers, Alípio and Telmo. We owned a grocery store and a house in the centre of the village." His nose is sharp, his fingers elegant and his nails manicured. "I was a farmer," he says.

"Do you remember Senhor Franco?"

"Of course. João was many years my senior. He never married, but he had children."

"And did you ever marry?"

"No, I didn't. I had a girlfriend, but she died, and I did not want anyone else. She lived in Lisbon. Her name was Marília. We would write to each other a lot."

"Was she the daughter of Franco?"

At the mention of this other Marília, Dantas seems suddenly confused.

"No. Marília was not my girlfriend. She never took the name of Franco. It was only when she was fifteen that he gave her his surname."

"And where does Marília live?" I ask.

"She lives with her mother. At fifteen, she moved into his house."

He does not mention Lisbon Marília again, and anyway, he only remembers the letters. His memory can no longer handle the mysteries suggested by two Marílias. Sometimes his answers stumble and fall.

"Ask if Marília was depressed," I suggest. Pedro remarks that it is a complicated question to ask the oldest man in Candemil.

"Then ask if she was sad."

"Yes," confirms Dantas, "Marília was sad during the years when her father did not recognize her." Pedro brings his ear closer to the mouth of the old man as if to hear a confession.

"But we were not together." He clarifies, "We were both single, but we were only friends." I ask him to describe the house where Marília lived. Dantas recalls the details and shape of the rooms with precision. "Franco may have owned more land than we did, but there was only one of him and many of us. So we worked in his fields too." He speaks of Franco as though he were still alive but concedes that he must be "ancient like his mother, though she has already passed away." It seems his brain chooses to ignore unfortunate things such as the death of his peers. His delicate physique is not typical of village folk, and is undoubtedly different from the image of the robust Franco who would beat impudent young men with a stick.

"My brother was huge," he says of the brother who lived with him.

Up until ten years ago, Dantas still lived by the grocery, in the house with the four seasons ceiling relief. He worked every day and built wooden toys for his brother's grandchildren until he was injured in a car accident near the house. He has been here ever since, and every year he gets colder. I touch him tenderly. He reminds me of my mother when she was in a nursing home and the same age, ninety-six.

After an hour, he withdraws from the conversation and drops off. A nurse stops to wipe his nose with her hand as you would with a toddler. I gently press his soft hand, but he does not respond, appearing to maintain the same pain-free posture. He does not express sorrow or sigh. His eyes remain shut.

Zé Paolo and the House of Granny Ermelinda

"I am nothing. I shall never be anything. I cannot wish to be anything. This apart, I have in me all the dreams in the world."

Fernando Pessoa

34

As **Pedro and I leave** the last abode of the village elders, I feel we have climbed out of the realm of Hades back into the land of the living. Even in a foreign country, one breathes a sigh of relief after a visit to a nursing home. Old age is a nation of which everyone eventually becomes a citizen, and the thought is saddening. But an autumn sun is shining on the cobbled street in old Caminha, and the window boxes are in bloom. I walk to the square and come across a ground floor apartment with large windows and a glass door facing the street. I glance inside: the space is crammed with old objects piled on top of each other, just as in Marco's shop. I glimpse chandeliers, cushions, old toys, typewriters, chairs and cabinets full of other delightful knick-knacks. Amidst this chaos stands a tall, bearded man gesturing for me to come inside. He lives directly above the antiques shop. These antiquated items are his passion.

"When can I come to the shop?" I ask.

"I am never here, but every time you come, I will be," answers the man in a line straight out of Pessoa. His name is Zé Paolo, short for José. The poet, too, was employed for a time in the antiques trade on São Pedro de Alcântara, Lisbon. Among old objects, he scribbled his poems and slept in an adjacent alcove. Paolo also lives with his antiques but is a graphic designer rather than a poet. He was born and grew up here in the house of his grandmother until the age of five - "because my parents just left me here." He casually mentions disturbing facts about his life. His mother was a cold woman who worked as a teacher, and his father was an irascible banker given to bouts of rage. But his good-natured grandmother, Ermelinda Gonzalez, raised him, and when she died, a grown-up Paolo returned to the house where he once loved and was loved. He has lived here ever since, only without a trace of the order that reigned during the time of his grandmother. Were she to return from the grave, she would be horrified by the chaos. While Marco Silva, the antique dealer from east Cerveira, is a villager with a tidy warehouse, Paolo from west of Cerveira is a wild anarchist, with a decaying, overflowing shop, consumed in part by mould. A line from Pessoa rings through my head as I look around: "I am nothing. I shall never be anything. I cannot wish to be anything. This apart, I have in me all the dreams in the world."

From the moment we meet, Zé Paolo speaks English in perfect, poetic phrases thrown around effortlessly. Sometimes sentences get tangled up in the process, reaching a dead-end, until he gets angry at himself and at the foreign language and becomes contemptuous of good order and the evil bourgeoisie. He is conscious of the prevailing status quo, the old customs of the Alto Minho: "to own land is everything here," he says. "If you do not own land, even a small *horta*, a vegetable garden, and have no family of your own, you do not exist. Like me, I have no home of my own, no permanent job, no wife, family or car, and certainly not a plot of land. So who am I? I am nothing," he says, echoing Pessoa again.

I make my way from the well-lit room at the front to a dark rear hallway, which has doors opening to four even darker rooms, windowless and replete with lifeless objects. When I shine a torch into one of the rooms, a cat jumps at me, its hair on end, hissing like a tiger. I recoil quickly, stumbling on a folding chair and coming face to face with a vintage round mirror. The rooms are full of mirrors, square and elliptical, frameless or ornate. I remember that Pessoa hated mirrors and always turned his back on them, refusing to look at his reflection.

The shop stocks Portuguese poetry books, amateur and religious paintings and many figurines of saints collected from the houses of old ladies. One cupboard is full of bankrupt business files. As I grab the corner of an old window frame to look at it more closely I suddenly hear what sounds like an air raid siren outside, but when I instinctively put it down and rush anxiously into the street, no one seems to be crouching down or looking for cover.

"That's the fire station alarm to announce the burning of vegetation before the rains," Zé Paolo reassures me. "Soon, there will be heavy rains." He is around forty, his face adorned with a salt-and-pepper beard. His nose is prominent but not imposing, and his eyes are warm and bemused as if he is about to laugh, or burst into tears. His coat is worn. I go with him to the apartment above the store, followed by his three cats in convoy: little Minnie, Amarelo, a large yellow tomcat, and fierce Dona, who scared me earlier.

The stairs are also full of things, as are the narrow corridor and rooms, where a ceiling relief is crumbling from the salty, damp ocean breeze. Here and there, iron scaffolding supports the edges of the ceiling. In one room, a cloudy glass ceiling stares down at an unmade bed. The house that withstood the hurricane which destroyed Caminha homes in the 1970s is slowly collapsing under the pressures of time that wreak havoc on everything.

After this initial meeting, I often return to visit Zé Paolo. I make friends with him and dig around the shop. He hates the notion of property yet accumulates objects, lives apart from his wife and daughter, and rarely sees them. It is as if he has forcibly disconnected himself from everything suggested by the term family: new possessions, status, ambition, progress and at times violence, rage and quarrels. Perhaps it is anxiety left over from childhood when he witnessed his home fall apart.

He shows me where his grandmother kept rabbits and the nesting places of the birds of his grandfather, an avid breeder of carrier pigeons for competitions. In the last room down the hall, he restores wooden furniture, exterminates woodworm and makes bird nesting boxes. Occasionally, like Marco Silva, Zé Paolo is invited to abandoned houses to rake up their entire contents like a whale swallowing plankton: valuables and rubbish alike. When I set sights on a mirror or some other object, he has difficulty deciding on the price. "Take it," he says, refusing my offer of payment or coyly asking for a paltry sum.

Paolo is one of those people you meet for the first time as if you have pulled on a magic string. I walk down his street, calling out, "Zé Paolo!", and his head pops up from the tiny first-floor balcony inviting me up; or I walk in on my own when the shop door is open. Sometimes he falls in love with a new purchase, and it finds its way upstairs into his apartment. It stays by his side for a while, like his women who come and go - thus evading romantic complications. He quotes the Austrian architect Adolf Loos who said that "memories are like a coffin. They will bury you with them."

And yet he chooses to accumulate things and memories and live among them, surrounded by a group of friends I come to know. Such is his neighbour, a fisherman's widow who lost her husband many years ago to the ocean. Or Isolina, whose father was the first Portuguese cartographer to take aerial photographs of the country and helped draw the first modern maps eighty years ago. Or his neighbour Cláudio who grew up with his grandmother next to Zé and his grandmother. He is a computer technician who loves to sleep and laugh. He likes to recount the story of Portugal's failed military exploits in World War I. And there is João Manuel da Silva Santos, a dealer in ancient Chinese artefacts and cousin to Zé. His shop is full of marvellous terracotta statues of 2,000-year-old soldiers, Ming dynasty rabbits and cavalry, which my heart desires but cannot afford.

The town of Caminha where Zé Paolo was born and lives is an old-fashioned treasure trove. Located by the Minho estuary, it was a destination for the rich of Porto for many years. Initially established as a spa resort due to its location between two rivers flowing into the sea, its waters are full of healing iodine. It could be the beginning or the end of the world. In 1890 a railway line was built to bring in English holidaymakers. Then everything went downhill. But traces of beauty can still be seen in the old streets, ceramic tiles and the beautiful fountain square.

A French friend passing through Carminha after a voyage to Colombia told me it resembles the legendary Cartagena de Indias, with its ancient houses and stone walls at the edge of the ocean. But the Colombian double is immense, wild and much more festive than its quiet Portuguese counterpart.

Below the old town citadel is a tunnel dug by Brazilians 130 years ago for local trains. They still pass with a deafening roar that shakes the ground. Paolo has another storage space near the tunnel opening close to the house of his mother, in whose forlorn yard fragrant daffodils grow. I locate and purchase a copper bell that sounds like a church chime for the house gate.

35

IN LATE OCTOBER, FRANKLIN FINALLY sends his workers to detach, disassemble and remove the roof. I receive this news on the other side of the English Channel as I sit in an old Oxford library, looking for books on Portugal. My phone vibrates to indicate a message from Gilberto. Initial photos depict three men standing on the roof of the house dismantling the slates. The image is as blurry as the one of the first man on the moon. They pass the tiles from one to another and pile them up in the yard. In another photo, a man stands on scaffolding smashing the chimney.

"The rain held back," writes Gilberto. "Just when you left, Franklin and his men arrived." Then another message arrives at Oxford Ground Control: "The roof has been removed." After the excruciating wait, phase one is complete.

After visiting the Oxford library, I return to Tel Aviv. I have some lingering obligations from the previous chapter of my life. A major organ that had been part of my body for thirty-five years - journalism - has been removed, and I am undergoing replacement surgery for my heart and my professional identity.

At Candemil, the workers use a small generator for power and lighting. They proceed to knock down walls, replace the water system and put in sewage pipes. For a while, only the lower wooden joists remain, like the illusion of a roof. By phone Gilberto consults me over different matters.

Gilberto photographs what is left of the upper wooden skeleton. From the top, it looks like an artist's impression of a cityscape: an image of towers and streets shaped by truncated planks rising from a wooden surface. After that, the builders demolish the lower ceiling and the adjoining bathroom where Marília washed in the sink. Doors are left without a wall -

windows without a ceiling. The builders smash everything with sledgehammers, dragging pieces of history into the yard.

By the time I return to Candemil, some of Senhor Franco's aura has already dispersed. The house is a naked skeleton: granite and concrete walls with an old wooden floor. The open rooms share a light blue ceiling. The soft Alto Minho autumn light touches everything that was hidden before, peeping into every dusty corner. Even what was once the kitchen is now a shapeless mess. Had the estate agent shown us the house for the first time in its present state, we would probably have been completely put off by this dismal ruin. A mountain of gnawed, sawn wood full of old nails lies in a heap in the yard.

We propose to install antique and ornate front doors and an old round window above the kitchen. Gilberto says: "You won't find old wooden windows or doors here. Anything from churches, old houses and palaces is thrown away unless picked up by aficionados. These days people install double-glazed aluminium windows." He recommends we use aluminium.

Perplexed, I recall treasures glimpsed during my wanderings and incursions into abandoned houses. I have found doors, lintels and windows of master craftsmanship lying about and have visited empty mansions where light penetrates through old but still functional shutters. I have revelled in the splendour of those wooden creations made by highly skilled and knowledgeable artisan carpenters. Inspirational baroque beauty can often be found rotting on floors. That all this is smashed and discarded when renovations begin is, to say the least, puzzling. A quick web search reveals, for instance, that similar items are valued and coveted in France, where every old window or embossment is considered a work of art.

The cement support for the roof has not yet been laid. I explain to Gilberto which water fountain we wish to install in the yard. We have seen similar fountains in Granada, where water emerges from an opening slowly flowing over a round rock. "What you describe are water cooling systems for patios which use fountains and channels," he says, deeply appreciative of the ancient design. "They came with the Moorish invaders from Africa to Andalucia, where summer temperatures rise to 45 degrees." He describes shaded areas designed to counter the heat, where the cooling systems create a natural air conditioning effect. In my mind's eye, I can see a water fountain gurgling where the debris from the old house now lies.

"When the rains begin, you will have your roof to protect the walls," the assiduous Senhor Franklin assures us.

Gilberto glances at the notebook, which lists the work in detail. Next up are the animal pens that need new windows and floors. Builders will use high-pressure hoses to clear soot, smoke and animal remains from the dark walls. A dilapidated stone wall, which divided the space into two rooms, will be removed stone by stone and piled up outside.

The ground floor of the roofless house is a dark space with granite stone walls and three narrow air slits. In the past, human excrement also poured down here. As the pig grunted in its tiny cell, sheep and goats would crowd next to the cow to keep warm during cold nights. The heat rose through the wood floor into the house, and with it lowing, lambs bleating for their mothers, and finally the screams of slaughter, the smell of blood, and a general stench of decay.

Neighbours recall that Senhor Franco, his father and his grandfather before him, dealt in livestock. When he died, the farm was reduced to two cows, a few chickens and some rabbits. The lives of animals leave no traces and are never recorded. They are born, fed, give birth, are slaughtered and eaten, smoked or salted. Only the neighbour Manoel Joaquim remembers the names of the two cows and commends them for being industrious creatures who produced many litres of good milk.

36

ONCE I RETURN TO CANDEMIL, builders seem to vanish like fairytale elves who only work when no one is around, as in the poem "Gnomes of the Night" by Hayyim Nahman Bialik:

> Hurry, gnomes, for the morn is approaching!
> The rooster soon summons the dawn.
> How quickly the gnome-troop arises,
> By sevens arrayed for their flight;
> And sadly they march and in silence,
> Returning - ascending the height.
> And when the moon, shamed, hides its pallor,
> And wraps its pale face drained of light,
> The gnomes march away to the shadows
> And melt like a dream of the night.[*]

Now that work has begun, I find an intoxicating sense of freedom and faith in the metamorphosis of the house. I often go on walks alone, get lost without a map or Google's help on narrow roads which branch into villages like Covas, Sopo and Campos. Car tyres rattle on the old asphalt and cobblestone streets like ancient wagon wheels. The forgotten glory of the past unfolds before me in all its worn-out beauty.

Visiting abandoned estates and country residences, I realize that deterioration always begins from the top down. The roof is the crown of the house, its head, its hat, its helmet. Destruction begins when tiles break because of fallen branches or stones

---

[*]   https://opensiddur.org/prayers/solilunar/everyday/nighttime/ bedtime-shema/gnomes-of-the-night-by-hayyim-nahman-bialik- ca-1894/

thrown by kids. Rainwater discovers gaps, penetrates and eats at the beams, slowly and patiently. Over time, the rot spreads through the house, from top to bottom.

Whatever the water does not damage, the woodworm devour. In no other country have I seen an army of worms so efficient. I can identify their signs, the light dust mounds left on every aged piece of furniture I see or purchase. They are the loyal tenants who never left, heirs to those who did, with a secret hold over all properties. They are the true, private owners of the land, who slowly and diligently chew at the wealth, consuming every wooden ornament. Often only a staircase remains intact; sometimes only the metalwork.

"At such different stages in our lives, we're undergoing separation anxiety and displacement," Orit writes to me from Tel Aviv. "The process is not without pain. Belonging to two homelands is hard on the spirit, at least for monogamous souls such as ours." She quotes the poet Lea Goldberg who, having emigrated from Russia to Palestine, knew the pain of displacement: "Perhaps only migrating birds know - suspended between earth and sky - the heartache of two homelands."

Fragments of my old life often appear in my dreams. I wake up in a daze in the mornings as if I have barely escaped some disaster and have been rescued. They are dreams of being uprooted. Like a baby breaking new teeth, I am growing a homeland or roots. I tell Orit that mixed in with the joy of finding a new and treasured place is a sense of loneliness that lasts sometimes for entire days. There is a deep, poignant sense of independence, alongside solitude and *saudade*.

Orit says it must be the language barrier. Language is also a home, a house made of words. One acquires a language from birth, inhabiting it like a warm coat, a comfortable apartment. It touches me personally as the son of a Hebrew teacher and as an author. At Candemil, I live with a foreign language, surrounded by words I do not understand. I get by in technical matters, but when it comes to meaningful conversation, my Portuguese invariably disappoints. Any radio programme, café chat, joke, laughter or baby talk are still impenetrable.

Faced with inscrutable conversation, one gets a sense of being invisible. Not understanding a word, I am not burdened with responsibility nor am I obliged to participate. It is a feeling of omnipotence, and there is also magic in that. A Czech writer who left for Paris after the Russian invasion once spoke of her liberating exile, of not being imprisoned by language.

I drive while listening to a local radio station, Rádio Cultural de Cerveira, broadcasting from a small building near the school. I do not understand a word, but the presenter, Diamantino, has a rich, slightly bemused voice, hoarse like a heavy smoker. Despite the language gap, I pick up on his mindset. I imagine a large man of about fifty on the microphone, who enjoys occasional vulgarities, which are old-fashioned, non-PC and provocative. The broadcaster brightens the road for me; he picks up the Portuguese songs, swinging them once in the air before sending them on their way to fly over rivers, roads and hills. With that husky voice, he is the Tom Waits of Radio Cerveira. Yes.

37

AT THE HEART OF A small square in the old part of Vila Nova de Cerveira stands a monument for some forgotten war surrounded by magnificent magnolia trees. Around the square are several dozen vacant yet expectant chairs belonging to nearby cafés. Like their owners, they are patiently awaiting August when the square should fill up with people.

When Gilberto opens his little black notebook, I notice pencil drawings of family members, our house, unanchored bookshelves, elaborate windows and more. He points to a green house at the end of the square. The Casa Verde, described in one book as "a nineteenth-century residence", is a two-storey building, spacious like a small palace or mansion whose façades are lined with greenish tiles. A regal crest hangs on the summit of its locked gates. The house dominates the heart of the town like the deserted home of a mysterious patriarch. No one has seen lights in its windows for years. "A Brazilian palace," Gilberto calls it. "Many emigrated to Brazil in the nineteenth century, following the Napoleonic invasion. After amassing fortunes, they returned to set up flashy dream houses, surrounded by exotic gardens of tropical flowers and Brazilian palms."

The grounds behind the house contain palm trees, a fountain and the remains of magnificent plants. "Years ago, they were considered bizarre, tasteless houses, extravagant and nouveau riche. But time has revaluated them, and now they are branded national treasures and heritage sites." Even Gilberto, who practically lives across the road, has never seen the interior of the house and does not know its history. Who were the last tenants? Why did they disappear?

Time is on our hands, thanks to Franklin, who finished removing the roof but never returned to lay the cement, and the other hard-to-pin-down workers. There is now time for good conversation. Our architect loves to delve into historical discussions of the great inventions of revered Roman builders. Such were the architects who, following Greek traditions, built bridges with underwater foundations from a material they learned to extract from volcanic lava. They noticed that this lava when solidified in seawater was durable. He speaks of books on Roman architecture found in a monastery in Switzerland that mention materials still in use today. Such are the green tiles of the Brazilian palace; the bright solid material which highlights the dazzling beauty of the emerald tiles was created in the late nineteenth century.

I wonder if similar building delays to those afflicting us existed in the old world; setbacks are, after all, human. Robert Harris' book about the destruction of Pompeii is filled with the hardships, corruption and negligence preceding the volcanic disaster which engulfed the city.

Gilberto admires the Swiss architect Peter Zumthor and his modest and simple designs. Zumthor is an artist who works on a few select projects, making precise use of materials, adhering to simplicity and environmental conditions. He quotes architecture critic Paul Goldberg, who reveres Zumthor as "the messenger of the gospel of the true".

The greatest feeling a building can confer, Zumthor has written, is of "a consciousness of time passing and an awareness of the human lives that have been acted out in these places. At these moments, architecture's aesthetic and practical values, stylistic and historical significance are of secondary importance. What matters now is only the feeling of deep melancholy. Architecture is exposed to life."

Gilberto mentions one of Zumthor's projects: the thermal baths in Vals, Switzerland, a grey rock-like structure carved into the mountain, "as if it had always been there. Both artificial and natural, the baths seem to rise from the ground, like the black monolith in the film *2001: A Space Odyssey*." Gilberto, especially frustrated during this tedious phase of no-show builders, says that Zumthor "never compromises, only takes on what he wants".

He recalls how he once designed a comfortable, honest house suitable for its surroundings. It was for the mother of a Portuguese friend. The mother sold the plot with his plans to a German couple who requested so many changes that he grew sick of the project. But when he wanted to resign, the couple pre-empted him by expressing their immense satisfaction with the project. "For people to be comfortable and happy in a house, is to comply with a central principle in architecture. But I will never show you that house," he laughs softly. Everything about him is quiet and restrained. His eldest son is the same. This polite boy accompanies him everywhere, wearing a white safety helmet as if he were already a practising engineer.

We part, and I leave the square up an alley to look for a barbershop. My hair is growing wild, and I contemplate cheating on my Tel Aviv barber. On the right side of the street, I notice a hair salon called Big Zao. It has only one chair, so there is clearly no Small Zao. Big is a clean-shaven man with a Lenin-style beard and the leather apron of a butcher. He gestures for me to sit in the solitary chair and busies himself for a while, silently snipping at my white hair. The walls are red-brick like an Irish pub; the ambience is small-town America, and in the background Radio Cerveira plays. An old man with time on his hands sits around, not waiting for a haircut. He has come to talk, but Big Zao only nods his head, listening carefully and clicking his scissors near my ears. Here in the land of talkative folk, I have never met a hairdresser, or any man for that matter, as silent as Big Zao.

Conversations with Horses

"That majestic and sweet falling asleep of things. The blackening of the hills and groves, the light couples melting into the shade, a dormant bell ringing through the ravines, the whispering of the waters among the low grasses - they were for me like initiations."

Eça de Queirós, "Civilization"

38

A **SILHOUETTE OF DENSE TREES HIDES** a low wooden house. Occasional rays of light filter through the treetops, igniting its windows. As Zadok and I make our way down the steep path, a bare-chested man approaches us with an axe in his hand. Augusto Canedo - for that is who he is - has the look of an angry Viking prepared to defend his home. He is an actor, artist and teacher with the soul of a Robinson Crusoe and the physique of a lumberjack. Some of his previous work includes installations of Madonnas and other provocative representations of rural rituals of worship.

His estate contains stables, orchards, beehives, an ornamental pond and a vegetable garden, all of his making. It stretches beside a vast forest-kingdom of studios, warehouses and residential buildings belonging to his dear neighbour Henrique Silva.

The Henrique empire spans over forty years, since the first biennale when he discovered the wooded area of Gondar and established himself here. Then Margarida came into his life, followed by the younger Canedo, his daughter from a previous relationship and Teresa, Canedo's partner. Also across the road is Zadok Ben David.

Canedo is wearing a light shirt over his muscular torso as he gives us a tour of the property. He introduced tadpoles into his small pond to hear the wonderful cacophony of frogs' mating calls at night, and in the mornings, enjoys listening to the birdsong. "I have been the world over and never have I heard birds as in Gondar," he remarks as three horses trot towards us in a leisurely fashion. Their stable looks like a mountain lodge and was built next to a muddy pond where five ducks wade.

Canedo teaches in Porto four days a week, and the rest of the time works at perfecting his extraordinary farm. While sipping on *vinho verde* in the stable yard, we chat as the horses stand among us, forming part of the group and lowering their big heads as if to listen in. They stare at us with friendly eyes, sniffing at the wine goblets and rubbing against us as if they had called this fortuitous meeting. I have never felt such tangible proximity to nature, as if the human family has expanded to include animals like horses.

"The light grey mare is Wanda," says one of the riders, Canedo's daughter, introducing her protégés. Silver, the grey, is seven years old, and Cigana, meaning gipsy, is a chestnut colour and youngest of the trio. They stay with us peacefully until Canedo locks the gate behind us. Their big eyes are full of emotion in parting as if to say, "why are you leaving us with these silly ducks?"

As night falls, we make our slow return through the vegetable plot, and Canedo invites us to stay for dinner. I sink into an old sofa in the yard, recalling the words of author Eça de Queirós in his story "Civilization". Jacinto, a rich, urban, depraved heir arrives at his neglected country estate. Still under the spell of the city, his heart is nevertheless already beginning to note the charms of village life. On his first evening, he watches from a window alcove at dusk, noting "that majestic and sweet falling asleep of things. The blackening of the hills and groves, the light couples melting into the shade, a dormant bell ringing through the ravines, the whispering of the waters among the low grasses - they were for me like initiations."

Like Jacinto, I only wish to sit quietly on the red sofa in front of the slowly darkening grove, with a choir of sleepy birds and croaking restless frogs in the background. I enjoy our slowly rolling Portuguese, English and French conversation, mingled with *vinho verde*, the distant barking of dogs and a solitary cat brushing against us. The seventeen-year-old daughter tires of the adult conversation and escapes for an evening gallop on Cigana. Its hooves clatter on the pavement as we walk the distance back to the house, the song of water in the background. From a distance, we hear the neighing of the horses and the buzzing of a lost bee.

This entire region is covered with waterways visible and invisible: dripping, pouring, gurgling. They form a network of canals, pipes and aqueducts that carry mountain spring water to fields and plots, like the vascular system of the Earth's body. Near my property is a stone reservoir where giant white waterlilies grow like funnels. I come from a land where water is scarce and must be used sparingly. Drought constitutes a real threat, and there are monitoring systems in place to ensure water is not wasted. The idea of digging a well in one's backyard or independently redirecting a channel to water a plot is alien to me.

"It flows with virgin spring water, which everyone loves," says Gilberto of the public fountain near Casa Marília, pointing to another advantage of our house. The fountain, shaped like a cone on a flat stone base, was built in 1921, the year of Albano Dantas' birth. Mountain bikers stop to enjoy the water. Henrique and Margarida like to fill up containers because they are suspicious of their own well due to its proximity to the septic tank. The idea of immediacy between drinker and urinal, ripeness and decomposition, food and digestion, forms part of the local culture.

Even fifty-year-old seeds thrown in the garden and mixed with old animal excrement from the pens germinate in the muck through sunlight. It seems that we are not only buying a house, but also the lives of previous generations. This is what most appealed to my heart about this house on a hill.

In my country, hills are often the archaeological sites of towns or of ruined temples buried after wars or fires. Here too, in the Alto Minho, where there has been a continuum of life without periods of destruction or prolonged absences, were I to dig under our house, I would find another house, and under it yet another. House upon house and only the upper one sees the light, glimpsing the world.

"To buy (a house) is to choose where the future will take place," writes Frances Mayes in her book, *Under the Tuscan Sun*. And I would add, it is buying a share of the past. I visit the roofless house, go down into the cellar and fall in love again with the old weaving workshop. It is a simple structure that appeals to all who see it because of its authenticity and the breeze flowing through its two windows on warm days.

My set of keys includes a large, rusty key for the heavy wooden door of the cellar. It is so heavy that I leave it under the step. I return to the house daily, still amazed that I own a house in a place so unknown to me a few months ago. Not a property, a home. When I am thirsty, there is water; when I am hot, the breeze cools me. Intoxicating smells are everywhere: the yard, the house, the forests and the fields.

In the evening, on the way to Gondar, a flock of sheep appears on the narrow road, accompanied by a black and white sheepdog and a shepherd with a crook. She mounts a Vespa and smiles at me as I stop the vehicle to let the flock pass. The sheep surround the red Fiat 500, rubbing against it like big bath sponges, and when they disappear, a trail of dung pellets remains on the road, a rite of passage between pasture and pen.

39

THE NAME OXFORD COMES FROM the place where oxen could cross the Thames and is reminiscent of the old way of life that existed in that part of the English countryside. To this day, narrow waterways and canals continue to be used for recreational, if not economic, purposes, and the landscape is rich with ancient estates, mansions and churches with their graveyards.

At the 150-year-old Blackwell's bookshop, which has several floors and contains tens of thousands of titles, I find an entire section on the Iberian Peninsula. Most of the books are on Spain, especially the civil war, which fascinated Europe as a precursor to World War II. Portugal is a mere footnote to the peninsula, half a shelf.

Even in the travel book section, the bookseller mutters to himself, as if trying to recall: "Portugal, Portugal..." He comes up with a handful of books, a tiny number compared to the stacks that fill the shelves on Italy and other Latin countries. "Here is *Wild Guide Portugal*, a guide to its rural areas," he says waving a tourist picture book. Next to the history section, I delve into *The Portuguese* by Barry Hatton, a journalist and colleague who has worked and lived in Portugal for years.

Hatton laments the absence of Portugal from world media reports: "Wider recognition is owed to its fascinating history, which includes the first steps towards globalization; and a spell as the world's richest nation; its climate which is as agreeable as the gentle and hospitable Portuguese people; a captivating variety of countryside within a relatively small space; and food that is so good that overeating is always a temptation."

According to Hatton, it is difficult for a foreigner to penetrate social circles or to glimpse authentic Portuguese life.

He refers to the country where he has spent many happy years as "the enigmatic corner of Europe". "My Portuguese colleagues have expressed their astonishment at my refusal of job offers in New York, London, Brussels and Madrid. They think I am mad." Hatton is among many intrigued by Portugal 500 years after its great ventures. The mystery lies in that a tiny Mediterranean country on the edge of the Atlantic produced great explorers who made significant discoveries despite meagre resources. Also puzzling is the disparity between its great past and the land it has become today, a remote European province.

Hatton describes with affection a diligent, warm and compassionate people, supportive and helpful. He notes great differences between the country's regions that render them almost separate entities. He distinguishes between a progressive "red" south and a more conservative and religious "blue" north. Exemplifying this difference are Porto and Lisbon. Comfortably sinking into my English armchair, I am struck by his words in spite of my relatively short acquaintance with the country.

Portugal views itself as irrelevant, says Hatton, but the Portuguese accept modern hardships with stoic serenity due to its history. Dire times do not rattle them. It is precisely due to stagnation that the beautiful variety of natural life has been kept almost intact. Rural areas, such as the Alto Minho and other regions, have preserved their agricultural nature, unchanged until the second half of the twentieth century.

Across the road, in the Bodleian Library, one of the oldest in the world, I read a copy of a memoir by Helen Cameron Gordon, an English woman who often documented her travels around the world. With the skill of a great travel writer, she describes how in 1932 she sailed to the country of the young Salazar, hoping to encounter warm weather in one of the least known countries in Europe. Departing from the port of Liverpool on a cold, rainy June day, she arrived five days later at Porto and came across a rare spell of frost, the first in forty years; "but that always happens to me". Gordon stayed in a British guest house, had five o'clock teas, and rode in the trams that had replaced horses and carriages.

She describes iron bridges and an aqueduct of 999 stone arches. She visited a secret stone chamber where nuns would find shelter during dangerous times, entering through a rock that only they knew how to move aside. Staying in Póvoa de Varzim, she found a charming fishing village fast becoming a fashionable holiday resort with hotels and a casino. She remained in Portugal until November, repeatedly wondering about the weather. She was promised a pleasant November, and yet it was cold, wet and miserable like in London. Upon her return, she did not recommend Portugal to her English friends.

40

Eɪɢʜᴛʏ-ꜰɪᴠᴇ ʏᴇᴀʀs ᴀꜰᴛᴇʀ Hᴇʟᴇɴ Gᴏʀᴅᴏɴ experienced her unusually chilly journey, November skies are clear. The Alto Minho air is cool and dry, and the concrete roof foundation laid by Franklin when I was in Oxford is drying. It is a thirty-five-centimetre thick strip made of an iron skeleton and concrete, enclosing the house like a thorny grey garland. It rests on top of the solid stone walls. It also serves to fortify the rear wall, which proved not to be made of granite like the rest of the house, but of two charred brick walls with a space between them.

This strange discovery clarified the origin of the pile of stones to the back of the house. They constituted the original granite wall. Until 1951, no records of the house exist in the municipal archives - an employee could only locate two documents from the first half of the 1980s. One is a request to decorate the place, and the other is an application to restore a collapsed roof. The applicant is one "Marília Franco. Single. A Housewife." Neighbours confirm that there was a major storm, walls collapsed, and roofs blew away. Several villagers were killed.

At the time, Marília had been living on her own in the house for four years. Did she wake one stormy night to terrifying creaking sounds as the wind and water shook the ancient foundations? Or did the strong wind tear off parts of the roof and the rafters causing the wall to collapse? In any case, it must have been a night of terror for the solitary villager. The granite wall with its large stones was never rebuilt. A cheaper double brick wall was erected in its place, and the date of its construction, 1984, stamped in the concrete at its base, where two stairs made it easier for Marília to go down to the courtyard. The roof was later repaired, and the wall whitewashed. The pile of stones has since remained behind the house.

The concrete strip now crowns the walls, drying out and waiting for carpenters to lay the roof. The team of carpenters has as its patron the veteran eighty-year-old master craftsman who handles all negotiations on their behalf. On the ground, work is managed by his right-hand man and second-in-command, Jorge. Jorge said he would arrive sometime in November "for sure", and then on the tenth of the month, "absolutely for sure". He then became "unsure" regarding the fourteenth. His words are uncertain as if time itself is shaky and his promises are as hollow as the brick wall.

Yet autumn perseveres in a miraculous spell of good weather protecting the roofless house. A flexible sense of time is the other face of the relaxed Portuguese personality, but for me, as someone who comes from a fast-paced country where everyone strives for instant gratification, the roof becomes an obsession. Gilberto is delaying the issuing of his Iranian visa to be present when the man from the electricity company comes to connect the new meter and zap energy back into the house.

"Once they reconnect the electricity, everything will go much faster," Gilberto reassures me as if revealing the cause of the setbacks at last. "It is impossible to work without electricity." But the old counter lies in its wooden box, and the utility man does not show up to connect it. Everyone is so polite that I dare not raise my voice. I wonder if they, too, lose patience sometimes and go berserk. Do they relay their rage to strangers or bottle it up until they become sick? Maybe this is the cause of the intense back pains plaguing Gilberto on occasion and forcing him to rest.

I am irate and yet surrender to the promises and the illusion. It is human nature, after all. Builders make promises with a pleasant smile: this week they will come for sure, or on Wednesday at the latest, just not today, not right now, sometime soon.

What is more seductive than hope? I recall my immigrant parents, who were nice, decent, polite, considerate and clean. But my father used to say: a man must keep his word, and he always kept his. That is something I miss here sometimes.

41

In the morning, fog cascades from the hills onto the house, turning it into a nest of clouds. I stare anxiously at the exposed walls waiting for the floodwater, then leave, escaping the alarming prospect. I pass by the church. Someone has posted a death notice for an old lady from Candemil.

From a side window in the low building next to the church, I see an elderly sacristan in a grey sweater throwing an emerald green robe over the shoulders of the priest. A song of prayer rises from the building. I push open a side door to find myself among a dozen or so old worshippers. In the front row, three men stand before the green priest conducting a ceremony that seems to me, the outsider, like a series of conjuror's tricks. The *padre*'s hands are never idle. He swings and lands a shiny silver goblet; grabbing a white napkin, he covers it and picks it up again. I wait for a pigeon or rabbit to come out of the magical cup, but he pours water and drinks wine. Wiping his hands, he raises them to the magnificent wooden ceiling and swings a white disc to the sound of a vibrating bell, blessing the small congregation and bowing as he walks.

With his flowing movements and wide robes, he appears to turn like a mechanical doll on a greased axis. The worshippers reciprocate the complicated dance by standing up or sitting down on cue. They kneel before approaching the altar, mumble as they cross themselves: amen, amen, amen. I suddenly recognize the submissive figure of Maria, the wife of Manoel. When the ceremony is over, I wave, but she seems to turn pale as if seeing a ghost in her Holy of Holies. What is the *Israelita* doing at the funeral? Everyone disperses, the priest disappears into his office, and Maria attempts to avoid me, but I corner her, asking after her husband.

125

"*Le cœur, le cœur,*" she holds her hands to her chest to illustrate. "He is done for. He is wounded," she says of the man who once seemed so robust to me. I ask if I can come to visit them at their house up the hill and talk about the old days, but she says, "We're running from one hospital to the next getting tests. We do not have a minute." She disappears and I drive away past figures wrapped in coats by the side of the road. In the fog, everything disappears as if it has never existed.

Pedro, my translator, is immersed in his studies, so Gilberto finds another English-speaking student, Valter, to help me with interviews. He is a young man from Caminha who studies art in Cerveira and works in France during his vacations. I tell him about Marília and my findings so far. Valter says that his mother was likewise born to an unknown father from an illicit affair between a rich man from a shipping company and an office worker, his grandmother. She was not acknowledged by her father either. Only when her father's brother returned from an extended stay in the colony of Angola, where his rigid views were softened, did he discover that his brother had a *bastarda* daughter. He pressured the brother until he acknowledged his daughter. This story repeats itself in different variations casting light onto Portugal's Catholic past with its power dynamics, forbidden sex, secrets, hypocrisy and illegitimate children.

During spring break, Valter becomes my trusted guide to modern Portugal. Being an only child, he is disciplined and works during his vacations as a maintenance worker at Charles de Gaulle airport in Paris, working alongside other immigrants and "feeling free and happy".

"The Portuguese enjoy showing off," he says as I point out to him the gleaming marble tombstones, "perhaps a result of the economic crisis. Anyone who has any money immediately spends it on fancy tombstones, nice houses or fast cars, anything extravagant."

We drive together to the house of the green-robed clergyman, parish priest for Gondar, Candemil and Covas. He lives in Covas, the best kept and most English of the three villages. It is also where Valter's father grew up in relative poverty with ten other siblings. "Times were very different before the English, Dutch, and other expats came to live here ... of all family members, only one sister still lives in Covas," he says.

A woman leaves the church carrying a bouquet of blue flowers. She says that the name of the priest is Carlos Brito and points us to his house. But no one answers the door, and we cannot find him anywhere else in the village. We try the café past the bridge. A 1955 photograph of an accordion player hangs on the wall next to an aerial shot of the place. "Everyone around here has an aerial photo of their property," Valter laughs. "As if it's proof of ownership. Everything changes here, and yet everything remains the same. Suspicion and caution have run in our blood since the days of the dictatorship. The parents always tell us to be careful, not to do this or that, as if Salazar were still alive."

During the 1974 Carnation Revolution, his mother was sixteen and lived in Caminha. There was no television, and news of the revolution over the radio was fragmented. Locals remained undisturbed by current affairs, which only seemed to affect the big cities. His mother never missed a day of work during the time, and his father was almost deaf, "so he probably never even heard about it." Sometimes Valter himself seems amazed by events that took place here only fifty years ago, as if he were talking about the Ice Age.

A woman sweeping the courtyard by the church hands us the number of *Padre* Carlos. Valter rings, and I hear him explain to the man on the other end of the line that he is an interpreter for an author writing about the area. "The word *escritor* carries weight around here," he whispers to me as he waits for the priest to give his answer.

Father Carlos agrees and notes down the names of Franco and Marília. He promises to search the church archives where all the information about births, marriages and burials is kept. "He is very kind," Valter tells me, "he has invited us to the Candemil church tomorrow."

At five forty-five the following evening, the service ends and by six o'clock the building is already dark. Warm light pours into the plaza from the church office. A short man with hair as dark as his leather jacket turns on the alarm system. He then turns off most of the lights one by one. This is *Padre* Carlos, whom I have seen perform the magic rituals. Without his church garb he looks like a stocky mechanic. His manner is pleasant and genuine.

He has brought an old book with him from the church archives with a sticker on its cover. It is a book listing the dead since 1952. Here he has located death certificates for Senhor Franco and Marília. He was the priest who performed the last rites on Marília and knew her well during her later years. We stand in his office next to a tall wooden dresser staring at the paperwork for a long time.

Father Carlos arrived at Alto Minho and the surrounding villages in 2000 when he was twenty-five. It was his first posting. "She was a short woman, like everyone else around here," he smiles, "and very devout, always made donations to the church. She lived next to a woman named Maria who took care of her. Maria should know more about her. As a rule, the church does not divulge personal information." He points to a small official paper with a handwritten death notice dated January 2016, age ninety.

Yes, he was by her bedside for the last rites, the commendation of the dying which allows the soul to be cleansed of its sins and enter the next world. He heard the dying confession of the deceased, dipped his fingers in the fragrant oil and anointed crosses on her eyes, ears, mouth, hands and feet. According to the certificate, her soul left her body at ten in the morning.

The book records that she was baptized in 1925 as Marília Emília Barbosa after her mother. "Her father was not married to her mother," I tell him. "Let us discuss that later," he replies caressing the cover of the thick book. Marília passed away "single, childless", says the text. Her father was João Albertino Pires after his mother and Franco after his father. "As for her father," continues *Padre* Carlos opening the book of deaths in 1967, "I found him here. Church archives are not arranged according to names but by dates." No search engine. No Google of the dead. João Franco died aged eighty-five. Under family is written: "Single, Profession: Farmer" and "landowner".

He died at home, at six in the morning, a clear, crisp hour that usually saw him awake and active. The parish priest who served at the time came to prepare him for his last sacraments. "Who was he?" I ask. "It is written here that *Padre* António Cunha Ponte was by his side. He too must have died a long time ago." He was followed by four priests who served before Father Carlos.

"How and when did Marília and her mother receive his surname?" I ask. "Difficult to know," says the priest. "I will look for the birth registry from 1925. But it may be indecipherable due to humidity and other damage caused by time. Not everything is well preserved."

"I was told he had four children out of wedlock," I challenge him.

The priest clings to his book as if for salvation. He hesitates. We are treading on dangerous ground for the Church and its laws. "It is hard to know for sure," he says, "Franco was single until the day he died, so no marriage records exist. He died on 13 May 1967."

"Is it common around these parts for an eighty-five-year-old man to die single yet a father of four?" I ask.

He smiles: "A man can be a father without marrying a wife. During Franco's time, many fathers were not married."

"And Marília? What was she like?"

"Very devout and with a beautiful voice, she sang in the church choir," he replies.

"How did she pass her time?" I wonder.

"Like everyone else, in the fields. She worked hard but by the end was bedridden for several years. Sometimes," he recalls, "I would come to visit her when she couldn't walk any more but was still lucid. She talked a lot, had many stories." He smiles at the thought of the chatty woman.

Does he remember what the house looks like?

"Here," he grabs a sheet of paper and draws the interior of the house. "This was her room, where she was in bed at the end. He outlines two large rooms, a kitchen and a bathroom. One alcove belonged to Franco, and the other is where Marília lay at the end of the enclosed balcony. He traces a bed and a small window. "She loved to observe the village from up there, to feel like she was still part of it. She moved the bed so she could see the world."

"But the bed is low and the window high."

"She had an adjustable electric hospital bed so that her head was high enough to be seen even above the courtyard gate." His drawing is accurate.

"Did she come to confession while she could still walk?"

"Yes, absolutely." He is matter-of-fact, polite and seems to understand some English. Sometimes when I ask my questions, the priest is ready to reply even before he hears the translation. However, as befits his station, he takes time to mull questions over before answering.

"Do people still come to confession?"

"Yes. Every Sunday at two-thirty in the afternoon, people come in to confess," says *Padre* Carlos. "Each confession is allotted about half an hour. Three priests are present to receive members of the congregation. After mass, they go to the cemetery to pray for the ascension of the souls." I wonder if Marília ever lamented her fate to him. Did she speak of her father, her life circumstances, her loneliness?

"Some things are confidential," he says.

"Is there an old priest left who might remember her mother?" He considers the question, then tells Valter that one of the parish priests drowned in a river near Caminha when he had a heart attack, and another lives in a nursing home but is not cogent. And "there is also Father João who left the Church. I have no idea where he went."

He reiterates that "some things are best left between God and the faithful, the priest and the church. Not even a writer may hear them."

"Well, what does Portuguese law says about confessions from murderers, for instance? Do you have to report them to the police?"

"Neither report nor testify in court. It is between the believer and me. I can only suggest the person contact the police."

"And what if," I test him, "a little girl disappears in the village. And while everyone is looking for her, a man confesses to you that he has kidnapped the girl and is about to kill her?"

"Even then," says *Padre* Carlos, "all I can do is suggest that he turn himself in to the police and explain to him that if he does not do so, he will not be absolved. That is it. And I cannot tell you anything about the conversations I had with Marília, *escritor*, even the little I told you is too much." The tower bells ring seven times, a loud metallic sound as Carlos shuts the *Livro dos Óbitos*, the Book of the Dead. The three of us part with a handshake, and we drive away.

42

BY MID-NOVEMBER, DRY GRASS GROWING underneath trees becomes highly flammable. In cafés, locals are discussing a forest fire that razed an entire village in the south. A hundred and ten residents were killed by two massive fires in June and October; drivers were trapped inside cars. The café's TV screen flashes repeated images of charred houses, scorched water-fountains and riverbeds bare as dry bones. A displaced family say they had to leave behind all their possessions. This is the driest autumn Portugal has known since World War I, and also the most lethal. While an entire nation prays for rain, I form a one-man Resistance, secretly hoping that showers will hold off until carpenters install the missing roof beams, and Franklin lays down his tiles.

After that, let the deluge begin.

Even with the relaxed lifestyle I have adopted, I still get the occasional urge to break something: a carpenter's jaw, for instance. I lift my eyes to the skies where clouds are beginning to form and imagine the miraculous dry weather dissipating and the entire house flooded with water.

"Wood pre-dates us by millions of years and is therefore resistant to anything," Carlos reassures me. While driving through neighbouring Valença, I happened to glimpse a window display with pieces of wood and drawings of tile roofs. This is how I come to meet Carlos, an architect who speaks with an unparalleled passion for wooden houses and their material: "resistant even where concrete would crumble". "These days, everyone prefers aluminium because anything old-fashioned is considered repulsive: for locals, wood conjures up bitter memories of impoverished childhood homes. Also, aluminium is inhospitable to woodworm. Carlos is fifty and about to become a father for the first time.

"Given your penchant for all things wooden, be careful you don't end up with Pinocchio for a son," I say. He laughs for a moment before his face darkens. He points through the window at an adjoining reddish-wooden house left deserted. He is currently in a battle to save it from the grasp of greedy developers who have set their sights on it. The 150-year-old house was constructed as a temporary residence by a team of skilled builders put together by the engineer Gustav Eiffel. In 1860 the Frenchman was invited to design a steel bridge over the Minho River connecting Valença and the Spanish town of Tui, which stands to this day. It is one of several remarkable bridges designed by Eiffel at the time. A precursor to its better-known Parisian relative, it resembles a horizontal Eiffel Tower. Carlos agrees to try to find me a shop that sells old wooden doors and windows. Rumour has it there is one to be found across the border, somewhere in Spain.

Gilberto is also keen to stress to me wood's resistance to rainwater: he rings the carpenters incessantly, but "it's like calling an empty house". With nobody working on our house, I continue to arrange conversations with the locals, now without the aid of Valter, the student translator, who has returned to his studies. But goodwill eases the process of communication. I am in dire need of documentation for the house, I tell Gilberto. He explains that this would not present a problem if I had bought an old mansion. Registry existed only for the wealthy and educated who could read and write.

"Palaces appear in records; village dwellings do not. Almost no documents remain. Most villagers were illiterate, so verbal agreements were more common. Deep trust among people was indispensable for everyday life."

Gilberto speaks much of "trust" and "verbal agreements", of the confidence that locals have in each other. This is how it has been with him: not a single word of a written contract has been signed between us, yet everything proceeds better than it would with a hundred clauses and sub-clauses. For the Portuguese, suspicion is always something to be directed against the state rather than against each other.

43

I STOP IN A CLEARING BY the side of the road to Gondar and swing my arms in the air like wings, my eyes shut. I am hovering at low altitude above everything like I used to in my old flight dreams - and how I have missed them! In my youth, I could soar, stretching my arms and pushing my feet against the ground; I would let myself glide over the landscape. Now I have that feeling once again because I am writing and because I have found shelter. Rural Portugal is generous to the stranger, allowing one to simply be. It is not greedy, does not cheat, does not hurry, does not pry. She who has watched so many of her children leave, who has known scarcity and emigration, happily welcomes any newcomer as a small victory. The ghosts of its lost empire and orphaned children still haunt Portugal.

Sometimes loneliness settles on me, like traces of the famous *saudade*. The feeling resembles the phantom pains felt by amputees, a sense of absence and loss. *Saudade* can be collective: an intense longing for a shared past or a personal nostalgia for some private history. It is evident in the pain of parents who are forced to travel to foreign countries to support their families, leaving their children with relatives. *Saudade* lurks like a stowaway in abandoned buildings or even in the taste of some food.

It is in the *bacalhau*, which everyone eats. The dried and salted cod has been prepared in the same manner for hundreds of years, even today when food is usually processed or frozen. This, the most beloved of traditional dishes, is of a melancholy mindset. *Saudade* is also the forbidden longing for the colonial past, the African way of life which had to be abandoned. This specific type of *saudade* rears its head in a visit to the home of artists Margarida and Henrique Silva.

I sit in the kitchen of red-haired Margarida by the warm woodstove, with Canedo, Teresa, Zadok and Henrique, who at eighty-six and with half a lung is witty and dynamic. He always leaves the house in fabulous clothes, sometimes wearing a green coat over a light-coloured leather cape, like Mr Toad from *The Wind in the Willows*. Forever busy rolling one of his cigarettes, which consume his failing respiratory system, he inhales the smoke, coughs, laughs and continues to paint all night. In the evenings, he watches the news religiously as if expecting a new revolution.

When the jailed ghost of freedom broke out in 1974, Henrique was a charismatic young artist who together with other friends brought word of the new spirit to the edges of the disintegrating dictatorship. It was a wild initiative by painter Jaime Isidoro and his fellow artists José Rodrigues and Henrique. Together, in 1978 they established the first Vila Nova de Cerveira biennale. Even though the town is to many on the far side of the world, the biennale has since carried on.

As the last of the Three Musketeers still alive, Henrique Silva recalls how after forty years of Salazar, the town's streets were suddenly filled with an eruption of artists. With wild hair and beards, dozens of half-naked men and similarly hippyish women flocked to Cerveira from the cities. And how astonished the locals were by this whirlwind of the new era which hit them, stimulating unexpected appetites and lifting the boredom of puritanical tyranny. All the members of the founding trio, Rodrigues, Isidoro and Henrique, set up their homes around Cerveira and their disciples made pilgrimages to the small town.

Forty years later, Gilberto attempts to decipher for me the secret of the town's charms. He speaks of the artwork that has earned it the title "Villa de Arte" and which can be found everywhere. Sculptures fill the squares, and portraits by Rodrigues and Isidoro adorn walls, fountains and monuments.

Once fine art passes through a small place, it never remains the same. Something similar has happened with Van Gogh's adopted French town and the Spanish town visited by the young Picasso, where he caught sight of some cubist rocks that would one day become the symbol of an age.

"To this day, many visitors pass through Cerveira from Porto, Lisbon and other parts of the world, much like yourself," Gilberto once said to me. "A small number choose to stay. Many of those who stay are looking for something and have unique stories to tell. That is why chance encounters here lead to great conversations."

The two couples are now deeply engrossed and speaking Portuguese as if their foreign guests have been momentarily forgotten in the heat of the *conversação*. Their conversation is always enthusiastic and animated. I listen to the delightful sound of Portuguese as four dogs doze at our feet, occasionally pushing their paws at me: pat us, they say, don't be mean. I approach Teresa, pulling her away from the conversation. She is one of the *retornados* from the colonies who retreated to the homeland. In English, she recounts how she was born in 1967 in Lubango, Angola.

Formerly known as Sá da Bandeira after the marquess and political figure Bernardo de Sá, Lubango was established a hundred years before Portuguese settlers arrived. The population was as white as Teresa and her parents, who, driven by poverty, migrated to the colony at a young age, raised children, worked and sent money home. After the revolution, Portugal decided to withdraw from the colony; and hundreds of thousands of settlers were airlifted out of Africa.

"We were warned, fly or die." She recoils from the memory. "All we had time to grab was a suitcase. Ever since then, I just want to forget. As a child, I witnessed horrors, a great many people slaughtered," she whispers, finding it hard to rejoin the cheerful conversation. She speaks to me now as if a veil has been lifted off her forgotten memories.

"Every evening at six, the iron gate to our yard would be locked. I rode a bicycle in the garden, listening to the lions roar beyond the walls. Anyone who went outside would be pounced upon." She spoke the local language and sang local songs: "Now I only remember one."

"Please sing it," I plead.

She shudders as if lions stalk the perimeter of their house here: "No. I have completely forgotten the language." When they returned in the mid-1970s to a post-dictatorship Portugal, people like her father, once again in demand, became energetic entrepreneurs in the country's lethargic economy. "In Africa, we had freedom, but here time froze over. This country opened to the world again thanks to hard-working people like my father."

She has not returned to Angola since, but with the first rains when the earth releases the scent of damp rot, *retornados* smell Africa and miss it, with its wild animals they so feared at the time. Perhaps it was this longing that had uprooted Teresa from the city of Porto, where she lived for many years, to Gondar and its forest, where a moist, African-like scent is always in the air. Church bells ring ten times as we part.

Passing by the dark church, I see about a dozen parked vehicles and stop, expecting to see a vigil for the souls of the dead. All is quiet, everything is deserted, and lights are turned off except for some ceremonial candles and four lanterns, as if ready to search for the lost passengers of the vehicles. Only when I pass by the side chapel do I hear a muffled murmur and I push open the door. I am amazed to see the room full of mourners. In its centre is an open coffin where an old woman lies with her arms peacefully folded. A man rises from his chair, speaking to me softly in Portuguese. I nod my head and leave, then drive back to where I am staying.

44

I WAKE FROM A DREAM, BRIEFLY at a loss as to my whereabouts. My Portuguese dreams are detailed and vivid like a second life; past and present become an inseparable world. Through the window, the sound of a school bell beckons pupils into school. My room is bright and airy; I rent it from the notary, Cristina Cancela, whose eldest son Pedro helps me with my interviews. She has another son, a young football player with international aspirations. "If he is called upon to play elsewhere in the world," she says, "we will, of course, support him; we are conservative but also broadminded and not against him going overseas."

I go outside to meet Pedro at Café Rosa. He is a young man whose contours still bear traces of boyish grace. Sharp and attentive, he is open to the possibility that the course of his life will carry him away from his country. "In the Alto Minho, people are tougher than in the south," he says. He now lives in a city far away from his childhood home.

"Do you miss it?"

"No."

He interprets *saudade* as longing, but not necessarily for one's home. He first learned about it at school, in a Portuguese Studies class. In my country, they called it "Homeland Studies". *Saudade* is part of the school curriculum for all children here. "The *saudade* of Pessoa is something you learn about only at the age of eighteen. But the word *saudade* is taught at every level, according to age and ability. During the last year of school it reaches its climax with the Pessoa poems." Pedro considers *saudade* an adult preoccupation, which affects his own parents. It is a longing for the past, for childhood, for one's parents, for a simple, uncomplicated existence.

The country has eleven million inhabitants and about four million more living in the diaspora. He blames "Salazar, who was a dictator, but not murderous like Franco, Stalin or Hitler. As our introverted Portuguese nature dictated, all operations were covert; people were not murdered in the streets. Individuals were snatched from their homes and made to disappear in prison." Torture, prisons and the identity of security service people were all kept secret. Parents would say to their children, "whatever you hear at home, stays at home." Spies and informers were everywhere.

Cristina advises us to make further enquiries at the local café. Maria Elena Gonçalves, owner of Café Flor de Fontela, is small and energetic, yet seems somehow morose as if trapped in her own life. When I introduce myself as the new owner of Casa Marília, she immediately says that Marília was her friend, recalling that from her bed, the café and grocery store afforded her only view.

Maria Elena was born sixty-eight years ago, four miles from Candemil. At a young age, she married and left Portugal to work in France. Ten years later, she returned with her husband, two daughters and some savings. They purchased this house on the square in Candemil, and she has worked here ever since, morning to evening, weekends included. They set up home on the first floor and built a café whose sign remains lit until late, on the ground floor.

Her husband passed away. One daughter lives with her, and another in a nearby village. Her white puppy barks at passing cars from the balcony. A solitary goldfish swims in a pond. "Marília was generous and not at all lonely. She had friends, and she had the church," says Maria Elena. While Pedro translates for me, a neighbour with a round, smiling face enters. "Are you the one who peeked inside the chapel last night?" She laughs and tells me that the deceased was Aurélia, who lived in Lisbon for many years and returned here in her old age. She died at the age of eighty-four.

The smiling neighbour, Fernanda, knows that I am the new homeowner and, like others, confirms that Senhor Franco "was relatively rich. And that the mother and daughter were bedridden during their latter years. That is how it is with us. The older women remain alone. Their legs go weak, so they end up in bed," she says, perhaps contemplating her future fate.

"People used to walk everywhere. I would walk thirty kilometres to another village to sell a calf or buy a sheep and a box full of chicks to bring home. And the shoes we had were bad. The most common complaints with older people around here are high blood pressure and bad legs."

Marília no longer had cows when she met her. "She tended to her vegetable garden. She grew potatoes and tomatoes, and she had fruit trees. If she wanted to, she could pick apples for herself. She was fat."

"And would she speak to *Padre* Carlos?"

Maria Elena and Fernanda smile. "A lot. Because he would come to visit her house, she was devoted to the church. When they cut down trees from her woods, she would sell them, giving the money to Father Carlos. She donated more than most."

"And did she speak of the past?"

"People said she once had an affair with a man from another village, but that was over."

As I pass by the church, the office door is ajar. The man who spoke to me at the vigil smiles as if meeting an old friend. He is the grandchild of the deceased. Wreaths are placed around the coffin. Tall candles flicker in the cool room that smells of incense and wax. Trim and tidy as a child in her tiny shoes, the woman lies on her back. Her face is waxen, and her nose protrudes over a receding face, as happens after death. Above her head hangs a piece of black lace, protection from the flies.

45

"WHAT ELSE WAS THERE TO do during those years? People worked in the fields from dawn until dusk," David Leal informs me.

Before returning to his home in Viana do Castelo, he fills up a water container from the fountain while I tell him the story of the vanishing carpenters. As if to console me, I am invited to his sister's house, which has been in their family for generations. It is a one-storey white building, surrounded by a garden on the road to Gondar. Their parents were farmers all their lives. "That is what everyone used to do around here, adults and children."

"This is where our old house was," he says pointing to an area in the yard. He knew the two landowners, Franco and Dantas, but it seems that mere mention of their names dredges up remnants of suppressed anger over past injustices. During those days, most people were *jornados*, day labourers, in their own village. His parents had bowed under the weight of hard labour for meagre daily wages.

As a boy, Leal escaped harsh village life. First, he moved to Lisbon "because at the time anyone who tried to cross the border got shot; leaving was forbidden. And many of those who tried to leave," he tells me, "disappeared without trace. Some were killed on the river by soldiers. Others walked for a month through Spain to France and perished on the way from hunger or exhaustion, utterly hopeless." His older sister also left Candemil when she was young and lived with her husband in Porto for many years.

Half a century later, they returned to the Candemil family home, abandoned since the death of their father. It was in a state of ruin, so his sister opted to build a new house in its place, where we are now sitting. Leal tells me that he had planned his escape from Portugal where "Salazar wanted to keep everyone poor and so forced to work" for years. As a teenager, he worked in Lisbon for five years and never even visited his parents in Candemil because a train ride was beyond his means. He earned about a hundred *escudos* a month, and the trip cost twenty. There was no one to ask for help. "If we asked Franco for a basic work tool or groceries on credit, he would say, 'if you want them, pay now. No money - no groceries.' Only if you had a piece of land would he agree, then he would wait for the debt to accumulate so he could get his hands on the property."

"In owning land," says David, "you had vegetables and fruit. You had something to eat. Without a plot, you went hungry and had to leave. For years I had planned my escape to Canada. I travelled to Spain and came back several times until they trusted me. I saved up in Lisbon to pay a person who paid his contact in Canada to pick me up at the airport and instruct me on immigration procedures so as not to get deported. I fled there in the first months after the revolution when it was still difficult."

He left his pregnant wife behind, and while he was working washing dishes at some restaurant in Toronto, thousands of miles away, his wife gave birth to a sick baby. A year later, the woman and baby, who weighed two kilos and underwent complicated neurosurgery, arrived in Canada. In Toronto the baby recovered and "grew up to be a Canadian through and through". He still lives there. We speak as smoke rises from the chimney.

In the kitchen, lunch is cooking on the stove. It is cosy in the large kitchen where there are six people: a Portuguese nanny who lived in Toronto for years but does not speak a single word of English, David, his wife and her sister, his sister Adelaide and her husband Joaquim, who has worked as a truck driver for years. "Where there is food for six, there will be enough for seven," they say as they invite me to join them and show me a large clay pot with stuffed pork wrapped in thin slices of bacon and accompanied by small roast potatoes.

When I enquire about the past, they all stare studiously at the ceiling as if events from that past were projected onto it. The nanny remains silent, and Adelaide busies herself with the oven. From their parents, they know that Marília was born on this road to Gondar long before them. All those seated around the table were born in the 1940s or 1950s. "Her mother, Deolinda, was ill-tempered. You would not want her for a neighbour." The delicious aroma of the food spreads through the kitchen, loosening tongues and encouraging recollections. One person begins a story, prompting another to elaborate. "Deolinda was very devoted to the church, but not to people. She was hard on the girl too." It is possible that she was also illegitimate. Thus one miserable generation follows another.

"She didn't like human beings," concludes David Leal.

"When the child grew up, she moved in with Franco," or so they heard. "She would cook, clean and take care of her elderly father. At night she returned to her mother's house." When David's wife was born in 1950, Franco and his daughter Marília, who was then twenty-five, became her godparents, and she was named after the daughter. A godfather was usually chosen from among the wealthier men who would support the newborn and take care of their upbringing if the parents could not. Luckily for Marília II, she never required paternal input from Senhor Franco.

David remembers that Marília I, the neighbour, was inclined to sadness. She had a boyfriend from a neighbouring village, but he left because Franco disapproved of the relationship. This is how poor, sad Marília lived her life, between a difficult mother and a father she served. "Sometimes she seemed depressed." They make a compassionate gesture using their heads while Adelaide places the meat and potato dish on the table. "*Lombo do Porco*": they touch their backs to show which cut of pork we are about to eat.

In the years before Franco passed away, Marília II was already a grown woman and remembers him well. He was "an older man, short and stout. Not a bad man, but stingy. As godfather, he gave me pennies. His daughter Marília, who did not have much, would willingly buy me new clothes or shoes on holidays when it is customary to buy a gift for a goddaughter."

When Deolinda died a dozen years or so after Franco, Marília was on her own for the first time in fifty-four years. "She was childless but generous, donated to the poor, worked on her farm, raised animals and often went to church." They remember that one day she stumbled on the concrete steps by the house and fell. After that, she never walked again for the rest of her life.

"And who are Franco's other children?"

"One daughter is Florinda, whose daughter, Brisolina, still lives in the village. Her daughter is Madalena. Another daughter is Alzira, who has two sons: Horácio, who lived in Lisbon and was a used car dealer, and his brother Delfim, who may still live in Brazil." The sister clears the empty plates, and we move from the kitchen to the living room, where she serves a delicious sponge cake. "When we were children, we were given *pan d'oro*, which is made from flour, eggs and sugar, only at Easter." A solid grandfather clock counts time slowly, as the memory of past poverty materializes like an uninvited guest at this meal of plenitude. Under framed family photos, we drink *aguardente*, the digestif made from grape residue. The clear pungent liquid is served with sweet melon slices.

"Do you like our food?"

"Not the *bacalhau*," I say… and oh dear, what a mistake! Only one thing is guaranteed to infuriate the placid Portuguese: denigrating not their president, their favourite singer or even the pope, but the national cult of codfish with all its varied recipes. Unforgivable. And worse, it has happened to me more than once. The Leal family sighs; yet another stupid foreigner. They

145

all lean forward to take a closer look at the sacrilegious stranger. "*Bacalhau* is so delicious. Even the Italians and the French love it. We have a thousand recipes for it. You must like some of them." They try to comfort themselves; perhaps when I learn their language, I will also come to love their salted fish.

As I take my leave, thanking them for the beautiful food, Marília accompanies me for a look at the house of her godmother. As a child, she often visited the place, accompanying her mother who came to help Franco when Marília wasn't there. Now she is in awe: "here, in this small room, is where she used to lie. There stood the dining room table. And this was the living room. Here was the kitchen and in the corner stood a chair against the wall with a hole in it." She demonstrates how they would sit and points out the opening in the floor through which the excrement dropped. "The demolished house at the back belonged to a woman named Maria dos Anjos, many years ago."

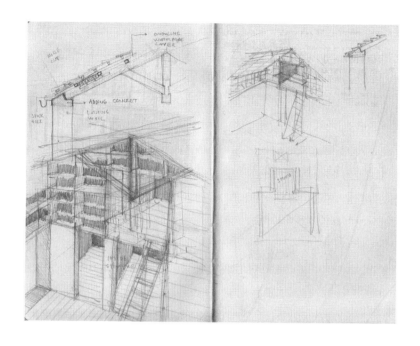

The Longest Dry Spell
in Ninety-Nine Years

46

THE EARLY MORNING AIR SMELLS of burning wood. When the fog clears, it is replaced by the smoke from bonfires, as if today was formally designated the date for burning branches and twigs, fallen leaves and other unwanted vegetation. These fires seem to be a way for the villagers to indicate to each other the changing seasons. The smoke curls upwards before the wind blows it sideways at a right angle and it dissipates. Like the fog, it also filters the sunlight, inspiring mystery. The burning wood produces a thin veil that envelops humans and trees, forests and waterways. In the background is the distant sound from the sawmill in the woods. It seems that everyone is preparing all at once for the delayed winter.

Several men sit sorting out a large mound of chestnuts in the low, grey Agricultural Union building. When I go inside to ask more questions, they pause for a moment pointing in the direction of the mayor's office. The same building also houses the Candemil Women's Cooperative. As I pass, I glimpse through lit windows the industrious seamstresses at work making padded steering wheel covers. A secretary points me to the office of President José Miguel Rodrigues Pereira, a grand title for a small village mayor. Senhor Pereira sits in a small office whose walls are entirely covered with shelves of colourful folders, sorted according to the various issues concerning Gondar and Candemil, which are united under a unitary council.

The president is tall and sturdy, young but with a weathered face. He is a hard-working farmer who, in his spare time, authorizes cheques and signs off invoices. He pushes his paperwork aside to make room for my questions.

"A very serene place," he says of his two villages. "Small, far from employment possibilities. Many have left over the years, but the landscape is unique, and the place is peaceful and trouble-free." He was born here. Through the window, I see a white cloud rising from a chimney behind the treetops like in a child's drawing.

"Is there much crime here?" I ask.

"*Nada*." He smiles. "Three years ago, there was a break-in - the council tool shed. That is all."

"There are a lot of abandoned houses."

"Yes, plenty," he agrees, "they belonged to older people who died. Now there are fewer. People like you are coming in to buy. There was a couple from Porto whose child became sick. They came to live here, and the child recovered on account of the fresh air. They worried about nosy neighbours but were glad to find that no one interfered in their life, and they like it here."

Above his head hangs a government poster totalling the population of Portugal in 2011 at 10,562,000 inhabitants, four million families and about six million homes. It is unclear how many of these houses are abandoned. Candemil is registered in the census as having 232 residents, almost one-fifth of its population in 1930. Its area is 8.64 square kilometres, and it has 164 dwellings. In 1864 there were eighty-four literate people out of about 500 inhabitants and 114 homes. That same year, thirty-six locals emigrated to other countries. Yet, in 1900 no one emigrated, and so on.

"Net migration rates are positive. Some of the older former residents are coming home to retire, but a younger generation is also slowly returning." Pereira says that the council offers 500 euros for each returning couple as a reward for their first baby and 700 euros for a second baby.

"So far we have given out seven such awards." He returns to his papers.

47

By **the gate to my** overgrown garden, I set up a makeshift table using a plank and some breeze blocks. I place a chair next to it and wait for someone from the electricity company to reconnect the power supply for the builders. I am standing guard, already prepared for a no-show. In place of the electrician, Antonio, the plumber, turns up; he is also called a *canalizador*, in reference to the old system of waterways. He checks outside in the street and returns bemused. "How are we to connect the sewerage system?" It turns out that what we thought was an inspection chamber is only an opening to allow rainwater to drain away. The village does not possess a sewerage system, so a cesspit must be dug.

The previous cesspit, which in turn replaced the older system that went down to the pigsty, was too narrow for the needs of a modern home. It sufficed for Marília, who washed in the sink as she had no bath or shower. Antonio says the new system will soak into the ground like in the old days. He also intends to replace all the plumbing and install a heating system with the option of gas. He recommends we use wood for heating.

"How many months a year will you be staying? Will you be here during the winter?" He asks because that will determine the type of heating needed. But the question goes beyond heating systems and has to do with something more fundamental and profound: will we be staying only during the summer holidays or are we planning to immigrate permanently? Antonio is impatient with my long-drawn-out reflection and recommends the Salamander, an iron stove that offers the pleasures of wood burning. Unlike many other workmen, he does not indulge in long conversations about the meaning of life and the history of drains but notes down the information and hurries on his way.

Two young, dynamic men appear; they are the aluminium people, bringing new material for my old house. They are quick at taking initial measurements but can only begin work after Christmas. "No chance before. This work can be done during the winter but only under a roof and it requires electricity." These are demanding conditions for a house such as mine.

After two and a half hours waiting for the company electrician to arrive, Gilberto promises to check. He is my lifeline, my only connection to carpenters, electricians, plumbers and the mysterious Senhor Franklin, who appears furtively only to disappear and never return calls. At six in the evening, as I kneel in despair on the wet sands of the estuary near Caminha, Gilberto calls me. Somebody from the electricity company is finally on his way to the house. I wipe off the black mud and seaweed from my knees and rush back home through the early winter dusk. No one is there. No sign of an electrician, but when I point my torch at the old wooden meter, a new red fuse box twinkles and a strange optical illusion makes the numbers on the meter appear to turn.

"Maybe it's good for the rains to wash through the house," says Orit over the phone when I give her the added information about the life of sad Marília and family. "Let the water wash away not only the dust but the accumulated loneliness and sadness. Let it purify the house." She is suddenly glad that the house has no roof and that all the old troubles have a means of escape.

She has had enough of old troubles.

48

I **WALK THROUGH A THICKET OF** trees, a lone palm, then a tangle of tall bamboo, sharp as swords. Two dark stone walls covered in damp moss like fine fur and a path between them. Someone once painted a rising sun on the iron gates of these walls. Beyond the gate is another; both are locked and yet recently painted like a promise of what lies behind.

Having wandered here at random, I stop my car to go inside to steal a look at the abandoned estate. I am examining some old metalwork when out of the darkness there suddenly appears a tall, slender, Giacometti-like man; his jaw is clenched, his cheeks hollow. I recoil like an intruder caught in the act, but his eyes light up, and he invites me into his house. It does not now occur to me that this man could soon become one of my best friends here and that the locked gates with the rising sun will open to reveal a tangled, painful story that unfolded right here in this peaceful town.

Next to the man, a small bouncy dog barks at me. "Quiet, Betty," he orders, and Betty relaxes, beginning to regard me as a friend. In fluent English but with a marked accent, he says his name is Michael and that he is Austrian. His house serves as a small hostel for pilgrims on the road to Santiago de Compostela. Ten years ago, after extensive travelling, he ended up in Cerveira and has been happily living in this paradise ever since.

Just as he engaged with me outside his home, he chats up pilgrims passing with their heavy loads; they usually stop to rest because of the steep road, and sometimes end up coming to stay a while in his house. "The pilgrimage to Santiago, which is about one hundred and twenty kilometres north of here, is probably the most mystical experience in Europe. It is a beautiful voyage free of preachers, each person to themselves. I meet extraordinary people hoping to find something, like me, perhaps like you too," he tells me.

"I am not a pilgrim," I say. He smiles and is silent. Betty wags her tail. Michael renovated this house which formed part of a farm, and realized that one of the Portuguese *camino* routes runs past his property here in Cerveira. He has since opened his home to hikers and pilgrims alike. He gives them a bed, and they, in turn, help ease his loneliness. He saw the stream of secular pilgrims grow stronger after Paulo Coelho's first book, *The Wizard's Diary*, was translated into German in the late 1980s. It documents a fictional/real/mystical journey along the miracle road in Spain and Portugal. As the book became an international bestseller and Coelho became famous, it sparked a renewed wave of walkers on the thousand-year-old pilgrim road. Michael quotes Coelho approvingly: "when you want something, all the universe conspires in helping you to achieve it."

He ushers the Israeli intruder inside, and I enter a spacious studio with a high ceiling. It is filled with spiritual paintings, lit candles at the foot of two Indian figurines and incense sticks spreading their scent of ritual.

My eyes rise to the wooden ceiling. Michael says a German friend built the roof: "strict and punctual... but the local carpenters tend to put things off. Such wonderful and humble people, but they always disappear when you're waiting for them." Ah ha. The man is well acquainted with the cause of my chagrin. He was born sixty years ago in Vienna, and his father is a wealthy Austrian businessman. His mother, who died many years ago, was an Estonian immigrant. He makes a living as a portrait artist, sometimes commissioned. On the easel I see an unfinished portrait of an obviously prominent man. "The President of Austria," says Michael. "My mother's brother. I am making a present for my uncle."

Michael has no children. His dog Betty, his companion, raises her adoring eyes to him, following his every move.

We soon enter into one of those profound conversations about the essence of life that sometimes occur between complete strangers at a random meeting. "At the beginning of my life, I conformed to the expectations of others," says Michael; "my life was laid out for me by my father." He studied law in Vienna but felt dead inside. His spirit was suffering and his heart aspired to something different, away from the soul-crushing wheel described in the stories of Hermann Hesse. At some point, he read about the rite of passage of Native American boys, who went out into the wild to decide on a way of life. Within four days the answer would come to them in a dream, in silence, or meditation.

"I set out on the road and moved from stifling Vienna to the highest monastery in Tibet. I wandered there on foot and lived in the high mountains for three months, in nature, without a hint of modernity. That is what made me who I am today. I returned to Vienna barefoot in white robes. My father went berserk." The dog is falling asleep; as she dreams, her legs twitch. The room is warm, and a vast glass window overlooks a green courtyard with two fig trees and an orange tree. Michael speaks of his father with the reverence reserved for a powerful patron.

"In Austria, I had the feeling that everyone was gossiping about everyone else." In speaking of his life today, it becomes evident that he has found peace in this land. "The world only knows the Portugal which lies south of Lisbon. But the north, the Alto Minho, is an unspoiled terra incognita. The Portuguese are sweet, soft and discreet. Here, in the Alto Minho, I am allowed to be who I am."

"The older people seem to be living under a spell. The melancholy, their *saudade*, is not a happy thing and is so strange. We live right on the border by the river, within spitting distance from Spain, where people are so different. Here the women are like shy Madonnas, and there they are fiery. Flamenco women. They are two close opposites. The Spaniards had Franco, much crueller than Salazar, and yet they are rebellious and disobedient. Here they had a mystical, clerical dictator who bowed his head before God and the Church, and they came out of it all submissively."

"Across the river in Spain," he waves his long, thin hand at the hill in front of his house, "they still have so many demonstrations and unrest." When we part company, he stoops to hug me. Betty, who has placed herself between us, seems concerned.

I know I will see them again.

49

THE AZURE COOL SEASON LINGERS this year in an autumnal dry spell unparalleled since World War I. The fire station marks 23 November as the official date for the beginning of the rainy season, which lasts until spring. Everywhere people are busy storing firewood, gathering crops, diligently repairing walls. The carpenters set a date, then another one, yet nothing happens.

I am comforted by the thought that while I wait for my house to be built, I am constructing another, made of words. I create in the only way I know how to, not with stones, slates, iron and wood, but with paragraphs and thoughts, observations and inquiries, conversations, and people's stories. I study the particulars of the house, the yard, the village, its roads. Getting lost on purpose, I get to know the location of hidden waterfalls, quiet pools in the forest and the side streets of Caminha and other small towns. This abstract, intellectual construct progresses well, while the tangible house waits and stagnates.

Gilberto no longer tries to console me. He shares our frustrations. I ask him to tell the carpenters in no uncertain terms that if the roof is not up by the first rains, they will have to look for another job. This is when Franklin makes his reappearance. He has done his bit by completing the concrete base for the roof. Now he wants to cover the skeleton, but the structure has not yet been erected.

The carpenters blame Franklin, and he blames them. Quietly, in a sort of phony war, blame shifts in a Portuguese game of ping-pong recriminations. Harmless bullets fly over my head, but I cannot bring myself to be angry with Franklin Brito.

He is a courteous, shy man, of average height, thin and weathered through work. He was born sixty years ago in a nearby village to a father who left a job in the sawmill and emigrated alone to France to support the family. Franklin was the eldest child, so his mother waited until he was thirteen to join the father in France and left him to care for his twin sisters. The parents only visited on holidays. Hence the independence and perhaps sadness that seem to follow him around. The Portuguese often seem to me like children, who even in adulthood miss their absent parents.

As we climb to the house, still open to the elements, Franklin explains that as soon as Jorge and his men install the wooden frame, he will place the boards to prevent the water from penetrating and put back the slates. He will do all this later this week, "if they come."

The "ifs" are stacked high like wooden beams: if this, and if that. And everything depends on everything.

50

Zé Paulo stands on the street in front of his funhouse, and I go inside to browse. I dig up another mirror. It seems I have yet to satisfy my hunger for mirrors. We then go to eat by Caminha's main square. The bustling Restaurante do Cais is his regular place, where all his friends meet. Six euros will get you a complete meal: soup, a large main course, dessert, coffee and a glass of local wine. The owner, head waitress and life and soul of the party, Paula, is also a country singer. Strong, temperamental and manically busy, she urges me to choose between two dishes and when I don't decide quickly enough, runs off to tend to the sudden influx of diners. She employs a younger waitress, who she says is *louca*, "everyone is crazy."

I have come across many such women here. Fierce and lively Alto-Minhans who can face any hardship, resilient in situations where men crumble. Like other local restaurateurs, Paula feeds people generously and cheaply, even by local standards. A friend explains that the power of these women stems from their Viking blood. The ancient tribe of seafarers reached the Alto Minho with their raids, and Viking women were fierce warriors who held on to their independent status. Zé Paolo cherishes the wild hypothesis that Paula is a descendant of the Napoleonic invasion. If so, the landlady is a Viking.

Rui and Rosali, a couple who are friends with Zé Paolo, join us for dinner. She is a smiling young woman with short hair which frames her round face, and he looks taciturn. She speaks good English and laughs at a joke I make. People with a similar sense of humour recognize each other like freemasons; Rosali laughs, and we immediately strike up a friendship. I tell them about the house, and they assure me that the rains at the beginning of the season are not heavy. Local builders always behave like my absent carpenters, they say. Rui restored a house on a riverbank a few years back. Together they both renovated their current home in the village of Dem. They are well acquainted with carpenter-related woes.

"We Portuguese have a problematic relationship with time." Rosali and Rui confess to having trouble being punctual, as if time is an insistent enemy to be eluded. Perhaps a rigid forty-year dictatorship exhausted the Portuguese patience with any law, rule, border or demand. They invite me to come one day to their home, a half-hour drive up the mountains, where herds of wild horses roam and villages seem to have been forgotten in time. We raise a glass of local *vinho verde* toasting friendship and choose a dessert from the fridge. Then we settle a bill that might cover a morning coffee and croissant in most other countries and go outside to the lovely Caminha square. A startled flock of grey pigeons rise into the sky sending a gust of wind at us from their wings.

51

NEAR THE END OF THE month it rains for three days on end, and the fate of the house seems sealed. In my mind's eye, I can see the rain seeping through cracks in the old granite walls, permeating the clay and rotting it from the inside. According to the weather forecast, an Atlantic cold front is approaching, so Gilberto sends a warning letter to the carpenters. I yearn for the artists Christo and Jeanne-Claude to come and wrap up the whole house, to protect this ageing newborn exposed to winter hardships.

There is no room left for any more Alto Minho miracles, and my sleep is agitated. Someone once wrote that dreams are our second life, but my dream world is submerged in water. I watch the Atlantic front from the window of my rented room as it hurls itself against Cerveira, scattering the fallen leaves which rested peacefully all autumn. The wrath of the wind blows them everywhere. The weather is fast becoming my enemy, and I feel betrayed by the carpenters. But a practical thought suddenly occurs to me as if sent by my late mother, who believed there was always something to be done. I am contemplating buying black plastic to wrap up the house myself, without the aid of Christo.

At the back of the Cunha hardware store on the way to Caminha are huge storage rooms stocked with plumbing and wood supplies, doors and screws. From iron rails on the high ceiling hangs a real paddleboat with three small holes visible in its hull. According to rumour, this smuggling boat, which once belonged to the shopowner's father, would transport tobacco and people across the river on moonless nights. Oars dangle from the upside-down boat. The holes were made by policemen's bullets that killed two border smugglers one night in 1975 before a young boy's eyes.

That boy is now the shopowner, and he is redirecting me to the care of a fair-haired and efficient young man who speaks some English. He takes me behind the store to a room packed with rolls of plastic sheets. We drag out a polyethene roll, and two workers spread out the double sheet to about twenty metres and cut. The forty metres I purchase weigh about ten kilos. For thirty euros, I may have bought myself a temporary roof.

I add to my purchase a utility knife and some nails to secure the sheet from strong winds, and by noon I am already climbing the sloping walls of the house on an old wooden ladder. I cut the sheet according to the length of the wall to wrap the concrete crown. I do not intend to cover the entire house because the rain and wind would blow the sheets away.

Ten metres above the inner courtyard, the ocean breeze is building up, bearing a light spray of water. The work is exhausting and I feel like a deck boy on an old ship sent to climb the masts to take down the sails. The wind beats down and I dangle over the abyss as the black polyethene inflates, attempting to carry me with it. I lay heavy rocks to weigh it down and find that Franklin's metal clamps are also helpful in fixing the material in place.

For three hours I move the ladder from place to place, stumbling and growing dizzy. I hold on to the deck of the house-ship in the gathering winds, clinging to the concrete strip that now covers where the avalanche of stones came to rest in 1983. After the helpless wait for carpenters, the act feels liberating. Black sheets now cover the decapitated ends of the house. Their corners flutter in the wind and are held in place by stones and clamps, tightened with hammer blows.

It is already six in the afternoon; the *tarde* has become *noite* and still no real rain. Only the strong wind blows away the light and warmth, darkening the sky. When it begins to drizzle, I go inside the Curt'isso Bar to sit among the warm cork walls. The place was built without any help from professionals. Its owners are two young friends from Cerveira, António and Nelson. They worked for a few years at the Café da Lenta by the waterfront until they decided to set up their own place, different from traditional Alto Minho cafés.

António, also called Tonino, had travelled to Austria, where he worked to save money and stock up on ideas. Upon his return, he began establishing the café with Nelson, near the small amphitheatre at the heart of the town. An old carpenter who was closing down his business sold them some good wood for making furniture that they constructed under his guidance. They built simple chairs and heavy tables that look both rustic and contemporary. They covered the walls with wood from local cork trees. My friend Michael from the *quinta* painted a mural in the hallway, and Manuel from Rasa brought old doors and *azulejos* from a Lisbon residence. António works in the kitchen, and two waitresses who look like 1940s movie stars serve at the tables. The place remains busy until the early hours of the morning, cosy and warm like the inside of a swallow's nest.

At a nearby table, a group of visibly intoxicated women celebrate a birthday. They laugh loudly enough to make the ceiling collapse. When one is alone, the sound of loud laughter exacerbates a sense of loneliness. The television news reports that oxygen in a missing Argentine submarine is about to run out. A sonar signal has been briefly detected from its metal body somewhere at the bottom of the ocean. The world is full of dramas much more significant than my own, but everyone sees only their personal version of my rooftop crisis. Amidst the hustle and bustle of the café, I feel a strong desire to go to the house of Jorge, chief carpenter, and pull a tile off his roof in front of him, to illustrate how he has left me exposed to the ravages of winter. "When the carpenters arrive tomorrow, don't kill them," jokes Gilberto over the phone.

Light rain falls on the house overnight, but the walls are still wrapped in the polyethene when I return, though I find puddles on the wooden floors. Soon the floor is bound to sprout weeds. In the field next to mine, a neighbour scatters wood ash to fertilize the pasture under dark skies. The carpenters assured Gilberto that they were responsible for everything and that they would repair any damage, even if they had to blow-dry the entire house or rebuild it from scratch. How light-hearted the promise, sweet yet fake, like a mass-produced dessert.

By noon I despair of Jorge and drive to the restaurant. My phone rings in the middle of the main course: chicken and eggs, rice and chips. "They are on their way to yours," announces Gilberto, and I abandon my plates half full and rush home to discover Jorge's white pickup parked in the alley. He extends his hand to me like an old friend, but I recoil. I point to the house framed in black sheets like a death notice and say in broken French: "By Monday. Or my money back."

A worker who speaks some French translates, and Jorge, stout and good-humoured, momentarily appears shocked by the fuss made by the uncouth foreigner in the face of slight delays and a bit of rain. With a triumphant gesture, he points out a dry spot in the warehouse where they have stored the fragrant wood. Parts of my Lego roof lie dismantled there and, in the yard, rests the longest beam, diagonally. The entire wooden framework is laid out. Everything will be cut according to size, and the timber skeleton assembled within a few days.

"And waterproofing the roof against the rain?"

"Ah. That's Franklin's job." He sighs with relief. When the interpreter translates, I look at the head carpenter and remember what a local once told me: "It's a mystery how this nation has survived this way for a thousand years." He also warned me: "Do not go against the workers, do not start a fight with them. They are nice enough and kind but can be vindictive and never forget.

They will change if you cross them. Respect local customs even when your carpenters disappear. This is their territory. You are the guest."

A desperate Gilberto is doing his best to negotiate and appease all parties, but he is already at the airport, on his way to the Architecture Conference in Iran. I am on my own now.

THE STRANGER'S HOMECOMING

Tiago: Under a Miracle Sky

52

COME EARLY WINTER, ATLANTIC WINDS blow even stronger through Caminha. The town was built by the massive delta of two rivers flowing into the ocean, the Coura and the Minho. According to marine biologist Dr Carlos, the vast marshes under the bridge at the entrance to the town are a protected nesting area for thousands of birds. A combination of reeds, natural water channels, tangled bushes, small ponds and protection from the wind forms a paradise for birds of many species. Some older houses still have a garret with large windows overlooking the ocean to spot lost seafarers during storms. I enjoy visiting Caminha, a seemingly remote corner that retains the beauty of the past.

One cold morning Zé Paulo is not at his antiques store, so I wander through the narrow alleys between occupied and abandoned houses. "For the most part, they are deserted places - treetops that lean against walls, blind alleys or front gardens where no one ever stops. In such places, it seems as if all that lies in store for us has become the past," wrote the great *flâneur* Walter Benjamin.

Behind the church, an old white two-storey building. A glance through its open window reveals the interior of a large, dimly lit room - an artist's studio. As I press my face to the glass, the door opens, and a man whose thick white hair frames a tall forehead invites me inside. Although alone, he is wearing an elegant blue jacket with gold buttons. The space seems ancient and the ceiling low, with terracotta tiles. On a tilting easel stands a half-finished watercolour. The painting looks like a giant jigsaw puzzle of all the other watercolours filling the room. Together they form a topography of clues, an aerial photograph of an imaginary land.

As if we have not just met a moment ago, the man generously welcomes me inside his kingdom. We climb up some stone steps to another studio, half concealed. The rooms are full of hidden treasures and old family heirlooms. He uses a pool table as a desk. Family portraits silently observe us from behind the glass fronts of wooden cabinets: men and women, luxury cars, old homes, paintings of birds of prey, terraces and the Madonna.

"I have been expecting you," Tiago Taron tells me.

"That mystical thing about meetings in the Alto Minho?"

"Not mystical," he reassures me. He is an artist, a painter and an established lawyer in Lisbon, a master of words in his professional capacity. As if arranged in advance, we settle down to our meeting, and he opens with a story about his grandfather who sailed from Lisbon to Luanda, the capital of Angola.

In 1894 his great-grandfather had met a lovely young girl on a trip with her father aboard the ship *Ambaca*. They both came from Gondarém near Cerveira. His grandfather and the girl married in Angola, but she died shortly after giving birth to their only son. The dead young mother marked the beginning of the "dynasty of the five males", as described by Tiago, a line of five generations in which no girl was born. Sometimes it was one boy, two or three, but no daughters from the girl's death onwards.

For more than ten years, he has been researching his family history. "I grew up in a family where the ambiguous, male-only past was never brought up, and only the future mattered." He is attempting to write the family history because "practising law is bad for the soul. It spoils one's use of language. Luckily for me, I have been painting for fifteen years. It saves me. It has helped protect both the way I express myself and how I feel." I listen attentively to the detailed family life of which I knew nothing only an hour before and find myself captivated by the magic of his storytelling.

I keep the stories he told me to myself as he asks and with a heavy heart. He intends to write his own family history. From that day on, and in every subsequent conversation, I appreciate Tiago's unique views of the Alto Minho, an area where he has lived most of his life.

On my way to Caminha that morning, I photograph the deserted Gondarém train station, where trains still pass but do not stop. Weeds are growing between floor tiles. Its *azulejos* are beautiful and intact, untouched by time. Gondarém, Tiago says, used to be a bustling town. The one and only Amalia Rodrigues even sang about it. He recites the lines to me in Portuguese; they translate as: "I came to Gondarém to die. The land of contrabandists, but don't dress me in the smuggler's cloak."

The song refers to what others have also mentioned: the dark past of the secretive river crossings when the border was closed. Now it has become a tourist attraction. Before the revolution, there were many *contrabandistas*, river runners of refugees and fugitives who crossed the water under a hail of police bullets from both sides of the river. They would smuggle tobacco, drugs, maybe weapons. Locals single out the larger houses on the banks of the Minho - bought with fortunes made during those times.

Tiago is a great storyteller, a wise lawyer experienced in capturing the attention of the court. It is only in speaking of his father that he stops and sighs, "He was not a prime physical specimen, but looked like a combination of Jack Nicholson and James Dean. He taught me discipline and gave meaning to my life." Tiago was born a year before Salazar fell ill and had to withdraw from public life. Forever etched in his memory are the wonderful weeks at his grandmother Olga's summer house in Gondarém during childhood vacations. It is the main house of the dynasty and "my childhood paradise".

Before his death, his father ordered him to return to

Gondarém, and Tiago carefully complied with the will of the man he so admired. He returned from Lisbon to Gondarém and Caminha. He renovated and restored the two houses. "And here we are, sitting and talking about all this." His speech is easy, eloquent; he assumes complete control of the narrative. With his vocabulary and sentence structure, he seems constantly to be ready to address a courtroom panel of judges. In his youth, he was an aspiring actor. He then studied law and began a career as an attorney in the entertainment industry.

At times he is loquacious but then is more cautious as if the personae of the storyteller and the lawyer are at odds. "When my father fell gravely ill, he only said, 'Fear Not.' This is what the deer says to the hunter chasing it in a Cerveira folk tale. 'Fear not, look a person in the eye and do not run.' Deer do that sometimes. They stop and turn to face the hunter with a noble gesture of acceptance and an expression of resignation that looks like an unspoken plea." As he reaches the end of the story, a gentle knock on the door emphasizes the point. When Tiago opens the door, a handsome man with an aquiline nose enters. He is an old friend who is due to call by. My time is up, and I rise and return to Candemil.

53

My neighbour Miguel Dantas watches the black sails flutter over the decapitated house from a window overlooking the alley. He invites me inside his garage, where in a nook by the ceiling hides a remarkable piece of architecture. It is a perfect swallow's nest made of mud. The opening is round and tight for protection but widens into a comfortable larger nesting area. Minute beaks have levelled the plaster to protect the tiny home from predators and rain. Miguel watched a pair of swallows fly back and forth for a month carrying the mud. He observed them from afar, not wishing to frighten the birds, thought to be an omen of change and good fortune. Some time after the work was completed, the chirping of chicks was heard from the nest. Like these tiny birds, I wish I could build my nest with my own hands.

At forty, Miguel is thin and delicate. He resembles his grandfather's brother, old Albano Dantas, whom I met at the nursing home in Caminha. Dantas inherited the Candemil house from his father and grandfather. Had he inherited a plot of land in any other village, he would have settled there just as happily because "it is the land that matters, not the place." His wife Carla, their son and daughter live with him in what is a big human nest. He opens a metal gate ushering me inside the property, consisting of a large plot of land and a stone house currently undergoing renovations in instalments. He is friendly and shy and works outside the village, still tending to his land in his spare time. "My grandfather, father, uncle and all the generations before them have all done the same."

He shows me a small wooden wheelbarrow built by Uncle Albano when he was ninety for his son. The Dantas family worked in the fields from morning till evening. "They worked holidays and weekends and never hired anyone because they were tight-fisted, yet very honest and they never owed money, not even a cent." Like the other landowner, Senhor Franco, the three Dantas brothers - Alípio, Telmo and Alfredo - were born in the late nineteenth and early twentieth centuries. Alípio had daughters and a son: Fernando, Miguel's father. Alfredo had two sons, including the Albano I talked to at the nursing home, and Telmo had a daughter and sons.

Fernando became ill and died when Miguel was twelve. His mother was left to care for two small children and often sent him to his grandparents, who lived by the grocery store in Candemil. There, in a small room of his own, the bachelor Albano Dantas also lived for years. Miguel loved being with the hard-working elderly couple. "A lot of children grew up this way with their grandparents. The grandparents raised the little ones because the parents worked in the fields or went abroad."

He finds it peculiar when I suggest that his grandfather and two brothers, together with Franco, were considered the wealthiest people in the village, big landowners. "Maybe we were called that because everyone else was dirt poor and our family was a little less so. We did own land, but we lived like everyone else. Yes, and a grocery store that was at the heart of village life. Distances seemed great because people had to walk everywhere," he says. "Until the 1970s, there were no cars here other than my grandfather's. No one went to Cerveira for shopping, so our shop sold everything, from potatoes, shoes, oil and gas to wine, cigarettes and tobacco."

At the Dantas grocery, people met to drink local wine or coffee. They would buy everything on credit and sometimes ask for a small loan when needed. They hung around to chat or check for letters from relatives who lived abroad. The postman dropped off all the village mail at the store. When someone needed to call a doctor or a midwife, that was where they went. Miguel Dantas recalls that sometimes his grandfather sent him with groceries or letters to Marília's house across the square. "A short, thickset woman with a broad face," he says.

When Miguel grew up, he married Carla, and together they left for the city, but he always felt a longing for the land that has never yet disappointed him. The soil is so fertile that it feeds you even during harsh times. "Land is everything; there is no substitute for that." For a dozen years he lived in the city, studied physical education and worked as a lifeguard in a municipal swimming pool, until one day he and his wife became tired of it all and left to return to their family home in Candemil. "When we came back to the house about ten years ago, I never saw Marília even once, even though she lived across the road. She was bedridden and never went out into the street. The house looked deserted except for Manoel, who would come with a tractor to plough the plot, or Maria, who came to take care of Marília."

To make a living, Dantas is a small-scale manufacturer of tables, chairs and umbrellas. When he returns home every day, he works his land, unearthing large rocks and marking paths, digging hidden pipes that pass under the earth. He knows how to calculate the sun's path and where the best place is to cut windows in walls. His rural genes are bursting with seeds of knowledge. As we stand in the soft autumnal light, Miguel indicates the path of the sun, sunrise to sunset, in the Candemil skies, instructing me in the different angles each hour in relation to our house. Casa Marília rests on a sunny hill. We chose well, unknowingly. "During winter, when the sun shines over Candemil, Cerveira is submerged under a big, damp cloud."

He explains how to measure the boundary of an estate, where a demarcating line runs along the slope of an embankment. He points out the edges of his own field: "Here, there, where two rows of granite pillars still stand. Once there were rows of vines here until one winter everything collapsed; only the rods remain as markings."

"I must ask something of you," he says pointing to the adjacent field, which belongs to his sister and aunt. "If ever you buy the plot with the flower pond from us, there is an old water pipe that runs across it diagonally, bringing water from a spring on the mountain and reaching the pond. From there, it continues to the smaller pond by the café and my grandfather's empty house. I never want the water to be blocked." As a child, he remembers kneeling next to his grandmother when she dug in this field repairing a cracked pipe.

Once a source of power for landowners like the Dantas family and Franco, land is sold today at a nominal price per square metre of fertile terrain with water. In the twenty-first century, the Dantas are just one of many village families with a house, a garden and fruit trees. "Of the whole family, only my son Valdemar will carry the Dantas name," says Miguel lamenting the shrinking lineage. His grandparents passed away about ten years ago, and for a while his uncle Albano was left alone in the large family home. He continued to sleep in his small room and did everything by himself except cook. Until he was ninety he pruned vines and bushes, picked fruit and cared for the trees growing in the large garden at the back of the house. He went with the family to church on Sundays.

One winter day, Albano came to eat with Miguel as usual at noon, and when they had finished, he came out of the alley to go to his house across the square. Miguel heard brakes screech and a scream. Horrified, he ran and saw the old man lying on the side of the road. In the fog, the driver had not seen him and hit him as he circled the square. Albano was taken to a hospital and never returned to Candemil. When he recovered from his injuries, he went straight to the nursing home where I visited him with Pedro and where we talked about the past and the two Marílias.

54

THE MORNING IS ICY AS if winter has descended all at once, yet the air remains dry. The bright but weak sunlight passes through naked vines, illuminating the bare branches. The house is still decapitated, and the pinewood rests in a stack next to some older recyclable wood, like a cache. I am without a home but steadily accumulating friends. Pessoa, who became a nomad after his childhood ended abruptly, never felt at home anywhere but in cafés. He wrote, "life had no face. We were outside and others." I befriend such *others* faster than usual, piercing the Portuguese shell of reserve. Zé Paulo's good friend, Rosali, invites me to give the autumn a send-off in the villages of the Arga Mountains near their home.

Overnight, frost builds on the windscreen and the wipers screech as if bearing a message. Yet the TV news still features images of parched soil and empty water reservoirs. There is not a cloud in the sky as I drive the twenty-eight kilometres to the village of Dem and continue from there with Rosali, Rui and the dog Felino (meaning cat), to the Celtic monastery and the mountain villages. The soil looks to be dark lava, the result of an ancient eruption. Between immense, black boulders, two storeys high and smooth like pebbles, stand tiny houses. Older villagers lead small flocks of sheep.

Rui shows me a grove of thorny holly trees with red fruit whose leaves are shiny like plastic. His last name, Azevedo, means literally a grove of these prickly trees (*Azevinhos*). The tree is sacred, an ancient symbol at the heart of Christmas celebrations. Rui Azevedo is silent by nature and a good listener.

He comes from a family of artists but has worked most of his adult life in the textile business. His heart belongs to music, however, and he is happiest when playing his guitar in the attic at night. Twice divorced, Rui is a guitarist in a band called Sem Nome, Nameless. It was there, in the basement where they rehearsed, that he met a round-faced singer and fell in love with her.

They were married, and after the birth of their son Miguel, Rui retired from the textile business and, together with Rosali, renovated a house and a watermill in the village of Dem. They rent the beautiful ancient watermill out to tourists.

Rosali, who has since given up singing, is a woman in her mid-thirties, short and lively, amusing and quick-witted. Born of a Portuguese mother and a Dutch father, these different tribes and her wanderlust and curiosity form part of her soul. She was an actress and a singer, sold retro clothes and theatre costumes, worked as a concierge and healer. Rosali is a person with a mystical worldview. She is fearless, proudly carrying her advanced pregnancy, gliding down a forest path to the spring through slippery ferns and treacherous soil.

Her first experience giving birth lasted all of an excruciating day, but as soon as Miguel emerged, she immediately cried out that she wanted another baby. In their backyard lives a pack of adopted rescue dogs. We inspect an old monastery courtyard and relax by the edge of a natural pond with blue dragonflies buzzing over its waters. "A blue dragonfly is a mark of pure water," says Rosali. Although she grew up in the city, she has faith in nature and bonds with the small hidden nooks, towering mountain peaks and massive godlike trees.

By the monastery are the villages of upper and lower Arga, and between them, a rocky path descending to yet another hidden natural pool with a waterfall. All around are giant boulders the size of houses. Quickly jumping in the icy water lest I change my mind, I let out a scream. I swim to the place where the water glides down the mountainside in a series of smaller cascades, surrounded by colourful shrubs. I sit in a small pool, hemmed in by vegetation and feel as happy as a flower.

55

ONE IS QUICK TO FORM habits, even in a place that was completely foreign only a year before. Such is morning coffee at the Café São Pedro or Villa Rosa, and such are evenings at Curt'isso Bar or Café da Lenta by the river. A simple routine can form protection against chaotic times or feelings of alienation and being away from home. Here and there, Portuguese words pop up like hesitant shoots.

This morning is no different. Driving home from the café and turning round the bend, I am hoping to see builders on top of the roofless house. Yet when I open the unlocked iron gates, no one is there. But I still manage to stumble over the large wooden girder laid across the yard with a few smaller beams next to it. There is also a portable generator that was not there the day before. The carpenters have returned, it would appear, laid down more equipment and wood and left. Before me lies the complete timber skeleton.

One of the girders has been replaced. "There was a problem with the first one they brought," says Gilberto, "it was thirty centimetres too short after we knocked down another section of the wall."

When I return to the house, around four in the afternoon, light is already fading, and my heart begins to pound; it is a virtual Candemil miracle. Two battered black Opel Corsas are parked in the alley by a small truck. When I raise my eyes, I realize that the girder has already been pulled up. It now lies tight between its two triangles. Two men are perched above the roofless beam, hovering in the wintry air like figures from a Chagall painting. They are energetic in their movements as if shaken from a long sleep and are being supervised by Jorge, who descends to shake hands when he sees me. He grins as though presenting me with a new and unexpected magic trick: the pulling of a roof out of a hat. His five workers skip up and down amidst the beams following his orders.

An electric cable dangles down from the roof to a small generator, and I hear the buzz of the saw and the drone of the drill. Without mechanical assistance, a few men, none of whom is under fifty, raise the heavy beam from the yard to the roof through sheer muscle power. The smaller beams are also being pulled up, and all five are dancing between them, a pencil stuck behind their ears, and hammer, protractor and spirit level in their belts. I stand there, indifferent to the danger, and keep on photographing.

The roof beams are smooth and pale, giving off the smell of fresh timber. The carpenters speak without raising their voices, using their protractors and drilling long screws. Sometimes they use bricks to raise the ends of the beams for balance. The ever-changing roof looks as if it is floating above the ground. Its strength is in its weight, says Gilberto. Its movement and flexibility - needed to handle the wind, the moisture and the different seasons - come from local timber, suitable for the fickle climate.

After an hour of watching this carpenters' ballet, I feel as if I am present at the construction of a large boat, bottom side up. The massive girder on top is the keel, from which the ribs of the hull extend. It is a large wooden boat sailing across the skies: its cargo, the old granite walls, the sides and the roof slates - there to block rainwater which is set to begin in a few days and last until April. I walk among the carpenters, my neck craning upwards. They joke around but never for a moment stop their work as Casa Marília is slowly transformed back into a home. Jorge does not consult the blueprints once, but gives short orders from memory and experience. His workers now lay down the wider girders to form the gallery over the kitchen. And he shows me his hand, which has been slightly pinched by the weight of a large beam. He does the lifting, pulling and hauling along with them. Almost everything is done by hand, ritualistically, like an ancient ceremony with rules known to one and all.

I take notes and photographs, sending them to Orit. I save a small sawn-off piece of wood and inscribe it with the date as a kind of cornerstone. I send photos to Gilberto in Iran and only leave when the carpenters wind up their electrical cord and take off in the evening. I feel like a condemned man given a last-minute reprieve.

56

I LEAVE FROM PORTO AND CHANGE planes in Barcelona to arrive early morning in Tel Aviv. A day later, Gilberto calls from Yazd in Iran and announces that Jorge will finish the woodwork and Franklin will need two consecutive dry days to cover the roof with sheets and tiles. As the wood is wet from light rain, he and his men dare not climb on it for fear of slipping. It seems that communications between Franklin and Jorge have been reestablished, and the imminent flood has reconciled all builders of the Candemil Ark. "Once they finish the roof," says Gilberto with almost audible relief detectable in short WhatsApp messages, "everything should run smoothly." Under the wooden umbrella, builders will be able to work even during the harshest winter.

In the pleasant Tel Aviv winter, I search a global weather website for Vila Nova de Cerveira's forecast. I see a cloudy sun hovering over it; temperatures are not very low. Weather is changing worldwide, the climate playing tricks everywhere. Berlin is frozen, Moscow is sunny, glaciers are melting somewhere, and the sun shines over Cerveira.

My neighbour Dantas sends us photos depicting the silhouettes of three men. Franklin and two other workers are walking on top of the wooden roof frame spreading flapping opaque sheets. They put in place cleaned up old tiles and new ones. None of the rooftop dancers is wearing safety gear, yet everything proceeds without drama.

In my bed in Tel Aviv, I dream that I am an elderly monk in white robes slowly climbing a very steep hill. As in many of my dreams, I am surrounded by a crowd of unfamiliar people, exhausted and at the end of my tether. At the top of the hill, I see a bustling café, but the terrain is so steep that my hands are by now digging into the ground as I climb. With one last effort, I crawl on all fours to reach the summit. When I get there, I find a fence protecting the café. I go over it and show my unknown companions the way. With every movement, my old body grows more assertive, and with a few steps I manage to jump over the fence and the railing to the café's balcony; as if shrugging off exhaustion and feebleness, I reach my goal light and fresh.

In the morning, I lie in my old familiar room and contemplate the dream. In a part of it I feel old and exhausted and in another I later regain my strength. I soar high like in early childhood dreams and even lead the way.

My phone vibrates near my head. Still in Yazd, Gilberto sends a photo taken by Franklin - an image of the new roof from inside the house. The completed ceiling is made of narrow light pinewood planks, waterproof and lovely. This is how our Candemil-Yazd-Tel Aviv social network functions. "The roof insulation is complete," Gilberto concludes.

After the first heavy December rains, a devoted Dantas sends photographs of the red-tiled roof. Gilberto, who has returned from Iran, finds some minor damage due to a storm; a single tile has fallen off the roof corner. "But the interior of the house is dry," he writes, adding: "the carpenters are very proud of their work but wish to make it clear that their initial quote only covers the roof. Additional work will require a separate quote."

"This misunderstanding is my fault," he adds, "since I see myself as responsible for the new expenses, I suggest we end our collaboration without further payment." It seems that he too has despaired of Jorge and his gang and has lost sleep over the thought that he selected them to do the work. "You are not to blame for anything," we reply in horror, attempting to dissuade him from any such premature retirement plans.

At the Jaffa flea market, we search for a round wooden window for the small attic. We locate two wooden arches, curved lintels over a hundred years old that once rested above Palestinian house doors. When placed together, they form a wooden hoop about a metre in diameter. They have shutters and grooves to hold glass. We pack the two twin arches for the journey in a large flexible black bag, a strange package which weighs over fifteen kilos.

At the airport check-in, an airline representative asks: "What is in the package?"

"A window."

"A window?"

"A window."

He calls his supervisor. She asks what it is. A window, I say. A window, she repeats and with a swooping gesture sends it on its way to Porto. According to this or that clause, wooden furniture does not require pest extermination. In Porto, the window passes unobserved and is welcomed into its new country.

By early January, the house stands intact and protected under its red-tiled top, its insides dry even after the deluge. I look up and marvel at the wooden ceiling. Tall and convex, it towers over the still unrestored house; it looks like a large boat from this angle.

I place the two window parts next to where they will be installed, in the concrete triangle under the tiled roof. I wonder, has Senhor Franco ever heard of Jaffa? Did Marília listen to the sermon about how God commanded Jonah, son of Amittai, to condemn the people of Nineveh for their sins? Do the people of Candemil know the biblical story of the frightened Jonah fleeing to Jaffa, and from there to Tarshish, getting lost at sea and finding temporary refuge from the stormy waters inside the stomach of the whale?

In the old weaving workshop in the yard, where I stock my purchases, the wind has shattered the window and rain has reached a pile of books. I fix the wooden window, and this sets my soul at ease. Smoke rises from the field next to mine. My neighbour is burning cuttings and damp grass, and the wind carries the smoke into my yard like the promise of a peaceful life. The roofing job has left its traces outside the house: a rusty cement mixer, a mound of sand, stones and bags of cement all tightly wrapped in my black polyethene sheets.

57

THE EIGHTH OF JANUARY IS a bright winter day. How lovely these glorious, clear days that seem like an unexpected summer. The sun dispenses gold into the gloom, revealing the beauty of the wet season and highlighting new shades of colour in the damp and cold. Taking one look at the sky, villagers act as if summer has returned for a day. Along the the road to Candemil, old women walk slowly on aching feet returning from neighbourhood visits.

Gilberto and Franklin arrive at the house to check that it is still watertight. They examine the two Jaffa arches, debating whether they should be connected horizontally or vertically. Franklin is not a man of many words. He is quiet and unassuming, apprehensive, practical and trustworthy. He often takes notes in his little book. He considers the old window a whim on my part. It brings a slight smile to the corner of his thin mouth. Why should anyone fit a cracked old window dragged from abroad into a storm-prone wall, when installing a double-glazed, airtight aluminium window is an option?

"Here we could leave the old stone wall exposed," Gilberto suggests. "And here, where it is too thin, install insulation."

As we strip off old layers, more and more is revealed: we discover weak or dilapidated walls and then ancient granite walls that formed the original house. Plans change as we go along. When some plaster happens to fall off at the beginning of Franklin's work, a section of the granite wall with large, well-carved stones is discovered. The chiselled watermark of the stonemason can still be made out, a cross engraved over the door lintel. Wood buried under the lintel is exposed.

I would like the archaeology of our home to remain visible rather than hidden under a new layer of insulating walls. Together with Gilberto, we decide to change the original plan and alter the insulation layout so that the ancient front wall at the heart of the house remains fully exposed. I also ask them to leave the kitchen wall unplastered, as it is made of small, uncarved stones. Franklin and Gilberto examine the wall, exposed when the chimney was removed, and discover it to be carelessly built of rocks and dirt. "If the wall stays this way, moisture is likely to infiltrate. It is poorly built and faces the sideways storms of the Alto Minho, which smash into any openings," says Gilberto.

As the removal and demolition of the interior walls progress, I find myself falling in love with the old, uncovered fragments. I want the mementoes, raw materials, the craft of builders long turned to dust, to be kept as they are. The different colours of stones and their mineral arteries form the spectacular fresco of time. Diametrically opposed to this, my passion, stands Franklin, the experienced builder who strives to erect white, straight, functional and insulated walls. He finds my love for traces of the past - which his contemporaries worked so hard to disguise - amusing.

I examine leftover sections from the new wooden ceiling installed by Jorge's workers under the roof's frame. They are thick, ready-made pallets formed of three layers: compressed wood-like material, soft blue insulation and wood. Here and there remain a carpenter's pencil marks, unnecessary gaps and slight flaws. I love these too, traces of human thought in the natural materials. Regarding the kitchen wall, I accept the decision of the architect and contractor to insulate it for reinforcement. The small stones are to remain hidden after all. We decide that the old wooden floor of the enclosed balcony and the bedroom should remain. It is battered and scratched; the wood darkened through years. Time has carved the whole history of the house on it. The floor shall continue to fulfil its role and bear witness.

58

ONE PARTICULARLY EVENTFUL DAY, THE house is unexpectedly filled with all the workers who have previously promised yet failed to return. A team arrives to measure the openings for the wooden windows and heavy doors that will be fitted in the former animals' quarters. The boss Vitório and his worker Sérgio note down the measurements and pull out an impressive catalogue of aluminium items with a wide range of sizes and colours. I ask that the window of the ex-pigsty be built into the outer edge of the wall, so that the niche forms part of the room's interior.

I opt for red aluminium. Vitório explains that it will take a long time to arrive, the green too. Black, on the other hand, can be obtained within two weeks. The voluminous catalogue shrinks before my eyes while the waiting grows longer.

The Portuguese have a primal fear of committing to specific dates; it is a fate to be avoided at all costs. The metalworkers promise to submit a quote. The first duo who came to the house measured and vigorously noted down everything, soon vanished and were never heard from again. Often it seems as if local craftsmen enjoy visiting potential building sites, just as my parents enjoyed touring luxurious nursing homes when they reached the appropriate age. Even though they knew they could never afford them, they would drink the coffee, eat the cakes and explore the lavish rooms and sea view studio apartments. Refreshments were delicious and free, and the customer service was excellent. I estimate the actual work done on the house at just over a cumulative two weeks since we bought it six months ago. Gilberto is despondent as if responsible for the reputation of all Portuguese workers. He assures me that under the auspices of the new roof things should soon change.

The same day, Franklin returns with the man who will install the gutter. They climb up to the roof with all the agility of chimney sweeps. After measuring the corners, they decide to bolster the last row of slates, two of which fell off during the storm. Witnessing all the action, I manage to calm down.

The Portuguese are charming even when evasive. When asked if they have time to meet, they claim to be extremely busy, yet conversations last an eternity. When Gilberto and I meet, he seems to have all the time in the world for his least significant client. "Time flows slowly here," says my Austrian friend, Michael. "I have been gradually slowing myself down in the ten years since I arrived." It took him eight years to construct his house. As an Austrian, he believes in punctuality as a force of nature, "yet somehow it all functions here without preset schedules. Everything is clean and tidy, and trains run on time." He concurs with the idea that the Portuguese see time as the form of government they must oppose. The painting of his uncle, the President of Austria, has not yet been completed, and Michael is pressed for time, but, like a local, still makes time for small talk.

In the evening, Michael shows up at the Curt'isso Bar with his dog Betty and a bearded, fair-eyed boy with hair like an Aryan Jesus. Dominique has walked the 800 kilometres of the Camino de Santiago three times. Once from France to Spain and twice from Portugal. This time, as he followed the route through Cerveira and walked down a steep alley, he saw Michael's sign, went inside and decided to stay. As he muses, we pick his brains like the parents of a taciturn son recently returned from a long journey. Dominique says he has always felt the need to wander on his own. Many nights he has spent under the stars. "That is when I sleep best. Even during storms."

His father was lost to him at some point, so since childhood he has moved and travelled with his mother as if they were the only two people in the world. "And when you get used to travelling, you can walk long distances. I once walked fifty-four kilometres in one day, but the next day I couldn't move." A warm smile flashes across his face. When money runs out, he stays somewhere and finds work. He has waited at tables and fixed roofs. He has no profession other than wandering: "My whole life is travelling and working to travel." Through the window, Betty stares adoringly at Michael and whines at the forced separation. She approaches the forbidden door then shies away. Michael considers whether he too could set off again on a journey with Betty. He has long dreamed of travelling but dares not leave the dog and so lives the nomadic life only through the stories of his guests.

"But a dog is a great companion on the road," says the boy, "it guards you at night, barks if anyone approaches. It can ease the loneliness that sometimes grips your heart when you are alone. It's better to talk to Betty than to yourself." He laughs but quickly falls silent as if remembering something. When he forgets a word in English, he checks in with Michael, for example, courage, *Mut*, in German. "You need *Mut* and luck," he exclaims. "It takes courage to venture into the world beyond an existence of slavery."

I take leave of them. Making a beeline through the caravan park, I pass Cerveira's small train station. It is still lit, but the last train from Porto has already passed through. The old waiting room is deserted. Inside two dustbins I spot the remains of discarded windows from recent renovations. Four slow-moving country trains depart daily on the old Porto-Campanhã route, stopping at twelve small stations, until 116 kilometres and two hours in yesterworld later, they reach Cerveira. It has been this way for over a hundred years.

Tonight, perhaps because I am intoxicated by the wine and the conversation with the travelling boy, my mother appears in my dream. In the dream she complains that her life is boring while her son is having a good time. She accuses me of preferring leisure to work. Indeed, throughout her life and even during her last years, living in excruciating tedium in a nursing home, she worried whether I was making a decent living. She wanted to know whether I still had my job, fearing that I might lose it and starve.

I wake up from the dream in my Portuguese room and think that if I could speak with my dead mother, I would tell her about her local twin.

She is an elderly village lady who lives alone in Seixas with a fluffy puppy for company in a small terracotta-painted house on the bank of the Minho River. Once I saw her busy in the garden with the dog beside her. She worked slowly, digging a hole around a rose bush, scattering a handful of fertilizer from a small container, then gently covering the plant's roots with soil like she might a baby on a cold night. All these gestures bore witness to a lifetime of tending a garden. Her small yard by the doll's house was neat and well-kept. She reminded me of my mother.

59

I TAP THE CHISEL WITH THE hammer, and as the old wall resists, a smell of burning spreads through the house. Sparks and shards fly before my goggles when the steel hits the stone, stripping off the plaster garment. The coat mostly breaks easily away from the stone body, but sometimes it clings, and I knock at the cement to separate it from the granite. I learn how to penetrate the chink between the two, to make an entire wall section fall off in thick pieces. The pattern of the hundred-year-old rocks remains imprinted on the plaster. Was it created during the era of kings? Or in times of anarchy? No one knows for sure, and no documentation exists.

People say that Franco's father, Caetano Luís Franco, born in 1830, built the house. He died in 1905 and was buried with his son under the same headstone. Perhaps Caetano Luís built the house when he married in the second half of the nineteenth century during the struggle between the monarchy and the republic. Peeling away the plaster has all the magic of archaeology; with each blow, another age is revealed when you reach the layer created by your predecessors, a burial cave of the past. Sometimes the chisel only scratches the surface and at other times it gets to the bottom of it all, to the very core.

In the middle of the inner granite wall, formerly the outer wall, I feel a soft spot between the stones by the window onto the balcony. A stone is missing, and as I continue to dig, the chisel sinks in effortlessly to reveal a square opening. I push my hand inside and explore what feels like a bird's nest inside a chimney. The cavity leads to a small tunnel running through the interior of the granite wall. It is full of leaves, sawdust, ash and sand. I wonder if it served as a small storage space for corn cobs or an oven chimney.

"It was a niche for laying coals or a candle," explains Gilberto, so not a chimney. They would pick up glowing coals with tongs and put them into the slot to heat the house for the night. He points to soot marks on the stone. Ash residues. But there is also a light, dusty substance. The softer plaster, he says, was once made of limestone, which is porous and flexible and therefore does not crack. Gilberto is a young man with vast knowledge that ranges from the behaviour of the local wind to building materials used in the past. And yet he is never overbearing and always listens patiently.

I continue my efforts, and the stone wall begins to emerge from the plaster as if shedding its skin. It is made of solid stone lintels, shaped stones and smaller uncarved pebbles. The mortar placed inside joints is now pulverized. On the other side of the window, where there was a smaller room, I discover a second niche and decide to leave both alcoves as they are and install a concealed light arrangement. In exposing the wall, I feel I am unravelling a secret, an old essence that has been covered up. Through the removal of the plaster I connect with the first builders of the house.

Today's builders working inside the rooms are knocking down old partitions. Occasionally they come to assess what I am doing. One of them hands me an old chisel more suitable for the job at hand and demonstrates how to use it. I leave a multilayered piece of plaster on the wall as a historical memento. I am taken back by the enormity of the exposed stones, wondering how they were carried back then without modern means of transport. And how were the immense gate supports positioned? They weigh tons.

"They moved them with song," Zé Paulo tells me.

"Song?"

"Yes, they loaded them on ox carts and drove them to the site. Then they propelled them into place using iron bars, ropes and pulleys, singing all the while. The song gave their work rhythm and united them like the spirituals sung by slaves."

It is early January, and the wind, rain and sun are playing tag. There are brief patches of blue sky, and the cold is less penetrating. We decide to forgo insulated aluminium for the new house entrance and look for old wooden doors salvaged from demolished buildings. I continue to peel plaster around the door of the old entrance and reveal the stone lintel of the sturdy wooden doors built by Franco's father.

By the river, we glimpse an abandoned house with all its doors and windows intact.

60

Passing through the old quarter of Caminha, I notice Tiago's car parked in an alleyway. It is a thirty-year-old white BMW convertible purchased by his father. Tiago uses it to shuttle between the different stages of his life: his childhood home in Gondarém, his father's house in Caminha and his own home in Lisbon, where his wife and children live. The car is outside a restaurant that his friend Jorge opened some thirty years ago.

Reviews for the Duque de Caminha are mixed, anywhere from "fantastic" to "never set foot in the place". Some customers feel neglected as the owner tends to engage in long conversations with favoured tables. One reviewer mentions that Jorge has specialized in the restaurant trade in Belgium but "is more of a clown than a chef", yet others are full of praise for the food.

Jorge is happiest when standing next to a table he likes. He acts as the generous, talkative host, a charismatic joker, waiter and chef. As with many of these family establishments, his wife Olimpia - who hides in the kitchen - is the real chef. Tiago is a welcome guest: home-grown royalty whom Jorge hovers over as a bee would a nectar-rich flower. "Look at this," says Jorge when I join them, showing me the photo of a customer he will never forget:

"Marcello," he sighs, wiping away a tear, "Marcello."

Jorge is a character actor: expressive, wild hand gestures, a combination of Bourvil and Louis de Funès. His most distinguished guest, Marcello Mastroianni, came to Caminha twenty-two years ago to shoot his last film. Portuguese director Manoel de Oliveira filmed and directed his *Voyage to the Beginning of the World*. Cast in the role of a dying man, the actor was indeed dying of pancreatic cancer and took comfort in Jorge's food as a condemned man eating his last meal with gusto. In the photographs on Jorge's wall - as in the film - Mastroianni is emaciated, yet traces of his legendary masculine beauty are still evident on his wrinkle-worn face. Sometimes he would take time off between shoots to come to the restaurant. Other times Jorge would drive to the set to take him food. When they said their goodbyes and "Georgino" (the name the Italian gave him) invited the actor back, Mastroianni laughed: "I won't be returning anywhere, ever." Jorge's eyes fill with warm sentiment as he recounts the tale.

In *Voyage to the Beginning of the World*, Mastroianni starred as an ageing film director who goes on a last voyage through northern Portugal accompanied by an actor named Alfonso and two others. He seeks out important figures from his father's past. It was a literal farewell journey for Mastroianni, who was parting with life itself through director de Oliveira's own journey through childhood. Marcello was already dead when the film came out, and Jorge mourned him as if he had lost a lifelong friend.

"This place really marks the beginning of the world," remarks Tiago, who is a great patriot of the Alto Minho region.

"Here rather than southern Galicia?" I ask over a plateful of food.

Tiago is appalled. "Galicia? This here is the birthplace of Portugal. Have you ever *seen* Galicians? They are as short as field mice. Compared with them, we are Goliaths."

"They look nothing like mice. They actually look quite a bit like the locals here."

Tiago protests: "Compared to them, our locals are Vikings. We have blonde women here."

Tiago reminds me of my friend, lawyer A. from Tel Aviv, with his natural gift for performance, a brilliant man who tends to go over the top.

"Yes, us lawyers, the same the world over," he quips when I let him know about his unknown twin. "We tend to lose touch, you know, head in the clouds. This is because we trade in logic. Our ethics are logical. It's such a delightful and crazy whim of nature to have created something so unnatural."

I drag the conversation back to the topic of Portugal, and Tiago holds forth: "My father believes that only here, in the Iberian Peninsula, could Quixote have become such a great literary legend. In other parts of Europe, Quixote would have been considered a criminal." He tells me that his grandfather on his mother's side, the philosopher Francisco da Cunha Leão, wrote of "The Portuguese Mystery", musing on how this nation, with no apparent skills or particular talents, has persisted for so many years.

"Humanity goes through eras of fear," preaches Tiago to his small congregation (consisting of Jorge and me, who listen in awe), "after which it collapses, and then through dream eras, where it soars higher and higher, only to crash again." The theory echoes similar ideas I heard from an Angolan author who dreamed of independence - and paid for it dearly. It also reminds me of another conversation I had had with a Portuguese film director.

Conversations here have a way of sharing a common thread since all the participants are Portuguese raised in this imbroglio of tradition, memory and diminished history of greatness. They have all navigated the same hardships of the second half of the last century. When I mention how much pleasure I take in being here despite my carpenter-inspired woes, he says: "you, my friend, are in a state of grace, *estado de graça*, when a person is under a miracle sky. You did well to come to this place. You have found refuge in the safest place in Europe. Up north, by the great river and the Atlantic Ocean, this is where it all began, and we will be the last place to fall." Jorge is listening, his eyes sparkling, his restless hands relaxing. If there is one thing he loves more than serving tables, it is good conversation. Tiago has a way with words that makes Jorge feel they have come from his own heart.

61

THE WHIRRING OF HELICOPTERS IS a sound rarely heard on the peaceful banks of the Minho. Lifting my eyes to the sky, I spot one hovering above my head, back and forth, scanning the river scene. On the Cerveira side of the river, divers in rubber suits prepare to enter the water while rescue boats comb the river and television crews are poised on a stone jetty. The search is conducted in utter silence and in an atmosphere of despondency. Following a Spanish-Portuguese triathlon, which included swimming across the Minho, it was discovered that one of the younger participants failed to arrive at the finishing line. He is currently declared missing.

When the investigation gets under way, it turns out that he never emerged from the river onto the Portuguese side. Although the river part of the race was clearly marked with rescue boats, buoys and observers, he was apparently caught in a midstream whirlpool. Rescuers now calculate the direction and speed of the current to locate the body.

River deaths are rare these days compared with when the Minho was declared a closed border with its smugglers and fugitives. Corpses floating on the waters were then a routine matter. Even bathing is considered safe today, provided it is done in allotted spots marked with buoys and attended by two lifeguards in season.

I take frequent walks through the park by the banks of the Minho. I walk alone or am joined by Michael and Betty. At times the river flows rapidly and can be tuirbulent; other times, the water is low and calm. For someone who comes from a relatively arid land containing one lake and a few parched streams, the Minho is like the Amazon. Its opposite bank is so distant that it belongs to an altogether different country. The waters are benign near its shores but deadly at its heart. During low tides, ocean water penetrates forty kilometres inland into Valença, so water is saltier in the summer. During tidal months, the river overflows into the sea, making the waters fresher. "The waters ebb and flow, to their conservation no doubt. To teach us that we should ever be in motion," wrote the Englishman Robert Burton four hundred years ago. He studied melancholy and considered travel a possible cure for it.

I study the pattern of the tides, enamoured of the sinuous traces left on its muddy banks. Lines are curved like a work of art, entirely made of alluvial materials. They form a monogram left by water swelling on the floodplains. The waterline forms a continuous strip of small stones, branches, waste wood and objects swept away, polished and smoothed by the waters. I sometimes collect polished driftwood as abstract sculptures or even reshaped plastic debris.

In one of Cerveira's parks is a modest museum that is at the heart of new research into the Minho River. It is surrounded by reedbeds where cheerful frogs enjoy one long fiesta. About fifty species of fish live here, small and large, round and long, swimming in huge aquariums. Marine biologist Dr Carlos Antunes, the director, is an avid fan of the river. He was a student of the German biologist, Professor Mike Weber, who during the 1980s initiated research on the Minho, a river which until then flowed in relative anonymity.

During their research, Weber, Antunes and a few other young researchers lived for a time on a large, deserted farm with iron gates, now Michael's home. Weber arrived in the early 1980s in the wake of the revolution and the opening of Portugal to the world. He came to write a doctorate on the Minho and discovered a 300-kilometre-long European river, fascinating in terms of aquatic life. Until then it had been almost unknown, perhaps because it ran through two enemy countries.

Fortunately, Antunes was a field researcher, and the area was also where about a thousand fishermen, Portuguese and Spaniards, made a living. The young Antunes joined their fishing expeditions. He learned from them the secrets of the river, which they, in turn, had learned from their forefathers. "They were river experts and my second university," Antunes informs me with typical modesty. Fortunately, the entire fishing industry was under regulation, and all Portuguese fishermen were registered, perhaps for surveillance purposes. Thus by the 1920s, every fisherman had been issued a licence with a photo. These photographs are exhibited in the small museum with other fishing gear in tribute to the water people he loves.

The marine biologist leads me down a dimly lit tunnel through large aquariums where river fish stare at us with round, cold eyes as if we have dived into the bottom of the Minho. He shows me a transparent eel, whose existence was unknown until a Danish explorer discovered it a hundred years ago. The Dane found that although this fish lives in rivers, it migrates to the ocean, travelling 4,000 kilometres to the Sargasso Sea near the Caribbean as an adult. There it lays its eggs and dies at a ripe old age. Its offspring swim for about two years all the way back to the waters of the Minho. I stare in wonder at the almost transparent fish, which totally ignores its new admirer.

"The fishermen could never understand what I was searching for. There is a gulf between them and the world of science. So I began popularizing the river to a Portuguese audience."

The thousand registered fishermen lived on both banks, from Caminha and La Guarda by the estuary to Cerveira, Gondarém and Monção in the east. They were both fishermen and farmers because they could not fish throughout the year. Antunes discovered that there was a thriving fishing community all year round in Caminha. Due to its location, the town benefited from both the ocean and the river, living from both saltwater and freshwater fish. There was a ban on commercial fishing in the river during those years, and fishing was allowed only for individual consumption in order to preserve fish stocks. Wealthy families owned parts of the riverbanks and fish, like they own private woodland and all the animals that live there.

As I visit this small but fascinating museum with Antunes, his love for the river folk is evident. They were his first teachers, a breed of hard-working, brave people who still carry on today despite the dangers. They have a solid connection to the water as a livelihood and a way of life. But their numbers have shrunk to about three hundred. The museum display cases are packed with their paraphernalia: fishing rods and nets, wooden traps for fish and crabs, sailing boat models and even the first petrol engine.

The state monitoring of fishermen and fishing proved to be of added scientific value. Since 1914, the authorities have recorded the daily numbers and types of fish. Thus, a contemporary researcher can learn about the quantities of salmon and lamprey, eels and crabs, species that have become extinct and others which have suddenly appeared in the area. I also discover that a writer, the son of a Porto fisherman, visited the area about a hundred years ago. His name was Raul Brandão, and he travelled along the Portuguese coastline, documenting the fishermen and their families in a detailed diary. In August 1921, Brandão reached Caminha, the northernmost fishing village. He noted that the fishermen's wives were mainly dressed in black because a father, son or husband had been lost at sea in every family.

"The Minho is the most important, most populated river in the Iberian Peninsula," Dr Antunes tells me. "It is beautiful and well preserved with dozens of dams. The largest animals in the region are the wild boar, otters and the exotic mink brought here for its fur. There are also deer, the emblem of Cerveira. But these are rare today. Some deer have been spotted near Candemil."

"Candemil?"

"Yes, close to your house. And on the mountains behind your house, there are packs of wolves and herds of wild horses."

As he speaks, I recall hearing my father's wondrous stories about European rivers. He grew up on the banks of the Wisla and remembered dense forests, abundant springs, fish and bathing in the river. My heart, too, is drawn to the river.

Together with Orit, I discover the magical Seixas riverbank en route to Caminha. A narrow path diverges from the main road by an abandoned mansion. It leads to an inner coastal enclave where the river caresses the feet of long abandoned homes of the wealthy. Between the houses, on sand and hyssop dunes, there are potsherds polished by the water. Some still carry the factory stamp, a coloured stripe on the edge of a plate, a mug handle. Sometimes a tiny porcelain piece tells an entire story.

We collect the fragments as if they were precious stones. Sometimes after a storm, we find large tree trunks sculpted by the Minho. The ropes of vessels moored on the river stretch over the sands, and the water licks the sides of the boats humming a river lullaby. "Water that runs and sings, It's water that makes you sleep," wrote Pessoa of a different body of water. I struggle with a large, fragrant and moist piece of wood, but it is soft and has grown a thin fur, so it slips from my hands back into the water as if it were alive.

"For many years, the river was a no-go zone which the authorities attempted to close off," says Zé Paulo. "But people always found a way in. You can't imprison people inside their homes. In trying to put an entire river into lockdown, you are encouraging people to cross it. Smuggling is not seen here as a crime, but a living," he says, sympathizing with all who disobey laws, rules, regulations and idiotic ceremonies and so expressing typical Portuguese tolerance towards all ways of life and also opposition to arbitrary state authority.

"My grandmother would return from the river with boxes of Spanish soap smuggled under her dress," he laughs. During the Spanish Civil War, smuggling increased due to shortages on the Spanish side. During the 1950s, when there were shortages and poverty on the Portuguese side, the number of people fleeing across the river to Spain significantly increased. The river was both death and salvation. They lived and died by the river; living on the banks of the river, you never went hungry. There was food from the fields, the trees, the water and smuggling."

62

AT MIDDAY, FRANKLIN'S WORKERS DOWN tools and head off to lunch. True to my newly acquired habit, I drive to Jorge's restaurant in Caminha. I find Tiago engrossed in his trout, prepared for him by Olimpia. "I could pick at this wonderful river fish for hours," he says. "When a person is hungry, he carries with him the hunger of generations, an ancient hunger." In all of the Alto Minho, I have yet to meet a man as preoccupied with his forefathers as Tiago. It is as if he finds existence to be valued only as part of a vast tree, holding on to its roots. "The past is the finest component of any man. And in these parts, the past is king."

"Was the world of your grandfather and father very different?"

"Absolutely. It was a fiery world, sensual, dramatic. One led a real life unhampered by this constant fear of death." Tiago scans the room disdainfully as if anachronistically thrown into a bland, vaguely repugnant age. "Life during the fifties and twenties had that particular flavour that prevails after a great war. In the wake of brutal wars, life is infused with meaning. It is a dream-era following a nightmare. When you dream, you become human. When you live in fear, you become a beast."

He grew up in the Alto Minho at the same time as Franco, Dantas and Franklin, yet he differs from them significantly. In his family, nature meant pleasure, not hard labour. He still remembers his joy as a child when one glowing summer day he sailed on the river in a light boat called Breeze. Few people were to be found on the water back then, discounting smugglers at night and daytime fishermen. Cruising for leisure was a pleasure pursued by a few wealthy families. He recalls the sight of the riverbank from the boat, the mysterious view of one red-brick house standing alone among several large trees not far from the Cerveira cemetery. Its balconies faced the river, and its back was to the town. To this day, it stands there on a hill, deserted and ravaged.

I show him a photo of the opening I uncovered in the stone wall beneath the plaster. "It wasn't a safe," he says. "It is too small and in a poor house." After his father's death, he discovered a safe in one of the walls and decided to open it. How curious he must have been, being the way he is, about the father's secrets. He did not have the combination for the lock because his father went to his grave with that secret. He tried several combinations until he noticed that the colouration on some of the numbers was lighter. He tried them, and the key turned, but eventually he had to break the lock for the door to open fully. At the bottom he discovered another opening from which he pulled out a metal box with an old gun inside. A crown was engraved on its butt.

Jorge adds a piece of wood to the open fireplace - a large stone slab dark from years of use, and with a chimney opening above it that seems to listen in to the flames. "A fire like this once burned at the heart of every Portuguese home," says Tiago, "but we are losing the fire that is the beginning of everything. We sat in front of it for generations until the first cave drawing, the first few words which formed a conversation. It protected us, warmed us, saved us from stagnation, chased away predators and protected us. Now the fire is gone, like other things of our past."

Olimpia arrives triumphantly from the kitchen carrying a dessert.

I tell Tiago about the round window, and he recommends his joiner, Paulo, as someone who can combine the two Jaffa arches into a window. His shop is across the bridge from Caminha on my way to Cerveira. And when I get there and mention Tiago, Paulo, tall and well-dressed, descends from his office above the premises and examines the old arches. He touches the wood, rubs it, brings it close to his nose to smell it, and examines the nail-free joinery. He asks if it once formed an entire window.

No, I say, two arches. Only once the work is complete will the *janela redonda* be created, a round window installed near the roof. Paulo calls on his foreman to plan how to join the pieces and design the window opening. The wall faces the sun but is hit by heavy diagonal rains during winter.

"A near-horizontal rain," warns Gilberto. "The wind comes to Cerveira from the south and not from the north-west as in the rest of Portugal." It is a strong wind carried with great force through the valley of the Minho. The round window will face challenges once inconceivable in Jaffa.

Paulo and the carpenter decide to connect the window with a horizontal axis. Glass should be cut at the glazier's to seal the shutter slits, and it will be sent to the locksmith to make the iron hoop to hold it together. This chain of events requires coordination between three different artisans, so there will be inevitable delays. In his well-lit office, Paulo lists the expected costs. The price of installing the window with all its new parts will be double its price in Jaffa.

"I would do anything for a friend of Tiago's," Paulo promises.

THE STRANGER'S HOMECOMING

The Round Window
that Sailed from Jaffa

63

FRANKLIN, WHO HAS LEARNED FROM bitter experience, will only agree to carve the circular window opening when the window arrives ready and finished, not a moment sooner. Now that builders have begun showing up to work, the house gradually rises from the ashes to take shape. Gilberto manages to find time away from his family, students and other projects to accompany me to a part of Viana de Castelo across the river. It is a vast commercial area with hardware depots selling building, electricity and water supplies. A person like me, fancying himself as a Robinson Crusoe figure on a romantic renovation adventure, can be overwhelmed by the incredible abundance of modern consumer goods. The shops present me with hundreds of kitchen and shower fittings, concealed cisterns and rain showers, thousands of kitchen tiles, handles and pedals - a fantastic selection.

I discover things I never intended to know about different types of toilets and showers, some costing as much as a house and others going for pennies. I learn of translucent kitchen sinks and steam cleaners, electric mirrors which diffuse steam. I hear things I never wished to hear about the differences between washing appliances, sinks, heaters, ovens and tumble dryers.

From bathroom supplies, I move on to a marble factory, whose vast yard is a geological garden with colossal slabs. There, I am required to decide between a sparkling black mist marble, snow-white marble or pink marble with red streaks, local or Italian, from Portuguese mines or the depths of the Italian soil containing beautiful minerals and remnants of ancient lava.

Such choices are usually made early on in a married couple's life, when the young still look at the world as a giant emporium, with goods there for the taking. Myself, I am a senior citizen, yet I must master that sort of enthusiasm so that we can make ourselves a home from the still shabby, leaking chaos that has yet to take shape. I message back and forth with Orit, sending photos and waiting for the ensuing discussion and argument.

Then, to recover from an excess of consumerism, I return to Marco's shop to breathe in the invigorating scent of the old. I am looking for a vintage pink marble sink that I am sure to recognize as soon as I see it. I refuse to settle for a modern one from the vast plumbing supplies stores. I help Marco unload unsold items from his red car and drive with him to another warehouse at the edge of town. He leads me to an unfamiliar yard, flips open a trapdoor and we go down into the bowels of the earth.

For a moment, I recoil from the damp darkness, but he turns on a switch to light this new pirate cave. Old children's toys, a carriage with a rusty horse, a round porcelain sink with a rusty drain hole. How different these venerable objects from the sinks of the megastores, how charged with history and memories. My eyes scan the room, searching for the object the very sight of which will strike an internal chord, telling me that it has chosen me.

Compared with the muteness of modern artefacts, in this basement every old item has its story to tell. An old coffee box from Porto decorated with a painting of an African woman touches me deeply. An iron carriage for a child with pedals. Small figurines kept as amulets for the health of a child or livestock. The miniature world of rural faith. Also, battered pots and black pans, a plough, scales, a rabbit feeding device, farm tools passed down through generations. "The patient, obstinate, reliable things that we use and get used to, the things we live by," wrote Ursula Le Guin affectionately.

64

AFTER A CLIMB THROUGH EXOTIC gardens around an alley is a small art gallery called Café dos Poetas, and on its wall is a plaque commemorating Luis Pedro's ex-bookstore, 1968-2009. Most days, the place appears devoid of visitors, but on certain nights it fills with people coming to hear a visiting author or poet. Only then does the gallery assume, for a time, the role of a sophisticated poetry café. On several occasions I have noticed an older man with thinning white hair and the ageless dignity of the artist or a man who sees clearly through life. Sometimes he leaves the café to slowly wander the streets, stopping to enjoy a meal and a glass of red wine, always alone in the same restaurant, seated at the same table by the window with the same attentive waiter. There is something about the man that commands attention: an austere figure surrounded by the commotion of noisy family groups. I come up to him one day and introduce myself as an Israeli author.

"I am an Angolan writer," says the man and I am taken aback. In my ignorance, I thought that during the era of the *retornados*, all former citizens returned from the colony to Portugal for fear of death. I was unaware of the existence of white Portuguese fighting beside Africans against the old country. As in South Africa, some white Portuguese viewed the independence of Angola as worth risking their lives for, even at the cost of taking up arms against their own countrymen. Even José Luandino Vieira's gait has something defiant about it; defiance clings to anyone who has fought in a battle of the few against the many.

When we sit down at the poetry café, of which he is the owner, he recounts how his parents emigrated to the African colony. In Portugal, his father was a poor shoemaker and his

213

mother a fieldworker in the service of others; impoverished tenant farmers whose own country held no future for them. Like others, encouraged by the authorities, they set out for the colonies in the hope of a better future.

"In those days, entire areas of rural Portugal appeared deserted. Many people left," he says. "Living here, sometimes I experience a similar sensation of desolation," I tell him. "Driving in the area, or here in Cerveira, there are so many empty houses, abandoned estates."

Vieira was an infant when his parents emigrated in the thirties. "They left Salazar's Portugal, at the time an impoverished feudal country." During those years before World War II, it seemed that the whole world was prone to dire premonitions. My parents also left Poland during that time and came as young students to build a new life in the Palestinian colony.

"Once in Angola, my father continued his work as a shoemaker but employed some locals and lived as a free man," says Vieira.

"What was your Luandan childhood like?"

His eyes light up: "Wild, free. As poor European immigrants, in Africa we found freedom. Freedom from oppressive Catholicism, from the heavy burden of universal poverty, moralizing and rigidity, Salazar's dictatorship, the silencing of voices. Then suddenly, Africa, Luanda: a port town with Portuguese architecture and a black population. And jungle Africa, exotic with all the wealth of the land. For us children, both black and white, it was a Tom Sawyer and Huckleberry Finn life, with the sea for a Mississippi, warm weather and with no parental supervision."

His impassioned speech reminds me of the words of Albert Camus when describing his Algerian childhood and of language other Portuguese such as Teresa use in speaking of their wild African childhood: voyages at sea, leopards on trees, terror and bliss. When he speaks of his lost childhood paradise, Vieira loses the habitual cynicism and restraint of a man who has lived a full life, and his face brightens as if returning to that seafront, to those childhood games.

Adolescence was a sobering time for him: a changing world was invading colonial life. Newspapers came to Africa, and with them information and calls for the freedom lacking throughout the Catholic dictator's empire. Vieira was a white boy in an African colony that began to long for independence, with no knowledge yet of the suffering in store.

"Horrendous suffering," he stresses, then falls silent.

He was thirteen years old when Angola attempted to negotiate its liberation from the imperial yoke in 1948. When these efforts came to nothing, an independence war broke out. The land was awash with blood. Vieira, a boy who worked as a mechanic, secretly switched sides until he eventually joined the Angolan resistance. He wrote and published several short stories on the life of black people, even winning a Portuguese literary prize. For a time, he led a double existence, but while in Lisbon, aged twenty-six, newly married and with a newborn baby, he was forcibly taken off a plane heading to London and brought in handcuffs before a judge, accused of participating in the resistance, carrying firearms and opposing the Portuguese regime.

"At the beginning of November, I had finished my first novel, and ten days later, I was already a prisoner." His novel, *The Real Life of Domingos Xaviar*, was a heartbreaking tale of the life and death of an Angolan tractor driver living under Portuguese oppression. When the book was published in Paris, Vieira was already into his third year in Tarrafal, Cape Verde, Salazar's notorious prison. The camp was formerly used in the slave trade. "There were eighty of us prisoners in the dry heat and immense boredom, waiting for Godot. And I went on writing."

As I sit across the table from him in his beautiful café, surrounded by poetry books and drawings of freedom fighters, a photo of Marilyn Monroe and work by the late local artist Rodrigues, Vieira spins his African tale in such a quiet, contained voice that I find myself shocked. It would never have occurred to me that this old man, so suave in his appearance with his white hair and trimmed beard, was for many years a prisoner on a distant island, a character out of a Dumas novel.

"When they took me, I was just married with a new baby - and I disappeared from my small family's life for twelve whole years."

"The camp where we were being held at Ilha de Santiago was set up six kilometres from the small village of Tarrafal and named after it.

Of all the men who were there, about forty survived and are living in Luanda and Lisbon - we keep in touch to this day." Only with the death of the dictator did things begin to change; Vieira was set free. Sometime later, his provisional terms were lifted, and he chose to return to Angola as an activist and journalist.

In 1993 his ageing mother asked him to come and live near her in Fátima, so he returned to Portugal to be by her side until her death aged nearly one hundred. "I have good genes."

For fourteen years he lived close to Cerveira in the same monastery where Biennale artist José Rodrigues resided. Vieira published books while in prison and wrote several others, gaining renown in his old homeland once so set against him. "In '92 elections were held," he says. "It seemed as if everything was going to settle down in Angola, but war broke out again, and it was the war of all wars in a country armed to the teeth - a bloodbath. The fighting only ended in 2002." His wife, who stayed faithful to him throughout his prison years, had died, and the child born before his arrest remained in Africa, where he lives to this day.

Each year Vieira travels to visit his old comrades in arms. The battle did not end with Angolan liberation; it just grew tougher. "In the end, there is no such thing as independence," says the former fighter who in his eighty-two years has seen it all. "A man is always a slave to the interests of the past, of his tribe, of external forces, wherever there are natural resources and wealth to be had. And anyway, dreams are made to break."

65

In mid-January, as the rain softly patters on our multi-layered roof, the house fills up with the hustle and bustle of workers. Franklin and his men put up and take down scaffolding, using cement and polyurethane to seal the last cracks in the roof. Inside the house, they wield sledgehammers to destroy the interior wall of the old kitchen; they uproot rickety flagstones. All the while I continue to uncover the stone wall. An electrician arrives to take measurements and verify the location of the power points, and the practical plumber António also makes an appearance. The aluminium people announced that they would start soon, and then the carpenters should arrive to finish the attic, the ground floor and the cellar. The insulator also shows up with his wife to inspect the house. He will bring drywall and light metal frames and coordinate everything with the electrician and plumber. Their work interlinks as he is to cover the pipes they will put in place. Marco Silva, the antiquarian, calls from Gondar to let me know that he has located an old sink. He invites me to his parents' house.

I arrive, but Marco is not there. An older man who looks as if he must be his father is waiting for me. Silva senior takes me to the yard behind the café, and I realize that hoarding is a hereditary condition. He takes me through a massive labyrinth of sheds and warehouses, rooms and courtyards overflowing with used objects. A large black dog is barking near a pile of shit, and Marco's father pushes the animal aside and points to a collection of old and unattractive sinks and troughs. He does not seem unhappy when I signal no, and drags me from warehouse to warehouse until we reach a small winery. He kindly gives me a bottle of home-made *vinho verde* as compensation for for my frustrated scrap journey.

In a tarpaulin-covered shed I find relatively new sinks. No. Our guided tour turns to a room full of mattresses where a young woman is working on a sewing machine; further down is another storage space with old furniture and bed parts. All this time, Silva senior chats away non-stop, until I feel that at any moment my head might explode like a watermelon. I thank him for the wine and make my escape, accompanied by the dog's barking. Searching for the past through objects suddenly seems tasteless and futile; instead of a holy grail, I have found a used cistern.

I escape in my car, driving to the river to calm myself down. I then sit in the Curt'isso and write until Michael, Betty and the fair-haired boy join my table. Dominique's beard continues to grow expansively but he remains largely mute. Only on his second glass of local beer does he begin to confess to his interrogators, describing some of the souls he has met on his travels. Once, two large dogs approached him and around their necks hung the scallop shell, emblem of the *camino*. He was glad of their company and bent over to make a fuss of them until their owner arrived. "That man came to exert a great deal of influence over my life. If he had continued in the same direction as me, we would still be together," says Dominique.

The dogs' owner was an elderly Czech with a massive beard like an ancient prophet. He explained to Dominique that he left his old life when his parents died, and inheritance disputes over the family farm broke out, an all-out sibling war of greed, hatred and envy while the graves were still fresh. "It's all yours," said the Czech to his grasping relatives and set out on the path of miracles.

They walked together a significant section of the road. The Czech spoke and spoke, poured out his heart and listened to the boy until they parted ways. "There are people like the Czech who pop up on the *camino* as if they were just waiting there for you, another stage on your crusade."

219

I tell Dominique that after thirty-five years as a journalist interviewing people, I realize that anyone will open up if you listen carefully. Even those sworn to silence like to be heard. "And sometimes it's the first step in falling in love with a woman." He listens to me as if taking in helpful advice for the future journey. Perhaps his memory from this café conversation will be of the short man who spoke of the magic of interviews, something to recount to others later in his travels.

Peals of laughter reach us from a nearby table.

"It's the Luncheon Club," says Michael, "the local weekly meeting of expats - English, Dutch and Germans. It has been taking place for twenty years. They usually meet in a large restaurant on the way to Valença." He smiles but I recoil, recalling what George Orwell wrote in his novel of his days in Burma and of the parochial white-only club with the boredom and narrow-mindedness of its members. It was the consolation of exiles whose only common interest was their distance from home. Michael moves over to the noisy table so as not to appear to be snubbing them.

The boy Dominique continues his story, telling me about a woman he fell in love with on the pilgrim route. She was a few years his senior and gorgeous. She appeared on the road one fragrant evening. It was her third pilgrimage towards Santiago. The first time she set out after realizing she was in an abusive marriage. The journey cleared her head, but when she returned to her country she fell in love with another violent man. Determined never to find herself involved with a monster, she set out on yet another journey. She confided in Dominique for an entire night, and his hungry soul became attached to hers, but when he woke from a short sleep in the morning, he found that she had already gone.

A year later, during the winter, he stopped on his way in a small Portuguese town. Seeking warmth and shelter, he entered a church and went to the confessional booth. The priest listened to him and said, "Well, this is strange because a woman with the same story came to me once." Dominique and the priest then realized they were talking about the same woman. "I have good news for you," the *padre* told him: "She continued on her journey and met a man who had set out because he wanted to put his abusive past behind him. She fell in love with him, and they were married here."

"I think they have a child now," says Dominique and looks at me with his bright, innocent but wise eyes. "Tomorrow, I am going back on the road," he informs Michael.

From a nearby table, "the Pirate" greets me with a wave. He is a tall man, skinny, with craggy facial features and a mane of grey hair like a windswept sea creature thrown ashore. Tiago refers to him as Clint Eastwood because of his looks. He is a well-known carpenter and wood artisan in the area. "A true Minho man," says Tiago approvingly as if he is the offspring of an almost extinct species. According to local legend, he fell over on the steps outside the Quinta da Malaposta after drinking too much and then had a breakdown. Since then, he describes himself as "down and out but happy". His name is Carlos Costa.

"What is it about this area that people like it so much?" we ask.

"Great *vinho verde* and border smugglers," laughs the Pirate.

66

"MY FRIEND MANUEL MARRECA HAS some traditional doors from old, demolished Lisbon buildings," Michael tells me. Over the phone, Manuel agrees to show me his gems, so one day Michael, Betty and I climb up the road to the place where the doors are kept. The abandoned mansion is set in the rolling hills beside the road connecting Cerveira and Candemil, near the Hotel Malaposta. I remove a wire holding the gates together. The drive within, lined with soft grass, winds between the different features: a watchtower, a pool, some sheds and a winery leading up to the house. The place is wide open to the elements, the tile roof shattered during a storm and by the whirlwind of time.

The staircase at the back of the house leads to a massive kitchen with a stone oven and chimney, a table and a few utensils arranged as if the family had been taken by surprise in the middle of supper. A plaster relief depicting a battle scene has dropped from the living room ceiling onto the wooden floor. We find a single bed with a straw mattress in a narrow space, straight out of a World War II field hospital. It seems as if time froze here fifty years ago, which fills this ghostly abode with a sense of mystery. Traces. Crumbs. Leftovers. A library full of bags. A briefcase. A velvet loveseat that was once blue.

Behind the mansion towers a wooded hill with stone terraces. We reach its summit out of breath. A huge cork tree grows from the cracks of a boulder. Beneath the treetop is a stone plaza like a roofless temple. Betty skips excitedly on a low stone wall as if a new scent is in in the air. The place is spectacular and open, infused with the spirit of nature. We rest beneath the tree for a long while, and I feel that Michael is watching me closely, trying to make up his mind about whether to confide in me.

As we return to the bottom of the hill, we spot a figure supporting a drain pouring into a basin once used for washing clothes, a colourful wooden sculpture untouched by time. In the past it must have been an avid listener to the conversations of the washerwomen at work by its feet. Next to it rises an external spiral staircase leading to the main entrance of the house. The stairs are covered with a crimson carpet of fallen camellia flowers. The walls are painted a live green moss as if nature alone is tending to the house. It decorates, envelops, covers and consumes it.

I rush from one structure to the next, opening doors, peeking inside a locked warehouse. I find newspaper clippings from the nineteenth century. Clues are everywhere. A pile of hand-painted *azulejos*. A wine cellar complete with wooden shelves, shattered glass and dusty, sealed bottles, the earliest from 1965, their contents long gone sour. Under ceiling supports, empty elephantine wine barrels lean against each other, like rotund fellow sufferers seeking support, and there are dozens of doors. This is the treasure trove that I had been looking for and unknowingly passed by daily. All the doors are from another century. Inlaid glass, ornate, Art Nouveau, double, triple or quadruple, pink, yellow or green, damaged or whole. They are the work of artisans, brought here from demolished mansions in the capital.

All the doors are very tall, though they were made back when most people were shorter. At the time, doorways were more prominent in wealthier homes because class was measured, among other things, according to ceiling height and door size. Some are grandiose, beautifully decorated masterpieces. Michael holds up a door, and I move another under it to test how solid it is. Some of the glass is shattered. I drag others about, pick them up and turn them over to find the perfect pair for the doorway of my house.

From among the dozens of doors, I find a matching pair

that are white with horizontal transom windows above. They are delicate-looking doors for internal rather than external use. Segments of painted glass lie between delicate mullions. Manuel names a modest price, and when I ask, he recalls the house from which they were salvaged. "A large bourgeois house in central Lisbon from the 1930s." After living its life, it was emptied of occupants and stood abandoned for years until it was knocked down to make room for a new building. He salvaged the doors and windows. "These are Art Deco doors," he says, "made of wood and glass lace in wonderful geometrical shapes. They served to partition rooms."

67

IN THE MORNINGS, CASA MARÍLIA fills with the sweet melody of hammers like birdsong. The builders are finally at work, and I am grateful. With each team of workers it is immediately evident who the boss is and who is the paid hand, whom the boss will blame when they run off to another job. Some are entrusted with the more complicated crafts. Others, even at sixty years of age, serve as deckhands, doing simple tasks such as mixing the cement, carrying the buckets, moving rocks or clearing debris with a wheelbarrow. The boss sets the tone, sometimes talkative, at other times taciturn. All the work is carried out without legal documentation or safety gear. No helmets. They walk unperturbed on a sloping roof, several metres above the ground.

As I look up at Franklin's workers, a hammer suddenly drops at my feet from high above. Gilberto warns me to keep my distance, but after all the setbacks I enjoy watching the work: the careful tightening of a rope between two planks, the small scaffolding which moves from place to place expertly fastened to the wall, the rusty concrete mixer, the buckets, the wheelbarrow on its wooden track. A crowbar is used as a lever, a plank as support for a considerable weight. All that humble, hierarchical industry, in which everyone knows their place. Only rarely does a mild argument flare up. When Gilberto says that concrete must not touch the wood because it will rot, Franklin listens and at once orders his obliging worker to dismantle a low section of brick wall he had just finished putting up.

Downstairs in the dark animal pens, Franklin and his men begin to cut two windows in the ancient wall, eighty centimetres thick. The plan is to install windows in the rooms which have thus far only had air slits. The size of the windows must depend on the

225

thickness and weight of the stone and the simple tools at hand: a crowbar, a plank, a disc cutter, a level and a ruler. Franklin sharpens his pencil with a penknife and keeps it behind his ear. Occasionally he chats with another client using an old mobile phone. He never shouts or raises his voice. There is harmony in all their actions. I watch the builders immersed in their quiet work, and they look back, amused by my wonder at their simple methods.

As they begin to pull stones out of the ancient wall, it seems to me that it might at any moment start to groan, its mouth open, and the whole house collapse on our heads. Each stone props up the one above it, with no cement or support other than the arrangement of the stones themselves and the crumbling mortar. But they work in unison like coal miners underground. For someone who grew up close to noisy construction sites, this dismantling and assembling of the wall is like a silent film. The workers whisper or speak in hushed tones as if not to frighten the stones or to be able to hear if the wall begins to crack and thus prevent disaster. Miraculously, with a single support beam in place of the rocks, the wall does not break.

I quickly move away when they push their heads inside the expanding cavity like a lion tamer placing his shaved head inside the jaws of the beast. The gap they have created is jagged, irregular and appears unstable. On top of the opening, another support beam holds the floor above. Franklin and his men put iron bars in place to support the foundation. It is real stone masonry, and Franklin is like a master builder from a medieval guild. He learned the craft at a young age and progressed slowly through experience, without technical courses or degrees, until becoming proficient. Franklin now studies the rough opening and shapes it to fit the dimensions agreed with the window installers and to support the stones.

At the same time, above them, Jorge the carpenter and his two men are hard at work on the first floor. He is a skilled woodworker, but without Franklin's quiet intellect, he is more of a kamikaze carpenter, a reckless lieutenant risen to take charge in the absence of a calm older master. The carpenters are working on the floor of the second room upstairs. Between the two rooms remains a *tapique*, a partition built without blocks or plaster. According to local custom, it mostly comprises a grid of thin wooden laths with cement-like mortar between them. The upper part of this wall was repaired in 1984 due to the landslide and is thus made of heavier concrete. Jorge's workers use a sledgehammer on this top part to dismantle it slowly. They cut through the exposed wooden skeleton with a chainsaw and a disc cutter, and the wall begins to tilt sideways.

Then, suddenly, pulled down by weight and disappearing supports, the partition overpowers what remains of the wooden floor and collapses into the animal quarters downstairs, thundering through the air. The mass of masonry falls within a whisker of Franklin and his workers, who are delicately moving the window into place underneath, missing them by thirty centimetres. In falling, it also topples towards Jorge, hitting him on the shoulder. The Franklin party recoils in alarm and the disintegrating wall also brushes against the window hanging on its side in the opening.

In one careless instant, gravity has demonstrated its force. As the dust clears and the commotion subsides, the house remains standing despite the chaos below. Even the loose window opening does not give way. Only Jorge, the unlucky master carpenter, is left clutching his shoulder and groaning.

THE STRANGER'S HOMECOMING

The Baba Schulz
Ashram and 360
Parrots

68

THERE ARE FOUR OF US in Michael's yard at the outer perimeter of the *quinta* as night begins to fall. Michael and Margot have been neighbours for a long time, and so has Marco, who moves about like a shadow. One of eight children, he arrived here thirty years ago with his father, a Portuguese gardener who was mentally broken by the bloody civil war in Mozambique. Even then, Marco was an unusual child in a world of his own. After his father's death, he stayed on as a protégé of the *quinta*. He lives in a simple shipping container, taking on the odd gardening and landscaping job and creating intricate paintings. He lives a shielded, reclusive life.

Michael said, "Come and visit us this evening. I will invite Margot too." Many weeks after my initial incursion, the doors to the estate, the former ashram of Baba Shanti, open before me.

"We could mull it over for years as one might with a natural disaster or a war," says Michael. He sounds anguished yet relieved, like a patient delving into childhood traumas. "The *quinta*, or farm, was the spiritual centre for the charismatic German Baba Ulrich Schulz, who called himself Oliver Shanti, and his followers who called him Baba Shanti."

We settle back in the dim light of evening, eating simple food and talking softly. Marco listens. Sometimes he hums to himself or gets up restlessly, disappearing into the darkness, his container home or into the tangle of trees and reeds.

Margot says she was seventeen when she first met Oliver Shanti. "And everything, good and evil, was in him from the start. But no one could see evil at first because Schulz was a force. He was a spiritual leader who touched everything around him. When you met him, it felt like an alien abduction. After that, you became a changed person."

Forty years after that meeting, Margot is a slim, handsome, energetic woman. A gifted musician who no longer plays any instrument, she operates heavy machinery around the farm. She was born during the German economic golden era in a Bavarian village to a Wehrmacht infantryman who had returned from the hellish Russian battlefield. After the ashram collapsed, she was the one who took over the task of rescuing all that remained, instinctively assuming the role of saviour.

"The bitter end meant that people only remember everything in terms of ugly exploitation, the trial, imprisonment. But we got to know a special person who was made up of both light and darkness, not just the perverted Baba of the newspapers which destroyed him."

She grew up in Bavaria with parents who were brought up in the Nazi education system. Brainwashing was very effective. "My father rarely spoke of the past. Neither did my mother. He only said that Hitler had some good about him too and continued to support him in part. As a child, I slept in bed with my grandmother, and she told me terrible stories about what really happened and the cruelty of the Nazis. Monstrous acts committed on Jews. Grandma wanted to make sure that I did not grow up to be like my parents. She spared me nothing." Margot shivers in the darkness of the yard. She sounds genuine and a decent person, and I instantly take a liking to her.

Marco comes and goes. He gets up growling, says something in a low murmur and disappears into the darkness only to return later. The night around us is suffused with ghosts, fathers gone mad: her father who returned from the Russian snow, Marco's father who returned from the colonies. Descendants who pay a heavy price for the choices made by their parents. The memory of Baba Schulz, who did good but became a monster, still hovers over this area on the outskirts of Cerveira.

Margot saw Baba Shanti for the first time in 1980; she was a beautiful, kind-hearted German girl and a gifted musician. She came from a home where matriarchs assumed responsibility for everything, such as caring for the injured and those who had survived the horrors of war. These traits are ingrained in her: commitment, compassion, caring for the weak.

"How did you come to Vila Nova de Cerveira of all places?" I ask. Michael's gaunt face is barely visible in the dark. Betty whimpers in her sleep. A wind comes from the sea, scents from the river. "We had a Portuguese friend who heard that there was a farm in Cerveira where people were squatting and that a German biologist was living there and writing a doctorate on the Minho River," Margot recalls. Now I know she is referring to Mike Weber, who I heard about from his student, river biologist Antunes.

"He finished writing and left, but we stayed on. By the mid-1980s, I was getting to know Portugal, but I moved between here and Germany, back and forth. And it was only at the beginning of the millennium that I came to live here," she adds. "And what we went through is like *The Rocky Horror Picture Show*, something that started out very intense and ended up in pieces. For a long time, Schulz had demonstrated fantastic spiritual gifts derived from his years with Anandamayi Ma, who was an exceptional guru."

Margot speaks, and Michael joins in sometimes. They reminisce while opening their hearts to their new friend, a stranger, underneath a large fig tree. "After meeting Schulz, you felt like a changed person. When everything went down, everyone thought we were crazy, but we weren't. He only changed in the late '90s, when he was over fifty. By that point, none of us could stop him. He became too powerful and had too much control over too many people and matters. You could not speak out against him or make him stop, and things got out of hand. He even owned all the rights to the music we made. A sole ruler."

Anyone who knew Margot back then says she was the inspiration behind the music that Schulz appropriated. Music created here had worldwide reach. Even today, one can find YouTube videos of Margot playing and singing in her unique style. Margot was the humble force behind the lucrative musical adventure that enabled Schulz to establish his own kingdom of darkness.

In Cerveira, Schulz was viewed as the wealthy benefactor as he arrived during the impoverished 1980s. He made generous donations to win public approval. He was like the old millionaire in the story of Friedrich Dürrenmatt, who returns to her poor childhood town offering to make everyone rich for a small favour, establishing a moral dilemma: those who harmed her in her youth must be handed over to her for justice.

"In the 1980s, Cerveira was not the town you see before you today. It was a small, poor place forsaken like the rest of Portugal until the big European money arrived. People loved Schulz. He even donated an old German fire engine to launch a proper fire brigade. Local aristocracy came to his parties. It was wonderful to feel so unique and superior," says Michael with typical candour. "He made us feel special. More extraordinary than everyone else. We felt connected. Cerveira in the 1980s seemed to us like post-war Germany. There were no wide roads, no supermarkets. And sometimes you even felt as if you were in an African colony: women walked along the road balancing baskets on their heads. Bullocks ploughed the fields, and the mayor's wife had a vegetable shop."

"The whole of Portugal is alive with secret histories," Margot says, as if to say: we are not the only ones living on top of the now cold lava of a vast secret. Betty is already snoring gently. I rise to leave. It is not yet time for the full story to be disclosed, and Michael and Margot are already shaken by what little has been said in the dark courtyard. I get up and drive home, passing in front of the illuminated town hall where the deer statue donated by Baba Shanti stands next to Zadok's sculpture of the same animal. The horns of Schulz's deer are very sharp, but his name has been erased from the pedestal.

69

LIKE THE CONDUCTOR OF A blind orchestra, Gilberto attempts to coordinate the different parties. It is mid-winter, and despite all the commotion I feel that the house is still far from finished. The job of building a house is a manic depressive affair, as fluctuating in its moods as the local river. Franklin arrives on his days off to finish the windows. The wall that collapsed from the top floor is still inside the animal pens, blocking the passage, a reminder of the near-disaster. The workers search the courtyard for old stones. They do not have to buy anything for the windows; all the necessary material is found in the backyard. They locate granite stones from the wall that collapsed in the 1983 storm and search for elongated rocks to construct the stone lintels.

Under a fig tree, they find a granite pillar supporting the twisted tree trunk; they uproot it and carry it on their shoulders to use as part of the wall. By five in the afternoon, when the day is done, the first window is complete. Its new frame is made of timbers and stones from the yard. In front of the house, a circular saw spews red dust clouds as a worker hacks bricks of a later period, converting material from the balcony into doors. With a blowtorch I burn off ancient layers of paint from an antique door. Sometimes the fire catches the tree scorching it, or it consumes an unfortunate snail or a knot in the wood, and the scent of a living tree breaks free as if the forest spirit has been unleashed.

I spray water on the scorched tree so that no spark is left to start a fire. The Japanese burn oil over wood to strip it, but Franklin offers a paint remover for the job. All methods lead to the same result: exposed wood returning to life in a hundred-year-old door. Its age can be gleaned from the layers, the colour of the wood, green, white, charred. As rain falls on the house again, I stretch sheets over the broken front windows and secure them with nails.

"It is the work you do with your own hands that makes the house your own," declares Tiago when I explain about removing the plaster and the art of exposing and restoring doors. He feels a strong attachment to the houses owned by previous generations of his family. He renovates them with the aid of workers according to precise plans, then lives, paints and sleeps in them. One studio is in Caminha and another in Gondar. He has varied sleeping arrangements. Every time I visit the house in Caminha, I run my hand over the shiny wooden ornaments and climb to the second floor. I undestand the connection he must feel to the place, the oil paintings and the comfortable armchair where his forebears would sit by the fireplace a hundred years ago. Lit candles are everywhere. The room is always cosy.

"You only truly own things when you assume responsibility for them. This simple dynamic is the meaning of ownership."

"Times are hard everywhere in the world," he says as a log crackles from the heat in the iron grate.

The rate at which he produces paintings is so impressive that it seems that sometime in the future they could all be connected to form a Tiago map of Portugal. Some of them look like aerial photographs taken from a mountain top. He marks historical relics, forts, cities and villages, mythological figures, lost kings and princesses. They constitute essential layers of Portugal, traces on the landscape and soul of the country.

When the sun rises, we drive to the village by the sea where he was born, and I see the island of Ínsua, nothing more than a bare cliff. Although close to shore, it is cut off due to strong currents. "Now it is deserted," Tiago says. "In the past, people sailed across in boats to pick up stones and objects from the monastery and settlement." As winter waves collide with the shoreline, the gloomy island looks like a prison colony. It was the last Portuguese fortress before Spanish Galicia. A military camp, a monastery and a lighthouse were once full of life, inhabited by soldiers, monks and a family who maintained and operated the giant lighthouse oil lamp.

Sometimes he speaks like an aristocrat whose estate has been plundered.

"The sages have lost their legitimacy, and fools come to occupy the vacuum. Collectiveness prevails over individuality. And in the midst of it all, the climate catastrophe. The next generation will view us as worse than Hitler. They will say, 'you murdered the whole planet with your selfishness and negligence.' They will regard us with horror and judge us harshly." Sometimes he is optimistic, and other times he sinks into anger or derision.

When the fish arrives at the table, he forgets his anger and speaks of the food. "Many forms of art are coming to an end, and the art of food, cooking and gastronomy have come to replace them. Nothing better than great food, good wine and interesting conversation. It combines everything we need. It is the most human and cultural thing in existence."

He cuts the fish, carefully removing the thin skin and savouring the tender fillet, then returns to speak of his country lovingly. "For me, Portugal is the most racially diverse country. It is made up of the greatest number of races and past influences, a melting pot of Asia, Africa and Europe. For two thousand years, we have been mixing Arab, Roman, Viking, Visigoth, Celt, African and Chinese blood. All these tribes have landed right here on this coast. This is why tolerance here is not a slogan, but a way of life and our blood relatives are not the barbaric north but Morocco and Brazil, Angola and Mozambique."

I sometimes listen, asking questions. I am a wave in the Taron River. We drink wine and finish off with fruit. Tiago says Portugal's national debt to Europe ought to be reversed. "Europe owes us all the talented young people who left on the excellent roads it built. All our brilliant youth who drove away on the motorways to France and Germany." His own children live in Lisbon.

70

"WHILE YOU ARE AWAY, THE house will be full of workmen again," Gilberto assures me, suggesting that by the time I get back the house will be standing magically proud and complete. First on the list is the electrician, for whom Franklin and his team have prepared the infrastructure. On the exposed walls, between the stones in the cracks and fissures, at the back of the roof supports, behind the cement, the electrician will install arteries and veins in every fold of the house. In the same walls, António the plumber will connect the water pipes and drainage system. The insulation man and his assistant will return to install aluminium cladding, stuff the cavities with yellow polyester and wool, and set up drywall partitions to create a protective gap between the moisture-absorbing stone wall and the house's interior. Then, Gilberto promises, the tardy carpenters will arrive too.

In April and May it rains in Candemil, according to weather forecasting websites. The rains continue throughout spring. "Come back, bring the summer with you," my new friends from the Alto Minho write to me in Tel Aviv. Gilberto reports that the Franklin crew dug two cesspits until they reached a non-permeable layer of clay. They dug deep because pits must be porous all the way through, so that they don't fill up too quickly. During my absence, Franklin has also cleared some of the ruins of the old house in the yard and transferred them to another of Gilberto's construction sites to be used as building material. The two sites sometimes act in symbiosis. Gilberto says the rewiring is now complete and all the water pipes are in place. Water and electricity are the lifeblood of the house.

From a distance, everything appears to be running smoothly in Alto Minho.

Sitting at a café in Tel Aviv, my friend, the philosopher Yaron S., says that "ageing is also a form of exile, the destruction of a familiar place. The world gradually changes throughout a person's life, but one morning, they wake to find that *everything* has changed. Their own country becomes foreign territory. Through the window, you could always see three trees, a kiosk and a grocery store. But two of the trees have been cut down, the grocery store is now a bike shop, and you say to yourself: this is no longer my home. Time kills gradually, not with a single blow."

I look up from my excellent coffee, and here in front of me, on King George Street, which I have known since childhood, the old post office has closed down and is up for rent. An ancient sycamore that collapsed in winter has disappeared from the landscape. "We are a couple of exiles nostalgic for our motherland. All avenues of life you once knew are now lost, and if you resent such change, people look at you as if you are mad. Because our lives are intertwined with a place, we feed and nourish it," he tells me. "Especially someone like yourself whose writing inspires certain moods through the descriptions of places, but then suddenly a place is gone, and there is no one left to listen to you."

"You are an exile in your own country," he continues, but I now also feel that I am exiled from my new country. I tell him how when I took my elderly mother once on a rare journey from her nursing home to a Tel Aviv beach, she looked out of the car window, her wheelchair fastened to the floor, and mused as if returning from the dead: "I once lived here."

"In Portugal, my alienation affects me in what is essentially a foreign place," I tell my friend, "so it is more natural and forgiving than the separation I now feel in the city where I have lived all my life."

One sunny day in Tel Aviv, I take off, land in Porto and drive away in a hired car. Within an hour I arrive at my Candemil home and discover that in my absence nature has gone wild like a child whose parents are away. It is a festival of blossoms, buds and tall herbs. The yard is a bedlam of pavement stones, uprooted when the cesspit was dug and the sewage pipes buried. Rainwater has accumulated inside the hole, and last year's pears and apples are rotting on the ground.

There is a commotion in the square in front of the Dantas grocery store, and as I approach, I see a large group of adults and children celebrating the return of summer. This is the feast day of John the Baptist, São João, born before Jesus to his cousin Elizabeth and her husband, Zachariah. Along with David Leal, who has come from Castelo, children and women decorate a pine tree trunk with hundreds of blue hortensia flowers like a colourful totem. Those who have returned from foreign countries like Leal have a renewed interest in the old customs, disregarded for fifty years.

When the pine trunk is entirely covered with flowers, they lift and carry it on their shoulders to a space between the houses where they thrust it into the earth, still soft from the rains. Manoel Joaquim, the house's previous owner, sits among friends in front of the Dantas house on a long wooden bench. When I ask about the state of his ailing heart, he unbuttons his shirt to let me feel a perceptible lump under the skin of his chest, where a modern miracle device has been buried to support an ancient heart. An entire pig is skewered over the fire, and chunks are distributed to all who wish to eat. Everyone is drinking *vinho verde*.

The sun fades late in the evening; at ten, final glimmers still remain, as if the light clings on, not wishing to let go.

71

"**WHEN YOU ARE AT HOME** here," Michael pounds his emaciated chest, "you are at home anywhere." He lives contentedly on his land on the outskirts of Cerveira. The sign on the estate gates by the Santiago *camino* reads, "Pilgrim Rest". He offers the weary a bed and a place to relax, a kitchen and nourishment. He waits for travellers to turn up.

I meanwhile sleep in an old Candemil house, which I share with a subtenant: a field mouse who lives by the kitchen stove. I feel more at home here than anywhere before.

When the river overflows with murky water, I visit Michael. He opens the gates before me into the site's holy of holies. The estate, purchased by Ulrich Schulz in 1986, covers about four hectares of forested land. We walk through a tall bamboo thicket alongside a wide stone pool, fruit groves, vegetable patches, bountiful tomato plants and a wild river creek. We visit paths and hidden nooks with Buddha statues. He shows me around the old accommodation and a well-equipped recording studio where the band played New-Age music, funding the entire community.

Arriving at a large greenhouse with massive stone pillars, Michael explains that this is where Baba Shanti kept 360 multicoloured parrots. They made a tremendous uproar which accentuated the jungle feel of the place. There was also a pair of exotic Hyacinth Macaws of a deep blue hue with a wingspan of over a metre, a rare and nearly extinct species that cost Schulz 30,000 euros on the exotic animal black market. He dreamed of setting up a zoo, similar to those he had seen in Tenerife and on a tiny island on the Minho.

The shrine erected by Schulz at the heart of his estate is well preserved, like a pearl in its shell. "A peaceful abode of natural harmony for disciples" is the definition of an ashram. Above a turbulent river creek, the building dips its long cement legs into the ground; the three-floor stone edifice seems happy standing in water. Michael opens the carved wooden doors before me. The marble floors are smooth and polished. Inside the library I find thousands of tomes on spirituality. The roof of the prayer and meditation halls is supported by magnificent girders made from imported exotic wood, resistant to Portuguese woodworm.

The ashram stands as well-groomed and lovely as on the day it opened. "Baba Schulz believed that he would leave his mark on the world. He did not realize that we live in transparent times," says Michael. "He did not understand that if he engaged in sexual abuse, and especially child abuse, the impact he would make on the world would not be the one he wished." I stand by his side, looking from the top-floor window at the treetops as if looking into Conrad's Heart of Darkness or the Coppola vision of the Vietnamese jungle.

Schulz, like Kurtz, took his dark passions to the extreme and ended up with the same God. Kurtz left behind a camp strewn with human skulls, and Schulz left an ashram of hurt and tormented souls. Michael tells me that he dreamed of Schulz the previous night for the first time in many years. In his dreams, the dead man floated peacefully above his *quinta* and above Cerveira, but when he came to earth, he was bleeding from his stomach and pulled out a terrifying internal organ.

"When I woke up, I felt as if I had been cleansed of the filth."

"So, you were a Pasha with children, dogs and parrots?" enquired sarcastically the German judge who sentenced Baba Schulz for indecent acts committed against the children of his followers. "When I visited him in prison, in the same old fortress where the young Hitler had been held, Schulz admitted that the parrots were a mistake. He did not mention the children. Like an ancient Greek philosopher, he was surrounded by a group of lover boys. We accepted that. But we did not know of the children. It happened during the last stage of his life here, and he kept it secret. Perhaps we did not want to know. When the parents found out, they went to the police."

And so it happened that seventeen years after Schulz's arrival in Cerveira, German detectives accompanied by Portuguese police stormed the peaceful *quinta* looking for the alleged perpetrator of these heinous crimes. Schulz, who was inside the shrine at the time, ran through the thicket and disappeared for years, living under a false identity among thousands of worshippers at the Sanctuary of Our Lady of Fátima. Inspired by Christianity, he became a devout Catholic.

"Schulz always said that he would die at fifty. Unfortunately, he did not. He only rotted from the inside. Instead of retiring from the world as a sage, he became increasingly coarse and fat, and his conquests younger and younger; he went insane."

"He did not leave on time," repeats Michael as if uttering a mantra formulated by the group of survivors. They had obviously discussed it at length and established an accessible account of what had happened. "He became a patriarch who abused his great power over lost souls."

"In the forest," says Michael with bitter lucidity, "the smaller trees need a larger tree to shelter under, but as they grow, the shadow kills them, and the larger tree must die in order for the light to reach them."

Open and candid, Michael speaks of a past of which he was also an accomplice and a victim. He speaks of all that was divine, captivating and attractive in Schulz, as well as of his irredeemable sins. He learned of the life of Baba Shanti from the man himself.

Ulrich Schulz was born into a wealthy bourgeois family in Hamburg under a strict, violent father who worked as a civil servant. At thirteen, he ran away from home, boarded a ship as a deckhand, and began travelling the world. In the sixties he opened a hippy bar in Berlin, Kathmandu, which formed part of the new Berlin. After that, he left for India like many and lived in the ashram of the Ma, who approached the level of Buddha and adopted him. Thus he became Oliver Shanti and the Baba.

"I can forgive him everything, just not the children. And when I brought it up during that one visit, Schulz dismissed me as if I were a speck of dust, and I realized there was no one there any more." The venerated guru, who pushed Michael to become a painter, was already trapped inside a world of paranoia where everything that happened was a conspiracy to take over his property. He had a plan to exact revenge on all who betrayed him and return to his greatness once he got out of prison. "But God had other plans. He died several weeks following his release. Only a few followers attended his funeral at the Hamburg cemetery."

The *quinta* was already deserted by then. All the followers were gone, the parrots sold, the music had died down. Of all his followers, very few remained, but among them were Michael and Margot, who heroically took on the debts incurred by Schulz. Purged of his evil spirit, the *quinta* hosts tourists, yoga classes and pilgrims, and grows tomatoes and grapes. It is run by Margot, the enlightened antithesis to the dead Baba.

72

NEAR THE OPENING OF A dark underpass, Gilberto stops the car. An ancient tunnel passes underneath the main road to Caminha, connecting Seixas to a coastal enclave, a narrow strip adjacent to the riverbank. The iron gates of the blacksmiths open onto the street. As we enter, we are hit with a strong smell of hot iron and oil. The place looks like a working coal mine from the Industrial Revolution, standing in stark contrast to the surrounding mansions. An old man in blue overalls, slightly bent from years of work, lifts up his soldering mask and examines Gilberto's design for three large window bars.

Gilberto wants to produce elegant metal bars to match the glass trapezoids of the Lisbon doors I showed him back at the farm basement. When light from the house pours into the yard at night, the silhouette of the bars will resemble that of the doors. He has outlined the shape of the doors and drawn the bars to match in thin pencil. The blacksmith, Manuel Cavaleiro, traces his scorched finger over the drawings. In the metallic space of the workshop, packed with iron sheets up to the ceiling, the delicate drawings seem lace-like, suitable for sewing, not soldering.

Yes, the blacksmith Cavaleiro will look over the drawings and give us a quote.

As we drive away, Gilberto mentions the second concrete coating of the bathroom floor and the slight gradation it has created. It demands a solution. There is also a problem with the direction of the door. Should it open onto the balcony or into the bathroom? Building a house from ruins is a slow miracle. Details gradually join together to create a living space that will one day be complete. At the house, I place a large porcelain tile of painted birds selected for the kitchen and bathroom on the wall to see if it complements the old door and its colour. Slowly everything takes form, but the rhythm is that of the Portuguese soul, to which one becomes accustomed. Nothing is urgent when you live in the present. The art of assembling a house is no less uplifting than its completion and the life to be lived there.

The round window returns to the house after being made ready by the carpenter, glazier and welder. It now looks like an old wood and iron carriage wheel; it can be rolled all the way to the house. We place it on a sunny day inside the opening made by the Franklin team. I push open its two vertical halves, like butterfly wings. From one half I can see the forest with the old sawmill, and from the other Elena's café, the grocery and the village centre. From the courtyard below, the hoop looks like a church window. The two Jaffa wings form a cross when shut.

After several sunny days, a hailstorm descends on the Candemil hills. It is then that Orit finally returns to Cerveira along with her Portuguese study notebook. At Café Rosa I listen in amazement as she enters into quick, fluent, if occasionally halting, conversation with the owner. I remember how my Argentine friend Marcelo spoke lovingly of the Portuguese language as "Spanish without bones" and sang me a few songs in Portuguese with its soft, whisper-like flow.

When Orit returns to the house, she scans the rooms in delight, checking out the new wooden floor in the living room, exposed granite wall, large front windows overlooking the countryside, concrete floor flooded with sunlight, and the kitchen ceiling made of girders and thin planks. The glass in the gallery window is scratched and hairy like the skin of an old animal, having endured wind and rains. Forever preoccupied with the hold-ups, it has been difficult for me to notice all the changes. Through Orit's eyes I can now see the long road that Casa Marília has travelled these past few months. As excited and full of renovation plans as Orit is, she is also seized by a desire to lay her massive mane of hair on the bed of the new house, to dive into a deep sleep and dream.

In the openings where windows have not yet been fitted, the insulating material is torn and fluttering in the wind. From the round window, old paint runs down the white wall like tear streaks. In the animal pens downstairs, where Franklin has torn openings, light enters like a new guest inspecting every detail. The collapsed bedroom floor and the wooden wall still form a monstrous pile of debris. Jorge says he will need four workers to carry the heavy beam and re-install it to complete work on the floor.

It is mid-spring when the rains return, the aluminium folk argue it is too wet to work, and the carpenters claim it is impossible to bring in the wood. The house returns to its state of limbo. House time is not human time; it has its own rhythm. But the new pieces of lumber are settling in their new home, shrinking, drying and sometimes softly squeaking as if suffering growing pains. In the damp former weaving room, pages of books I piled on a shelf curl up as if the fog has even invaded their stories. Trees that withered during winter sway in the yard. Violets and bellflowers emerge from that hidden underworld of tubers and bulbs, seeds and roots, larvae and rats, insects and rodents. Something is happening inside the ancient depths. Decay sprouts new life.

The rain begins to fall, then breaks off. A thunderstorm flashes across the skies and disappears, and the sun emerges from behind dark clouds. In the courtyard, uprooted old wooden beams lap up the water as if returning to life many years after their decapitation by guillotine. Flowers bloom over a mound of rubble while other shoots groan beneath it. I till and weed the ground by the studio, using an axe and hoe to fight against stubborn plants that bind their roots to stone crevices. We prune the vine shoots growing on the fence facing south towards the field, plant a red cherry tree and a seedling black cherry tree, tall as a toddler, and dream of an orchard.

When Jorge returns, he emphatically touches his injured shoulder to make it clear that he will not be able to lend a hand. His two workers cannot lift the beam on their own and return it to its place, so Gilberto calls on reinforcements from among the builders working on his house. Jorge's team finishes the work in the gallery, where the floor is made of wooden planks with rabbet joints slotted together. When they leave, we climb to the gallery above the unfinished kitchen. We are immediately entranced by the small upper floor, its low sloping ceiling, the smell of fresh pinewood, and the round window overlooking the mountain.

We carry our front doors from the farm basement together, gently laying them down inside the hire car. We drive up the hills to the house with the boot open. There Orit commences polishing the wood into a fleshy light pink. The wood is already exposed in part, as are the delicate, concealed, iron-free joints made by a now-deceased carpenter. "How amazing that the Lisbon doors are coming to life at the entrance to our house," Orit exclaims.

When Gilberto arrives with the ancillary crew, it turns out that the beam has already been moved. The two workers conferred while waiting then grabbed one end, lifted it slightly, slid underneath and, pushing it up on their shoulders, put an iron pole in their place as support. Thus, they moved the heavy beam agonizingly slowly like a cross, eventually lifting and placing it over the stone niche made by Franklin. Left to their own devices, Portuguese workmen seem capable of anything. With the ancient wisdom derived from manual labour, they can lift heavy weights without machines.

"Tomorrow we may finish the second room as well," says Jorge, smiling triumphantly as he reaps the fruits of others' hard work.

He returns a day later with one aide, but this particular magician's apprentice is swift. They finish work in the gallery, take away the saw and promise: "Monday". Gilberto goes up to examine the new gallery, as yet without stairs, and finds a defect where two large beams have a crack between them. The wood of the floor is also a shade darker than agreed upon. He detests imperfections, while I, on the other hand, am fond of the slight carelessness of the handmade rustic structure, the ageing carpenters who leave hastily inscribed pencil markings and the mismatched crack.

73

DRIVING WEST ALONG THE MINHO towards Caminha, Orit and I stop to eat at a small restaurant. As we return to the car, we find ourselves tipsy from the chocolate dessert soaked in red wine. Later, on the strip of sand by the Seixas seaside mansions, we kneel in our muddy mine of potsherds, where the river mouth continues to spew the fragments out. We find a mug handle with a hint of leaf drawing, the decorated side of a cup and a round coaster polished by the waters. Orit is moved by this beauty discarded on the shoreline.

My beloved was the youngest of four siblings of parents born in Baghdad. Her family was blue-collar; the father worked as a blacksmith, tinsmith, lapidarist and taxi driver, while the mother worked in a textile factory inhaling lethal fibres. Orit was still breastfeeding when she was separated from her mother, who was taken to the hospital; she returned pale and feeble until she disappeared again, never to return. The baby cried for her mother day after day until her aunt, who had had enough of the endless wailing, took her in her arms to her mother's photograph hanging in the kitchen and pointed at it. "No more Mummy. I'm your mother now," she blurted out with uncontrolled anger. Perhaps this was the moment when art was imprinted upon Orit's infant mind, and imagination came to replace reality. She remembers how she would often stare at the photograph. Sitting by the window at night, she searched for a voice, a clue, a sign from her mother with every passing light. She would converse with the glowing stars. When she was older, she enrolled in an art school and began documenting people who all had their backs turned walking away.

Now she collects broken fragments from the shoreline. The rocky riverbed is covered in hyssop, and the wind passes in quiet drifts through its fields of wild weeds. Flooded staircases descend from the entrance to every house down to jetties and mooring places built a hundred years ago. We assemble our treasures on the floor of the car, feeling the quiet satisfaction of gatherers descending upon us as if collecting twigs for the family nest.

Orit holds up an emerald green shard. "I will make an earring out of it," she says.

I find hollow bamboo reeds that the sea has smoothed into shapes like lamp posts. Farther down, by the Caminha waterfront, we come across large shells. They are spread open like the blue wings of a butterfly.

74

"**Bor-bo-leta,**" **calls out Zé Paulo,** "butterfly." He waves his long arms as if they were wings. "*Bor-bo-leta.*" At any moment he might soar above the Alto Minho, over the village of Dem and the beautiful house of Rosali and Rui where we are all chatting and drinking the fruity *vinho verde*. The wine was purchased from a neighbour, and Rui and Zé Paulo enter into a discussion over home-made wines. The locals have vineyards in their backyards, and families drink home-grown wine throughout their lives. The conversation goes on and on, stretches and expands. It is the *conversação* that I hear everywhere without understanding a word. As a spectator I watch a cast of people involved in lengthy conversations.

They go on to say that mothers who drink alcohol during pregnancy give birth to small, feeble children. Rui travels every year to the same winery where a wine and seasonal fish celebration takes place. This year he saw a ten-year-old boy stumble and repeatedly fall until his mother shouted, "Darling, remember what the doctor told you? No more than one glass of *vinho verde!*" They delve deeper into the subject and move on to another topic, still considering the same ideas and using synonyms to clarify things. What is important is the conversation itself, not the subject. Locals will describe some matter to me until we reach an understanding beyond the topic at hand.

"*Conversação* is not a purposeful activity," says Rosali, returning from the child's room. Conversation is not an act of putting forth ideas or being practical as it is in many countries. It is a social pastime. A state of mind. Conversation is a deep pleasure which persists. The digging of a pit that reaches deeper and deeper. This is why sometimes it is repetitive, like a chant.

It often begins with a slight argument until the interlocutors say, "but we mean exactly the same thing," and experience the joy of agreement.

"Agree and reconcile," Rosali adds, "so as to avoid liver problems."

By which she means not to store up anger. Not to get upset. Not to cause harm to a vital organ. "Converse so as not to be filled with toxins; a long and delightful conversation cleanses the body."

"Older people tell us that during the Salazar dictatorship the hardest thing for them was the ban on real conversation," says Rui, "the fear of speaking freely. Sitting in a café, one could not know who was listening in. Can you imagine a ban on *conversação*, the centre of our lives?" It seems that to this day Portuguese discourse remains cautious. Less political than elsewhere. "There are no protests here like in Spain. We accept things as they are, like the Church preaches: 'Kneel down and be grateful for what you have received.'"

Perhaps this is why the quiet, restrained Rui relates to small rebellious Rosali, who knows no fear and kneels before no one. Rosali, with her broad and expressive face, seems more like a daughter of the land of windmills than the land of watermills. Her great-grandmother was a member of the Kasper family. Kasper means clown. When still a girl, she left her native Poland to travel with a small circus, and when they stopped in the Netherlands, she fell in love with a guy named Van Duin, meaning "from the dunes", and had five children by him. One of them was Rosali's father.

She was born in the Netherlands to a Portuguese mother, but when she was five, her mother abandoned her father and took off with Rosali and her brother André, returning to her mother in Portugal. Rosali lived with her for some time, but by the age of thirteen, she went off on her own, travelled homeless, moving between her mother and father, changing countries and friends. "The Kasper circus blood flows through my veins." She was a wild teenager, angry at her mother and the world. When she left home, she sought love and happiness and a father figure. After studying theatre, she played the role of the unhappy girl in a play called *The Girl and the Soap*. The play suggested that adults should "let children play, not work." At the time, children were still full-time workers in many areas around this poor country. When she tired of the theatre, she travelled through Spain with an author many years her senior. To make a living, they put on a bar cabaret show under the name A.R., their initials, Arthur and Rosali.

This is how she became an actress, singer and artist, remaining open-minded, accepting of ambiguity, believing more in the invisible than the visible. She fears a routine life as she would the plague and is attentive to what she thinks of as her inner music. "Perhaps I am a magician. I was a neglected child and sick sometimes, so my soul left my body and connected with the world at large. I have seen things that others do not."

Her son calls her from the room again, and she leaves the conversation to put him to bed.

75

THE TWO WORKERS WHO WILL fit our aluminium windows are younger than Jorge's carpenters and Franklin's stonemasons. Energetic, they finish the work within a couple of days, installing a foreign yet resistant material into the ancient stone walls. They put in double-glazed windows insulated with a layer of mineral wool, like shiny porcelain teeth in an old mouth. Notwithstanding his love for all things traditional, Gilberto is an enthusiastic supporter of easy-to-install efficient materials. Dark aluminium doors with frosted glass replace the heavy, gnawed wooden doors with their rusty iron hinges removed from the animal pens. Thanks to the doors and with the openings created by Franklin, the former animal quarters are awash with bright, warm daylight.

When the installation of windows and doors is complete, carpenter Jorge arrives, conspicuously clutching his back to remind us of his pain. With him is one worker, and they quickly construct a new wooden ceiling in the lower rooms above an old beam, untreated for the ravages of time and woodworm. When I comment on the oversight, Jorge promises that everything will be taken care of on Monday and leaves. I wonder if the renovations will ever be over.

Someone is walking on the new wooden floor. The sound can be heard downstairs. I go up and find Luis, the insulation man who came with his wife. He speaks little English. Luis has made a previous visit to start work on the drywall. "I see the carpenters had to move some things," he says calmly and without resentment, staring at the devastation inflicted on some of his work by the collapsed wall which damaged the drywall.

In the evening, a new carpenter arrives, sent by Gilberto. He is a man in his fifties with a diamond earring in one ear. João examines the Lisbon doors, now stripped down and polished. Caressing the old smooth surfaces, João offers to fit a metal strip to protect the bottom of the doors. The same goes for the old bathroom door that I peeled with the blowtorch. He promises that together with his brother he will build new frames and install the doors. He climbs with Gilberto up the attic ladder, and together they examine the Jaffa window through which the rain has leaked. Bright light from the round window illuminates the ceiling. When the window is opened, the warm air evaporates and wind drifts in from the mountain, accompanied by scents from the forest and the Rodrigues brothers' sawmill.

The Lost Princess of Alto Minho

"May is the month when you devour the first cherries of summer by the dim coals of late winter."

A local proverb

76

THE IMPREGNABLE FAÇADE OF CASA Verde overlooks the square with blind authority. Like Toad Hall, it is wrapped in an evening gown of emerald tiles. From its detailed staircase, railings, windowsills and tiles to the decorated inscription below the plaster cornice, it is the work of master artisans. Yet all its windows are dark as if the master of the house is away on business, lost at sea or in a jungle. The building captures the attention of all who pass through Cerveira, but in all the months spent here I have yet to see its doors or shutters open, and the lights are never on. At nights the house looms mysterious, like a haunted mansion that stands in contrast to the brightly lit square and cheerful cafés. Only when I eventually go to speak to Isabel de Portugal Marreca do the gates of the Green House open before me, a warm light flooding the empty rooms.

"If you wish to speak to my mother, who owns the Green House, you should come on a sunny afternoon," her son Manuel, from whom I purchased the Lisbon doors, informs me. It seems the sun lifts her often downcast spirits.

From the road connecting Candemil and Cerveira, a narrow alley curves to the right. It passes between two stone walls reaching a small church. I walk through a large car park and up a metal staircase, then enter the garden through a small gate. The estate was designed by the architect Terra in the late nineteenth century. It now operates as a small family-owned hotel and is home to the "Lost Princess of Alto Minho", as she is sometimes affectionately called.

Isabel de Portugal Marreca reclines beside a stone wall under purple wisteria blossoms. She smokes a cigarette in a long holder while a dwarfish dog prances at her feet excitedly. "Vordel,

261

Vordel!" she calls as she lifts the pooch to her lap, cuddling him like a child. Her hair falls on her face, over dark sunglasses and ageing beauty, evident in the photos I am about to see. "Did you notice that they cut down the tree in the Casa Verde courtyard?" she spits out angrily as if she were still a little girl living in her grandmother's house. "A hundred and fourteen years old, it was planted on the occasion of the birth of my grandmother."

Isabel is spending the seventh decade of her life in this small, dozen-room hotel, owned by her family. She lives in a two-floor apartment painted in bright Moroccan shades and laden with precious objects like a private museum of the past. From an ornamental box she pulls out mementoes from her life. "I spent all my childhood vacations at Casa Verde. It was the home of my grandmother and her husband, Dr Bonifácio, and home to my great-grandmother, the wealthiest woman in all of Portugal." Just as Tiago glorifies the fierce male lineage of his family, Isabel proudly commemorates the female lineage of hers, where men are only an appendix to the main plot.

Through yellowing photographs, she gives me a tour of the rooms of the Green House, now hidden from sight. This part with high ceilings is where the family lived. The furniture. The round sofa at the heart of the room. The delightful tapestry. The ornaments. The family sold it to a Spaniard years ago. Here are boys on nineteenth-century bikes. Two family members sipping wine in the Cerveira of the early twentieth century.

"And this is my great grandmother, my grandmother and my mother." I get lost in the tangle of women. Here is the one sister who married. She also tells of nine brothers born at the turn of the century who never married but led very successful lives and yet squandered the family fortune. One photograph depicts domestic workers, and another the family farmland.

A near-century after these photographs were taken, I lounge in her rooms at the Malaposta Hotel, surrounded by sculptures and oil paintings, Art Nouveau lamps, embroideries and ivory or silver hairbrushes. The pup Vordel sits at her feet, as attentive as I am, as Isabel flips through cardboard photographs of past generations, uncles, cousins and children of delicate beauty.

As I have already discovered, though photos of poor villagers are rare, the albums of the wealthy are always thick. They include documentation of every family vacation, servants standing in rows on a hillside. One boy in a white sailor suit is as beautiful as a girl and as pale as the tragic Tadzio from *Death in Venice*. And here are the mother and daughter again, looking solemn, the bemused surgeon Manuel Bonifácio de Costa, the nanny, the sad Mademoiselle and the gloomy German Fräulein, teacher of the two boys. And again, the children with their precious toys.

Through the window I examine the small hotel garden full of flowers with its clay tiles and wisteria avenues spread out like a purple canopy next to the meadows. The old farmhouse, renovated by Isabel and her sons, João and Manuel, is an elongated, low-rise building with spires, small towers and a beautiful stone fountain. In front of a wooden dining hall stretches a modern swimming pool, blue as the skies.

I follow Isabel and her dog down through the garden to the water kingdom designed by the great architect Miguel Ventura Terra. Terra was one of the founding fathers of modern Portuguese architecture. He created some of the country's most significant buildings and private residences, including his own home, set in nearby Seixas. Isabel bends down to collect fallen leaves, pointing out channels, small islands and ponds inhibited by goldfish. A fountain shaped like a random stone mound stands among winding paths, red Japanese bushes, dwarf palm trees and small bridges.

For many years this glory was buried underground.

"When we bought the place and started restoring it about twenty years ago, an old man pointed to some rocks sticking out of the ground and said, 'Dig here.' The previous owner's child suffered from a fear of water, so he covered over Terra's water kingdom with earth. Everything was buried under mounds of soil, weeds and trees. We cleared the soil and restored everything. We flooded it with water and brought fish."

In the depths of the water flash the golden carp, much aged since those early days.

I return with her to the room and sit back on a small sofa next to her armchair. Drowsiness overcomes me, cushioned as I am by the delicate upholstery of the family narrative. Inside the old genealogical book of the Marreca family, Isabel tries to locate for me the first Marreca to set his house in Vila Nova de Cerveira. She shows me the most dominant family member of them all, her great-grandmother, whom Isabel got to know as a child: Rita Maria de Portugal. As mournful as a black raven, she stands beside her daughter and the smiling doctor Bonifácio inside the Casa Verde.

Isabel locates among the objects a notebook bound in a hand-embroidered velvet cloth, with a thin pencil woven on a thread to seal it. Her great-grandmother embroidered it as a gift for her husband João Carlos, born in June 1867 between Porto and Cerveira. On a decorated business card that slips out of the notebook is written his address: Vila Nova de Cerveira. The notebook is full of entries and dates. According to the book, the first of the Marrecas to have established his residence here was Lord Ernesto de Portugal Marreca, born September 1829, who later married Dona Clementina Rosa Gomes, made a large fortune in Brazil and upon his return was appointed judge in the village of Vila Nova de Cerveira by King Luís I.

The de Portugal Marreca family has been here ever since.

Eleven children were born to Ernesto and his wife. Ten sons and the youngest, a daughter Rita, born in October 1873. From her early childhood in the 1950s, Isabel remembers the ageing members of that generation: great-great-grandmother Rita "who was as regal as a queen," and her younger brother Alberto. But the Casa Verde, which knew extreme wealth, has also lived through its share of tragedies: at one time four of five children died, two in infancy and two, the beautiful brothers João and Ernesto, when they were still young men, as if cursed. The boys in sailor suits are riding bicycles, or staring calmly at the photographer, not imagining their fate.

From family stories, Isabel can recount everything that occurred before she was born. The talented João and Ernesto studied away from Cerveira in elite Portuguese colleges. One of them indulged in photography and painting: "I still have five of his cameras here." They both contracted tuberculosis and were sent to a sanatorium in Switzerland, like Thomas Mann's Magic Mountain. But they failed to recover and died there one after another, aged eighteen and nineteen. They were embalmed and sent by train to be buried in the family tomb in Cerveira. "One of them returned in a coffin with a glass window because this was during World War I, and the coffin had to be inspected to make sure that nothing was smuggled with the body."

Gradually the Casa Verde emptied of all its occupants and stood vacant. It was sold to a Spaniard for a meagre sum, renovated, and remains locked and lifeless at the start of the third millennium. Listening to Isabel's family histories, I am reminded of the remarkable Portuguese novel by Eça de Queiroz, *Os Maias*. The story centres on the rise and fall of an aristocratic family. The plot is imbued with the land itself, its palaces, upper-class women and men, their horses and carriages and their idle small talk.

The patriotic protagonists of this great novel, which I read breathlessly in Hebrew, are portrayed as idlers with a deep penchant for self-neglect. Their tragic fate reminds me of *One Hundred Years of Solitude*. It appears that Isabel's photographs from the Casa Verde are a glimpse into the Portugal of Queiroz: luxuries, ornamental windows, exotic gardens, private boats by the riverbank and inevitable decline.

Looking up at the nearby mountain, I say to Isabel, "there is a wonderful view from the hotel of the giant deer statue on the summit."

"The whole mountain is mine," she says, "all the land from the chapel to the top."

Several hundred hectares belong to them. It seems like the family owns half the town.

"Reminiscent of the plot of *Os Maias*," I say cautiously.

"A little," she replies absent-mindedly stroking the little dog's fur.

77

It is night and the light is on; the rosy Lisbon doors cast their ornate, delicate silhouette over the stone wall. When I set out on journeys, whether long or short, I leave a porch light on as a tribute to the ghosts who await my return. The old house retains an entity, a spirit, a memory, a notion. A passing shadow in the corner of the eye. Even after the changes, everything is immersed in Life. Call it ghosts, the soul of the house, memories from the past.

The hibiscus sports large yellow flowers. A small tree with downcast branches bashfully regrows its leaves. The cherry seedlings are waiting for the first leaves to drop. The first fruit appears on our fledgling olive tree. Apples and pears fall to the ground and rot, giving off a sweet, damp aroma.

João's new team of carpenters arrives to finish the work begun by Jorge's team, of whom I have despaired. The Joãos are more punctual and quicker than the Jorges. Sometimes only a single worker shows up and listens to the radio while working silently, or the boss, João, works while chatting with another of the team. After installing the front doors they build the staircase to the gallery at the back of the new kitchen wall. The stairs are steep for lack of space. They put in a round, smooth wooden bannister.

In the bathroom, the carpenters put in place the old door that Orit redecorated with chalk paints and a new door frame adjusted to the enlarged opening in the room where Marília died. I turn on the tap fitted by António and watch the miracle of the hot water flowing through a pump take place before my eyes. The pump has been placed in the former pigsty downstairs.

All the old wood from the house has been chopped and transferred to the storage room for heating. It is now filled to the

267

brim with discarded, chewed-up wood. The old house, separated into parts, is slowly disappearing from sight, some destined to be burnt and some to be consigned to the rubbish dump. Orit paints the old wrought-iron bannister a bright blue; it is the same one Marília held on to as she descended the concrete stairs. She patiently draws pictures of yellow-blue tiles on the courtyard gate facing the alley. Neighbours stop to marvel at a gate painted with Portuguese tiles.

Neighbour Manoel, who inherited the house and sold it to us, walks by in the evening and mentions that this iron gate was installed sixty years ago by Franco; before that, there were wooden gates. Here, he shows me, was an ancient vine above the courtyard with a wide trunk. He indicates with his hand the width of the trunk and seems amazed at its current dimished state. Where did it all go, all that universe of dark wine grapes?

In the second room upstairs, Orit polishes the old wooden floor that collapsed into the animal quarters, then has been reinstalled and reinforced rather than replaced. Cracks and scratches, signs of its previous lives, furniture dragging marks, table and chair legs are clearly traceable on the wood. The scars of time and the life that has passed through it. I drive around looking for pesticides, wood varnish, paint remover, drills and saws. Like a kid in a sweetshop, I roam the hardware stores, addicted to the metallic smell and abundance of mechanical inventions: a small garden plough, saws and lawnmowers with petrol engines, electric water pumps, leaf blowers, pressure washers and cleaners, very popular among the clean-cut Portuguese. If they were to set up motels in these stores, I would stay overnight.

I learn to work with intimidating tools such as chainsaws, where one careless movement can slice off a hand. I love dextrous tasks whose results are immediately apparent. I shy away from monotonous work like weeding a field for an entire day. In writing, like at home or in the garden, I work in bursts, half an hour or an hour long. When most Portuguese become restless looking for soup at midday, I look for a sofa to rest my head on.

At twelve-thirty everything stops. The radio turns off, tools are put to rest. Only after about an hour and a half do they return to the site, sometimes intoxicated from the midday wine, occasionally several bottles of beer and a glass of *aquavit*. A friend tells me that on one occasion he sat next to a group of builders amazed at the amount of alcohol absorbed between the cod and the coffee. And then, at the construction site, they had to measure the same beam three times. "Try building a house like that. The most dangerous time is after the lunch break."

That is when a wall could easily collapse into the room below.

78

LATE SPRING CASTS ITS PLEASANT weather over the fields, but flowers are still reluctant to bloom, wary of the forecast rains. "May is the month when you devour the first cherries of summer by the dim coals of late winter," says the Portuguese proverb. Villagers carry bouquets of yellow flowers picked from the woods by the roadside, separated into thin bundles. They attach a garland to each doorframe as a good luck charm against this month's devilish uncertainties. They cover all entry points, even doors and gates no longer in use.

I return to Michael's estate, and intimate as we have become, the conversation turns to the inner journey we make through life. "You know I was a neo-Nazi as a boy," Michael suddenly says. The sentence seems to burst from between clenched teeth. "We had a charismatic teacher who talked about rays of light and how Hitler was not a monster. We were three friends captivated by the magic of his speeches and became his disciples." He does not go easy on himself, even in the presence of his new Jewish friend. He has observed me during long talks and chooses to confide his life story to me. So he speaks frankly.

He describes his father, who is still alive, as an authoritative, charismatic Austrian businessman whom he admires and fears. His mother, of Russian descent, who died many years ago, is conspicuously absent from the story. After high school graduation, he travelled to India, where he proudly told local people that he was pure Aryan like them. "Until I realized that Hitler's energy was one of hatred and contradicted the values I began to acquire in India. I climbed mountains, lived for months in a monastery, absorbed spiritual principles and returned to my parents as barefoot as Sappho."

Pressured by his father, he began to study law until he felt that if he continued, he would suffocate. Then he heard about a Baba of German descent recently returned from India to Bavaria who established an ashram in the Black Forest. "I lived there for months. A group of young musicians gathered around the Baba, and I began painting. Without Baba, who supported my passion for painting, I would have had no confidence to create. There is not a person in the world who influenced my life like Baba Shanti."

Baba Shanti was looking to form a new ashram and heard of a farm in northern Portugal, at a place called Cerveira. The large farm was owned by Dona Felisbela. During the times of Salazar, secret meetings of dissidents from Cerveira were held there. Dona Felisbela sold the *quinta* to a Portuguese colonial official who worked in Macau. In the early 1980s, Baba Shanti and Michael travelled to Macau to purchase the *quinta* from him. They rebuilt it along with its walls and iron gates.

Ulrich Schulz was based in Cerveira but travelled the world. In the *quinta*, his followers set up a professional recording studio. Margot, who could play any instrument brilliantly, collaborated with other musicians in composing spiritual music still popular today. Michael recalls how everything ended abruptly after seventeen years of blissful existence. The *quinta* was lively and full of animals, families, children and music. In 2001, the police appeared, followed by a tsunami of reporters who stormed the place. A criminal investigation began regarding hundreds of cases of sexual exploitation of boys and children by the guru.

"And Schulz disappeared without a trace," Michael tells me, holding his jaw. His teeth are hurting.

"This is when everything fell apart. Everyone left. And I tell you, even today, many years after the devastation and everything I discovered, no one has touched my soul like Baba Shanti. But when one is truly enlightened, the ego evaporates, and with

Baba, the ego took over and destroyed him " It was then, after the disaster, when everything was deserted, that Michael took the decision to fix his home where the great rift happened and found peace at the foot of the volcano.

"Betty, come, come, Betty," Michael calls like someone returning from a long journey greeting his loved one. I head out into the alley and the Santiago pilgrim road beside his house.

After some warm rains, the evening is sparkling and polished, and the air is saturated with the sweet scent of blossom. I have recently found myself travelling back and forth between Cerveira and my old country, whose Air Force has been bombing Gaza. Cerveira is a new refuge, in which I still feel a deep sadness, a kind of personal *saudade* about what is happening in my country of origin. The immigrant is a divided person. One place discards him, another picks him up. Fifty years after my sweet sixteenth birthday, on the banks of the Minho, I feel like my new friend Michael: old and young, shrinking and growing.

79

Early in the morning the buzzing of a giant saw and the faint sound of massive tree trunks falling come from the direction of the old sawmill at the foot of the mountain behind my house. It rained all night on the yellowing grass, which now shines a copper-gold between evergreen shrubs and the dark and orange moss-covered road signs and fences. It is a wintery summer palette of prodigious colours. Around this time, alone or in pairs, old women gather and walk up to the cemetery, a meeting place for the dead and the living. They freshen the graves with new flowers, clean the tombstones, sweep the paths, pull up weeds, and converse. Then they walk back together to their homes.

At the Rodrigues Brothers, sawmill, the oldest brother João is overseeing the delivery of a tree trunk unloaded from a truck using a tractor. It is now being transported to the tree gallows, sentenced to serve as chairs and tables. The tree moves along tracks on a miniature train operated by João and heads towards the serrated steel blade. Another man operates a saw taller than himself, and yet another uses an iron rod to push the trunk into place. It is a world lined with sawdust that comes to rest on everything, even clinging to the cobwebs as if over the years, spiders have spun a garment for the sawmill.

Sometimes I stop by to observe proceedings, take in the fragrance, purchase a single beam for the yard or rough wooden planks for future shelves. Everything is raw and alive, sweet-smelling, and very cheap. From the mill, wood is transported to the carpentry workshop above the church. Jorge João Pereira Rodrigues inherited the sawmill almost forty-five years ago from his father Elídio, who purchased it in the 1930s. Before him, one man operated a single saw powered by a stream coming down the mountain.

João gestures for me to follow him, and we skip over rotting and new trunks, pieces of bark, planks and wood shavings. Among an array of wooden and stone structures accumulated over the years, my neighbour shows me a stone aqueduct that collected water flowing down from the mountain springs. It poured into a vertical pipe which operated a system of wooden wheels that propelled the saw.

Elídio, his father, was a lumberjack all his life.

The trees make three stops: lumberjacks in the forest on the mountain, sawmills at the bottom of the hill, and finally, the carpentry workshop for the more delicate wood processing and construction of furniture or floorboards. A lumberjack, a sawmill worker, a carpenter: each of them an ancient and separate profession. João was born here in Candemil, near this sawmill, in July 1954 to a family with two sisters who died in infancy and four brothers. The man next to him is his brother Candido, and there is another brother, Luis, whom I sometimes see, who looks like an identical twin but has a different character altogether.

Luis sits silently at the entrance to the sawmill next to some women in a shed engaged in chopping firewood. It is a more accessible, monotonous craft. His hand is paralyzed from a stroke, so he had to give up work. A fourth brother has passed away.

As a child, João saw his father bring in new mechanization: a diesel engine instead of a water-powered one, and later the electric motors that now seem like old accessories from the Industrial Revolution.

"Everything is yours; just pay for it," he laughs at my amazement, "I am tired." He dreams of retiring from his job and working as a woodcarver instead. In 1967 when Senhor Franco died in the house I am now renovating, the thirteen-year-old

João began helping his father at the sawmill, and his first job, like that of all the children in the house, was removing the bark from felled pine trees.

I examine his strong hands with all joints and fingers intact, and he smiles his ironic good smile. He explains that the most dangerous machine is not the saw with the serrated strip, the four-metre-long *fita da serra*, which is sharpened every four hours, but rather the innocent-looking sanding machine in the inner hall.

For years they all lived in the house that his father built over the sawmill. They used the same types of wood they do today: local pine, oak, eucalyptus, cedar and cork, now protected. Fires burned down the sawmill twice, and once a forest fire reached the house. They rebuilt everything and carried on. The mill is only closed on Sundays.

"Now, can I ask you a question?" he wonders.

"Yes."

"I was born here. It is a quiet place, I know, but that is it. But you? Why have you come to Candemil from another country, from a city life? And you paint your house crazy colours and leave the porch light on at night! Why did you come here?"

I tell him I adore the village and the area of Cerveira.

But the lumberjack shares a widely held belief: "You ran away from the big city," he says, "we know what goes on there! In the Alto Minho, you only die of hunger if you decide to," he declares, quoting a local saying.

80

A **DARK TILE OF NATURAL STONE** on display in a hardware shop captures my attention. It possesses a unique beauty that cannot be duplicated, a dark abstract painting of some violent scene, and I want it for my own. I buy six of these tiles and feel as if I am taking part in the work of creation. But on my return home, their beauty fades as if diminished through displacement.

I stop by an abandoned house and marvel at the loveliness of water running down the paintwork in a corner where the roof collapsed, the inimitable way the rain draws letters on the plaster. The house is dressed in moss, the dark old glass covered in cobwebs. If only I could duplicate these exact shades in my renovated home.

"Corrosion is the greatest artist of all," I tell Gilberto.

He agrees and mentions an architect who speaks of how climate, nature and time redesign buildings. An intelligent architect should add the time factor to his toolbox. I also love the way the industrious woodworm, which gnaw at what otherwise seems timeless, leave a record of their journey on the wood.

In the villages we drive by, I glimpse farmers hard at work in their fields. "They certainly live according to the seasons," I say. Gilberto laughs. "There is an old man who tells me every day what the weather will be like tomorrow. He never fails to get it wrong."

"When we were kids," he says, "there was a fisherman who knew how to look at the sky and predict exactly what the sea would be like the following week." Gilberto fears that the ancient knowledge of rural life is dying with the elders, and Google has come to replace it. I tell him how when the Chinese moved on to wood ploughs thousands of years ago, a sage lamented the end of the world as he knew it. "From now on," he said, "everything will change for the worse; the modern wood plough will efface the memory of the stone plough."

I watch the rituals of the changing seasons in the village. Elderly people without the internet light bonfires on the same day in different villages, collecting and weeding and disposing at the same time. They prune their vines together at the same time and in the same way. It seems that nature and tradition still have a role here and continue to determine everyday life. Being local, Gilberto disregards what a foreigner like me sees: the survival of such traditions. They escape native eyes.

The assertive presence of time can be felt everywhere. When I go in the morning to fetch water from the spring, I smell the woodsmoke rising from the chimney of my neighbour, former accordion player Henrique. His daughter is making breakfast. I see six sheep coming out of a low stone structure into the pasture. During the day, they slowly return to their abode. I hear the chop-chop of a neighbour's pruning shears as he works in the garden. All my neighbours carry on their business at regular hours. I hear spring celebrations. I watch Cerveira turn into a bustling town in August, only to be abandoned once more in September.

A wildlife photographer once described his favourite time for working: the battle between seasons, when a new season takes over from the one that has just ended. Sometimes you can see it in the giant but short-lived ferns. They dry up in the summer and are painted a fabulous golden rust shade, looking limp after foggy nights.

Every evening when darkness falls, I see the same woman riding a scooter at the head of a herd returning to their barn. The horse Prince and a pony, accompanied by a pampered puppy and a sheepdog, run in front of them. When I stop, a haughty giant goat with an air of authority arrives. It is followed by an apprehensive sheep. The head goat looks intently at the foreign driver and whispers something in the other's ear. They both turn in their tracks. But the woman calls out, "Anna, Anna," and says to me, "Pass, pass," you can pass.

I move aside at this wondrous sight, and the leading goat ventures forward once more. Following it, through a narrow crack in the fence, spills a white cascade of sheep. They want to catch up with each other so as not to be left alone, bleating lambs chasing after their mothers. They pass with urgency rushing in front of the car's headlights. The pony pushes between the dog and the horse, the horse trots by, the goat proudly leads and the sheepdog checks that everything is in order as the small dog climbs into the shepherd's arms. Only small droppings remain on the path.

One evening as it gets dark, I see the beam from a torch moving as if marking the boundary to my property. I approach and see a tall, stout man shining a flashlight on the ground and ignoring my arrival. He continues to examine something until he disappears from sight beyond the thicket. At that moment, as if orchestrated by a skilled film director, Zadok's employee, Jorge, appears on my doorstep, so I ask him to speak to the torch man. As usual, they converse at length, and it turns out that the issue at hand is that of water distribution. 15 June, says the robust man, is the beginning of the relatively dry spell that lasts until the rains, and there is a list of households that are entitled to draw water to their land from the central canal and specific times when this is permitted. For example, he receives water "from when the sun disappears behind the mountain". The man points to the distant ridge at the back of which the sun is already fading. This is how times were set before the advent of church bells. "For instance, your time is tomorrow from five o'clock in the afternoon," the man tells me.

He is from a nearby village but keeps some sheep here. He points to the field where every morning I see a handful of grazing sheep. They have a water quota too.

"How many sheep do you keep?"

"Six," he says apologetically, "but there will be more. They are pregnant."

He was passing through my land, he explains, to make sure that the wooden stoppers were blocking my sub-channel, and that the water continued down another course which passes underground to his pasture.

At night, sheep appear in my dream. I lie in the meadow, and they surround me, cropping the grass and sometimes licking me like dogs or gathering around me as if discussing my future. I wake up from the dream wanting to witness the birth of a lamb, like an echo of the intimacy with which nature surrounds me. Perhaps it is the call of the wild.

The Mystery of the Vanishing Glass Harp Player

"Wolfing the past like bread, without time like butter in your teeth!"

Álvaro de Campos, "Birthday"

81

Sometimes, when a tangle of wild thorny shrubs at the back of some abandoned house ensnares me and tears at my flesh, I ask myself why I find the empty and deserted so appealing. What is it that makes me search for phantom music, the seductive sirens of oblivion? Why do I return to the realm of spiders in attics, dark, damp basements and rotting stairwells ominously creaking under my feet?

Am I searching for the ghosts of my parents who fled Europe, their old country, the Jewish Atlantis of millions, including dozens of my family members who disappeared without a trace mid-century? Perhaps nostalgia for the humble farm of my maternal grandparents, from which they were banished to their deaths. Those erased and silenced old family memories are resurfacing now. The image of an apartment by the river above a wine shop in a charming village no different from Cerveira. I wonder, did my grandparents lock their home before they were uprooted, did they turn the lights off, ask a neighbour to water the plants, abandon a beloved pet?

Seventy-seven years after the catastrophe, I have returned to Europe to renovate an old house and lead a country life very much like my mother's on her father's farm. The Portuguese remind me of my parents: short in stature, decent, industrious, quiet, and very clean. I return to the past to find it a dynamic present. Maybe it is a case of the famous wandering Jew gene or a fascination with water and vegetation of which my parents spoke with longing, even in the desert habitat to which they emigrated. Every Saturday, they would take us to visit the sparse forests planted by the Jewish National Fund, a pathetic attempt to establish a small version of Europe in the hot Middle East.

We hiked through uniform pine forests planted in arid areas, where, after a rainy day, the air held a hint of European rot, and golden pine mushrooms thrived in the shade.

On the outskirts of Cerveira, beyond the river, between the stadium and the round swimming pool, I often pass a deserted red house, proud despite its desolation. A haughty beggar commanding its own hill with a stone turret like a giant chess piece. The windows of the house facing the river are boarded up like the eyes of a blind person. At the back is a garden with an avenue of orange trees and an ornamental pond featuring a shattered ceramic fountain.

Not a soul has lived here for years.

Bending, I squeeze through a small hole in the wall. I climb up a spiral staircase to discover two storeys from which even the tiles have been stripped. Water trickles down the roof to the stairwell. Locals recall that the tenant was "an Austrian and a homosexual". He fell in love with the Alto Minho and lived here alone with his dog. Each year he raised a flag that might have been Austrian. His dog would walk to town on its own to pick up the newspaper and bread in a little basket.

Venturing further, I discover a spacious central hall with a large fireplace, a kitchen and toilets, and a bedroom on the second floor with a balcony overlooking the nearby river. Someone has spray-painted "Death" in black on the stairwell. Squeezing back through the small hole on my way out, I see etched in stone above the gate an inscription in Roman numerals: 1963.

It is a lead into the past.

"The documents of Casa Tinta from the 1960s, please," I ask the archivist at the Cerveira records office, pointing at the house through the window. She knows.

The archive is a modern, beautiful, bright building whose rooms hide treasures. Occasionally they present a small exhibition. Now on display is Cerveira's role in World War I:

photographs of a local pilot, a brigadier, a soldier kissing a girl before parting. Objects on display: uniforms, weapons, a pilot's helmet.

A thin cardboard folder, like a treasure map, arrives at my desk. I carefully spread out the folded pages. As the engraving suggests, Casa Tinta was indeed granted a building permit in 1963. House blueprints also include an accurate and elegant drawing submitted in June 1962 to the local council. The house plan is on a 1:500 scale. It depicts the façade, interior design, floor plan, side view, garden plan and the railway tracks that separate the plot and the town. Also, the design of the windows facing the river. The round turret is a stone stairwell that contrasts with the red-brick façade.

The house name is registered under "Lusitania" - the ancient name of Portugal. One room with an area of sixty-five square metres is marked *Biblioteca*. There is a terrace overlooking the river. Also present are all the permits and receipts for fees paid; the bureaucracy of building a home. Everything was well documented towards the end of Salazar's reign.

And here is the lost name: Ejnar Hansen, and with him listed an American partner. Hansen is a typical Danish name. Not Austrian or American. The discovery sets off a chain of quickly unfolding details. I show the plans to the architect César Rouco Marques, whose office is in front of the Villa Rosa Café. Typing something, he points at the computer screen. In the past, he was interested in buying the house and immediately noticed a strange detail: it was constructed counter to its 1962 official plans, like a mirror image. He suspects that when construction began, the owner realized that he could have more privacy if he turned the house around.

The side with fewer windows faces the town, while the balcony and larger windows face the river. The entrance to the house and its lower-level garden face east, where there is no other construction other than the cemetery. This keeps the house and garden partially hidden. "Discretion," says architect César. He is an agile man from Porto, exceptionally knowledgeable in the ways of building.

I return to Isabel de Portugal Marreca with the name Ejnar Hansen. Oh yes. Hansen does evoke some memories. Specifically, she recalls an image from one life-changing and traumatic day about fifty years ago. Isabel remembers when Mr Hansen first appeared in Cerveira in the early 1960s, five years before the incident which happened near his house. She waves her hand as if repelling an insect from her face. "It is such a horrible memory. All I want is to forget."

When Hansen arrived in Cerveira, her grandmother and mother immediately befriended him. When they visited, the house still smelled of fresh paint and lime. She was a mere nine-year-old girl. "Very few got to know him around here, and all who did were upper-class." She remembers a handsome and talented man, a painter, an author and an art collector. Growing up in a wealthy home, she at once recognized the value of the precious objects and paintings in his house. There was a fifteenth-century chair in the upper living room. "Was he gay?" She does not know. She only remembers that he lived with another man, the man's wife and a younger gardener.

"And the dog?"

Sure. A great Irish Setter that Hansen would send to the store at the centre of town. "The dog went past by Casa Verde each morning and would return with fresh bread and an English daily in his basket; although Hansen lived here for many years, he did not speak the language and never mixed." She remembers a helpful detail: "Hansen was an expert glass harp player, a kind of xylophone made of wine glasses. He was world-famous and played classical works."

Isabel's miraculous memory, which loses no details, also

recalls that he did some travelling. Sometimes he would lock up Casa Tinta and travel for months to India or visit friends around the world. When he returned, he would raise the American or Danish flag. This way, he informed people that he was back.

"I will never forget how every time we came to visit, this polished society man would kneel in front of my grandmother and put a pillow under her feet. Such tenderness and respect. The townsfolk, they did not like him. Perhaps they could not understand him because there were not many foreigners around at the time, and he *was* very different. But people like my grandparents, and Tiago's father, did befriend him. Sometimes he would play music for us and then walk in socks over the wooden floor, brushing it with his feet." He would tell us about India, where his friends held terrific parties. He also mentioned elephants."

"What did he look like?"

"Like you, if I may say so. Average height, foreign, white hair, pale eyes." She regards me as if suddenly aware of a striking similarity between the two foreigners who appeared in town: non-Portuguese speaking, forcing her to converse in English.

Among all the paintings she saw in the spacious upper and lower rooms, she remembers a large picture of a palace that might have been Hansen's childhood home. When you evoke a memory, a sound, a name, or in this case, the image of a house the colour of raw meat, an old curtain is lifted. I ask about Hansen, and Isabel steps inside that abandoned Red House as she reclines on her colourful bed at Malaposta, surrounded by a thousand souvenirs and photos from her wild youth.

"He called this place his paradise because he was a man of refined tastes who coming here, fell in love with the river, the town, the sea and the forests. All that beauty. He was a nature lover who travelled a lot with his dog and always dressed like a movie actor," says Isabel, framed by the rich setting. "Always in a nice suit, a cravat around his neck and sometimes wearing a bow tie. And I would sit next to my mother and grandmother, on the balcony facing the river. The house was hidden. It could not be seen from Cerveira. Sometimes we sat in the garden to sip tea."

She remembers well what I only glimpsed in the deserted grounds. "On one side is a garden with a fishpond and a fountain and on the other, an arrangement like ours. Artificially arranged rocks, a small cave and a waterfall. The train passed by the end of the garden like today. The tracks separated it from Cerveira."

She shudders when recalling the Day of the Dead in the winter of 1968 when she was fourteen. The date has haunted her all her life. On the first of November, when people go to cemeteries to lay flowers on graves, Isabel de Portugal Marreca was riding in a car with a friend, Paulo, and his older brother Carlo. Carlo was driving. As they were crossing the tracks near the cemetery, there was a spot where the train would slow down and people jump off. Isabel sat next to the driver, and Paulo sat in the back, flippantly trying on her yellow hat.

"We were all laughing."

"A woman and a man were standing with their child by the tracks. The man motioned for the car to pass but then suddenly shouted: 'The train!' And we saw the locomotive bearing down on us so close that in a panic Carlo stopped on the tracks and we opened the doors and ran away. Paulo came out after me. For one split second, I felt the tip of his hand touch my back; perhaps he delayed a moment longer because he couldn't see what we saw. Then Carlo's terrible scream: 'I killed my brother!' And I saw Paulo crushed and dragged along with the train, my hat cast aside. Three months later, I was still sleeping with my nanny because of the nightmares."

The day after the disaster, Paulo's mother arrived from Geneva, and Isabel's uncle, Dr Bonifácio, came from the Casa

Verde and gave her a sedative as she was being told of the disaster; "It happened close to Hansen's house. I have not gone there since. And only from my mother did I hear that he came to a sad end."

82

Luis, the insulation specialist, has prepared a winter outfit for the house. Large rolls of yellow wool are unfolded, cut and stuffed into crevices between the old stone walls and white drywall. A warm sweater now separates the outer cold and damp from the warm interior. The smooth white wall reflects the light, breathing new spirit into the rooms. Luis and his assistant have installed a lighter wall where the heavy wall collapsed into the animal pens. They separated the two upstairs rooms by putting in balcony walls. This way, the house shelters the stone wall inside so that what was once a sturdy exterior wall is now at its heart, its beauty revealed through the exposed granite stones; it radiates the past and the spirit of Franco's time. One of the old windows has also been left untouched. The soul of the house still belongs to the rural nineteenth century.

Franklin's worker finishes the kitchen wall where cabinets complete with sink and a countertop will be installed. The pantry will be at the back of the wall, where there are hidden wooden stairs to the gallery. A worker is attaching colourful bird tiles to the smooth concrete. Thus, out of the remains of the old house, the new one grows. In the room overlooking the square, where Marília spent her last years, a yellow epoxy floor has been laid, a shower fitted, all the facilities that did not exist before. Gone are the scars on the wall where Marília's bed lay, but her memory has not been erased. It lives on through the house where I document her past. Hers to me a life of toil worth documenting in case it should be forgotten.

On lazy days, I write in the café and read Roger Crowley on Portugal, how the many voyages of discovery from the tiny nation on the fringes of Europe founded an efficient distribution of knowledge and commodities: gunpowder and bread for Japan, green beans for China, African slaves to America, tea for England, pepper for the New World, remedies for all of Europe and a genuflecting elephant as a gift to the Pope. Crowley describes how the Portuguese established new connections between different nations and parts of the world. This had a decisive impact and changed the face of the planet as a whole. It is surprising and strange to read about this global influence now, in the twenty-first century, in a café in Cerveira. I am residing in a humble country whose sense of greatness is long gone.

Only when immersed in nature do I feel the vibrations of the past, its grandeur, the mystery. It happens when the sun begins to light the horizon, and I glide towards the river entering like a blind ship into the fog. The world at my feet then resembles an ocean. No land. There is no road, river or village. Everything disappears as if a dam has opened, and the familiar is flooded with a milky fog. It is so thick that driving one's car, one floats inside it enveloped in moisture, and the moss glistens like algae growing underwater. I am reminded of the Arabic phrase "the green sea of darkness" and of all those valiant sailors who sailed with outstretched sails towards the unknown.

83

ONE MORNING VISITING CERVEIRA, I discover the near-deserted town suddenly bustling and awash with visitors. Not a free table is to be found at the cafés which have stood abandoned for months. The Alto Minho population seems to have doubled, perhaps tripled, and the younger two generations magically appear like a demographic miracle. Each local couple of a certain age has welcomed back children and grandchildren, all the young people who have left throughout the years to build a life for themselves elsewhere. Most of them live in France or other European countries and work all year round without a single day off; hard-working and frugal, they await the summer.

Bursting with pent-up energy, they piled their luggage into their cars in Paris, Marseille or some other city and drove for an entire day to their parents or to vacation homes built on family property. The younger people like to keep dirt bikes lying idle in deserted sheds or barns for eleven months, then use them to roar up peaceful mountainsides. The country roads swarm with Alfa Romeos, Mercedes and Peugeot SUVs overtaking more cautious drivers in smaller local vehicles. With the surge in energy, motoring behaviour in the sleepy countryside changes, and the accident rate goes up for a while. The holiday season does away with good manners and reserve, breaking the normal rules. The constant background noise is of a huge family gathering with the crackling of fireworks, the thumping rhythms of seasonal parades and the festive horns of village brass bands.

In the evening, as I sit typing away in the sleepy Café Da Carla under the *telenovela* screen, the door flies open, and a dozen or so loud and chatty family members march in, young and old. Their clothes and customs are different, and they inject a noisy and frivolous spirit into the tired locale. It is as if these flesh and blood families can keep the ghosts of the past at bay for a time. A fair-haired little child sits next to his grandmother, their resemblance unmistakable. He speaks perfect standard English, but when turning to his grandmother he converses in Portuguese. She is apparently appalled by his lax manners.

Six visitors from Paris appear as I walk in a field: sturdy young men and a woman with a pushchair, a girl and a dog. They surround a tractor driven by a local grandpa. The boys laugh as if taking part in a country show. Still quite smartly dressed, they swing hay bundles and load them onto the cart. The woman lifts up the little one and puts him on the grandfather's lap. He drives off, one hand on the wheel and the other wrapped around the toddler, who is jubilant with fear and joy. This scene will be forever etched in the child's memory: his Candemil slice of heaven, the paradise of summer.

Due to high seasonal demand, we are without a rental car and regress to a time when people used their legs to get to the nearest town. Walking by the side of the road at natural human pace, we observe things we otherwise miss when driving. Next to the bend at the entrance to the village, we turn onto a road which ascends sharply up to a eucalyptus forest. There stands a plain wooden cabin supported by four tree trunks, and when I look inside, I find a massage bed. In this Robinson Crusoe camp are sheds, a greenhouse and a caravan.

A woman is standing there with a baby in her arms. Her name is Alexandrina Lobo. "Lobo as in wolf," she says, "I am a lone wolf."

The wolf cub is called Ana Vitória. A cat slips inside the caravan to lie on the girl's bed. About twenty years ago, Alexandrina Lobo met a young indigenous shaman in Brazil. He introduced her to the secrets of the spirit world and married her. Thirteen years ago, their son was born. When she returned from Brazil, she lived in Braga but dreamed of a house in the woods and bought a piece of land in Candemil. The man and child returned with her. He helped her set up camp with the greenhouse, a vegetable garden and a rudimentary consulting room, then returned to Brazil. Lobo hopes that people will come to be healed by her, the local shaman. But the place is built under eucalyptus trees too acidic to grow vegetables underneath. At night a thick and damp darkness descends on Alexandrina, Ana Vitória and the cat Mica. Lobo has decided to return to Braga, and she asks me to keep an eye on the cat. Beginning everything anew has not been easy.

84

WHEN I TIRE OF MY empty promises to clear the debris in the yard with the help of a truck, and wanting a tidier garden, I decide to light a fire one morning. The yard still glistens from the early morning showers as I set fire to the pile of scrap wood and sections of wall consisting of old clay and wooden lattices. The fire grips the wall sections, and by nightfall it is eating away at the embedded timber, leaving intact the sturdier materials, the clay that held it together. I collect and sort the toxic construction waste into plastic, polythene and metal components, distributing it via many wheelbarrow journeys to different waste containers.

The sun rises behind damp hills and forests. Candemil is warmer, but Cerveira is enveloped in thick mist rising from the river; only its high ridges protrude from beneath, like sunny, exotic isles from the sea.

Inside the lovely Cerveira library, the librarian points to the two shelves of English books. I am looking for the three books written by Ejnar Hansen. It turns out that they were published in New Delhi, and all of them sport a handwritten dedication to the city library. Next to the signature is the name of the house: Lusitania.

For the first time, I am holding in my hands a tangible object, a book donated to the library. The dedication, in lovely, neat handwriting, belongs to a person with whom I now feel an affinity that transgresses time. He is a fellow immigrant who fell in love with the region's beauty, tied his destiny to it and settled down to write. He left behind a house, the sum of his dreams and fancies, and a mystery. Here you are, Ejnar; I am holding on to the hem of your ghostly apparel, embroidered with the cobwebs and dust of oblivion.

The three books mention different dates around the mid-1990s, some thirty years after the house was built, at a time when northern European money had already taken hold here. Hansen was in his mid-seventies. The Angolan writer tells me that returning to Cerveira in 1993, he remembers "the foreigner's dog going to the store to pick up the newspaper. I noticed it because our dogs were friendly, and his dog would come over sometimes to play with mine."

I pick up the three autographed books preparing to commune with the long-departed author, and settle down in the reading room next to two men looking through the daily newspaper. The first book, *Book Me Around the World*, describes Hansen's varied travels, from Cuba to Afghanistan, India, Haiti, Thailand, Japan and other exotic places. The inquisitive Dane seems to have set foot everywhere. "I have an aggressive travel gene," he wrote. In the second book, Hansen describes the life of a dog named Fidel from the animal's point of view, like *Flush*, only without the talent of Virginia Woolf. The third book is autobiographical; I check it out and begin to read eagerly. It describes the author's life from the time he was born at the end of World War I in the second largest city in Denmark, how at the age of twelve he was bereaved after his beloved father's death and was the youngest of seven children raised by "the best mother in the world".

The painting of the palace that Isabel saw on Hansen's living room wall does not depict his childhood home. His was a humble household barely surviving the frozen Danish winters. The book's title is *Storm in Some Glasses*, an allusion to the core of his creative life as a glass harp player. It is the story of a man whose life centres around playing Chopin and other classics with his fingers on the moistened rims of wine glasses. He describes how he discovered this eighteenth-century invention in his youth and learned to play, then travelled. He sought to make a name for himself abroad and made sure to hide his attraction to people of the same sex.

As is evident in the photographs, the owner of the Red House was a very handsome young man. He felt an emotional attachment to intelligent women and a physical attraction to young men, only implicit in his tales. During World War II, after his country was bombed and occupied by Germany, he travelled to Berlin and Vienna and describes the bombing, brutish military men and the music. In the Austrian capital, he experienced the horror of contemporary events and, according to him, even performed at the Gestapo headquarters. He describes a blood-curdling yet somehow comical scene in which a Polish noblewoman whom he revered, Madame Mici, attempts to save a Jewish girl from the clutches of the Nazis.

Upon his return home, Hansen discovered that his brother had joined the Danish underground. Nevertheless, he preferred to broadcast glass harp radio concerts. Four years after the war, he left Europe with one final concert. "Ejnar Hansen is a genius of wine glasses," "Hansen takes the audience back to the days of the Rococo," wrote enthusiastic critics of the thirty-one-year-old who went on to sail towards the American dream.

His first months in New York were as miserable as any immigrant's. Penniless, he worked folding envelopes at his country's embassy, survived on sardines and lived in a five-dollar-a-night alcove next door to an older Italian man called Frank. One day, after his neighbour had not been seen for a while, police broke down the door and found Frank's rotting body. He had died alone, like a stray dog. This incident was etched in Hansen's memory like a glaring warning of lonely old age, perhaps a macabre prophecy of the heart.

For a dozen years, he lived in the United States and made his mark in a relatively short time. He imported Danish cheese, worked at a bank on Wall Street, invested in stocks, and even appeared with his glass harp on television and radio shows. He struck up a friendship with the famous Danish entertainer pianist

Victor Borge. Hansen was a Scandinavian heartthrob: dark hair, bright teeth, smiling, bespectacled and talented. Within a few years, he was already thriving in the wealthiest metropolis in the world. He gave himself ten years to save up money to realize his dream of "retiring to a peaceful country life while still relatively young". Twelve years passed before he moved to Cerveira.

About sixty years later, I am sitting in my room reading about the glorious journey of the forgotten man. The autobiographical book omits his refuge in Cerveira altogether. Only a single photograph depicts the Red House as it was in the 1970s: a well-groomed residence arranged for a comfortable secret life with four chaises longues in the garden. The eye prefers to dwell on the plush details of this private paradise rather than on the ugly, skeletal remains of today's crumbling mansion.

Cow Shed Dreams

"There are some places here, thank God one finds them everywhere, where one feels more at home than anywhere else, where one gets a peculiar pristine feeling like that of homesickness, in which bitter melancholy plays some part; but yet its stimulation strengthens and cheers the mind, and gives us, we do not know how or why, new strength and ardour for our work."

Vincent Van Gogh to his brother Theo, in *Letters to Theo*

85

Bright light enters the new windows in the former animal pens facilitating the renovation work. Franklin's crew begins excavating a sixty-centimetre layer of soil, excrement and old fodder accumulated over a hundred years under the hooves of sheep and cows. The workers arrive with a convoy of wheelbarrows, shovels and hoes. Later, this rich compost is scattered throughout the garden. Seeds that have lain dormant for many years may germinate in the sunlight. The dung of long-dead cows will feed next year's apples and pears. The workers level and press a thick layer of pebbles on the exposed ground inside and pour a coat of uncompressed cement, thirty centimetres thick. The plumber installs the water pipes leaving openings in the wall, and the Frankliners cover them with wide plastic sheets again.

When the floor dries, they pour a layer of liquid concrete mixed with iron oxide powder, an iron pigment that fortifies the adhesive and gives it a reddish tint. They push an old-fashioned wooden plate on the damp surface in a circular motion. This device is used in confined spaces where a mechanical "helicopter", which polishes floors to a shine, cannot be operated. The floor is reddish and still shiny. "It is a type of floor that is coming back into fashion again after almost disappearing," says Gilberto. "Similar floors are only found in Brazilian houses from the early twentieth century. Concrete floors are usually laid in humid spaces such as bathrooms and kitchens."

In the middle of the reclaimed space, the plasterer has built a small kitchen. The room to the left opens onto a bathroom. The main area has been redivided into two rooms with a shared passage to form a small apartment.

Framed by elongated granite beams, the two windows cast light at all hours of the day. Each window has a deep alcove with a thick wooden board beneath. Cleaned with a pressure hose, the stone walls return to their original light colours, stripped of a hundred years of filth. The spaces between the stones have been filled with a soft material, but the granite is still damp because part of the wall lies below ground level, and the carpenters surround it with a wooden skirting board and leave a gap between stone and wood for the ancient moisture to slowly evaporate.

I turn on the radiator, slowly heating up the new rooms inside the old shell, and we fall asleep for the first time in our home. It is quiet in the lower quarters, which were once filled with damp fur, barking and the dreams of pigs, sheep and cows. Now it is a thick-walled, soundproof human residence with double-glazed windows and door. We sleep on a soft bed, embracing under the duvet. In our sleep, we pass through dream-filled corridors. As we wake up in the middle of the night and fall asleep again, the street light casts a faint glimmer on the wall. In the morning, soft light from the backyard peeps into the bedroom. What was once the property of Marília, Franco and, before him, his father, mother and grandparents is now our home.

86

With the evidence gathered from his books and from the internet, the plaster of time slowly peels off Hansen's story. The story of the forty-three-year-old who came to Cerveira in 1961 is gradually revealed. He arrived accompanied by N., a twenty-four-year-old American friend, tall and handsome, who still lives in Portugal with his family. Hansen fell in love with the region's beauty and its atmosphere, its "velvet air", as Henry James would describe it. He settled down in a town with white steeples, an ancient fortress and a green ceramic-clad house, where the extended Marreca family lived, including a girl by the name of Isabel who sometimes visited.

In Cerveira, he found the river, forests, hills, villages and ideal hiking trails for a man with a dog. "I have found paradise," he wrote to friends in the United States. He loved dogs and throughout his life favoured their barking company, free of judgment or criticism and infinitely loyal. He had at his disposal a large sum of money accumulated during his American years, which allowed for early retirement. Several months later, at the more desolate end of town by the railroad tracks, he found a farm with massive trees and large rocks. It had a fantastic view of the nearby river.

He decided to build a spacious, two-floor reddish brick house on his land, with no basement or attic, a prominent tower shaped like a chess piece, and a wide terrace. For a year, carpenters, stonemasons and roofers worked together on the house, generating novel and exciting activity on what was otherwise a lonely riverbank. When the house, garage and gardens were complete, Hansen filled them with precious objects: antique furniture and small, beautiful pieces, books and paintings by Marc Chagall, silk sheets, elegant clothes and plenty of shoes.

The Minho River constituted the border between two enemy states ruled by dictators and was an active nocturnal passage for smugglers. Sometimes gunshots or the sound of oars could be heard at night along with the shouting of policemen from the dark riverbank. Each year, about fifty thousand people were forced to migrate from the country in search of a livelihood. Still, Hansen clung to his new place because of its loveliness and perhaps the steadiness provided by a nation frozen in time. It was unique in that it did not take sides in World War II. Consequently, it was not bombed to destruction, and therefore not rebuilt with American money.

"The era of Salazar protected the landscape," the Portuguese say. The Old World never changed much here in terms of scenery, clothes, art and literature. Ejnar Hansen loved that, and it suited his fantasy of a remote hideout on the shores of a European river. Only the passengers on a passing train or those on the river, like the boy Tiago in his father's boat, could peek inside the house's gardens.

Hansen was a vagabond with romantic notions who wanted to grow old in nature, "far from the madding crowd. Engaged in reading, writing, music, gardening, and travel," as he wrote in his book. When he travelled from Cerveira to India or other countries, he left his dog with an English couple living in the village of Covas. He wrote his three amateur books, full of anecdotes, sitting in his house in which he lived, according to Isabel Marreca, like some form of refined, exotic, secretive Henry James.

"There are some places here, thank God one finds them everywhere, where one feels more at home than anywhere else," he wrote quoting a letter once sent by Vincent van Gogh to his brother Theo. "Places where one gets a peculiar, pristine feeling like that of homesickness, in which bitter melancholy plays some part; but yet its stimulation strengthens and cheers the mind, and gives us, we do not know how or why, new strength and ardour for our work."

This is how Hansen felt in Cerveira; I share the feeling.

Hanne Foighel, a foreign correspondent for a Danish newspaper and a friend, locates his nephew Henrik Hansen for me. He is the son of Ejnar's brother, Eric Hansen. Like their late relative from Cerveira, the father and son used to play the glass harp. The father has recently died, and his son Henrik is very eager to see his uncle's house. He writes to say that uncle Ejnar was "the black sheep of the family, who withdrew from the flock, maybe because of his sexual tendencies." He met his uncle in the 1990s when, in his old age, Ejnar paid a visit to Denmark. "We had no idea he was a property owner. He always looked thrifty, living with friends; he had so little to spend."

After Ejnar's death, none of his possessions, artworks or property passed down to his relatives. They imagined that he had left everything to his partner or had died penniless. Now that a connection with the nephew has been established, it seems that Henrik is resuming his interest in his late uncle. He contemplates coming to see the Red House. But after a brief correspondence, the line goes dead. The old curtain that for a moment lifted descends on Hansen once more.

In his autobiography, Hansen remained discreet about his sexual orientation. Until the 1970s, even Denmark, very liberal today, was an unforgiving place for homosexuals. "I am lucky," he wrote at the age of seventy, "I retired early to the south of Europe where it is sunny and joyous. If I had to live again, I would change nothing." He did not mention the location of the house anywhere. These days I pass by the house almost expecting to see the Danish flag hoisted on top, and an elegant man with a full white mane and a bow tie standing in front of the house with his dog. I wonder if during his last years in India, away from the Minho, old and destitute, Hansen remembered his old neighbour Frank, who died a lonely death in the next-door room in New York, his body undiscovered for days.

87

"The sky over the Alto Minho is always free of the clouds and smoke of injustice and war," says Jorge with the rhetorical passion of a politician at an election rally. "A land of clear skies," he calls the area to which he returned after many years in Brussels, "free from the contamination of unnecessary and bloody human actions." It seems that those who choose to live here, like Hansen, flee from prying eyes, greed or oppressive families.

"You are fortunate to have found this place," says Tiago, who returned to the area when he was nearing fifty. At the boutique hotel he is building on the family estate in Gondarém, he gives me a tour of a time capsule designed to preserve memories - a private archive of the five generations who originated there. The whole house is redolent of the past: objects, furniture, pictures, even the rooms which have names like Son, Father, Daughter. There is a communal dining area, a private chapel and a shallow pool in the garden to wash the dust off tired feet. Soaking one's feet in the water clears the head and relaxes the mind. After a long journey, it guarantees a sound sleep.

I tell him that since I have moved here, I have been waking up in the middle of the night, rising from my bed, eating a snack, reading and then going back to sleep. My sleep pattern is unusual.

"That is what natural sleep is like," Tiago says. "You are returning to the natural rhythm of the body: two sleep cycles. In the past, all people lived like this. They went to bed when it got dark and woke up in the dead of night after a healthy sleep cycle of dreams, vital for airing the soul. They would eat, do what they had to, and go back to sleep until dawn." I wake up in the middle of the night and avidly read the books I have brought, like a locomotive burning wood to reach the next station. I immerse myself in the thick volume *The Invention of Nature*, recounting the delightful life story of the fearless Prussian naturalist, Alexander von Humboldt.

Despite the restrictions of his time, Humboldt managed to undertake extraordinary journeys. Nature, he believed, is a wild kingdom whose system of checks and balances is based on diversity, from the humble insect and moss to the elephant and tall oak; each has its role to play and only together do they form a whole. He claimed that nature must be described scientifically but without losing the breath of life instilled by imagination. The Prussian left his mark on all natural studies, including Darwin's theory.

"Without losing the breath of life of the imagination." These words ring more true in Candemil than in my previous home.

As I emerge from my home each morning and walk the winding road down to the river, I contemplate how I would describe to a stranger, a chance visitor, or for you, the reader of this book, the nature of the place. The Alto Minho, northern Portugal's border region, contains the last stretch of a wild river flowing into the Atlantic Ocean. Due to its location, Portugal, this ancient country, ended up at the centre of a large empire, vast beyond its origins. Like a small port town venturing far away only to discover lands a thousand times its modest size.

How should I describe its impact on the psyche, this remote location, gorgeous, with its mild weather, sunny winter days and summer thunderstorms? A place where God is a devoted gardener who never lets his flowers wither; after a dry spell, the divine irrigation system is always activated and quenches the thirst of flowers, shrubs, trees and grass. In this place, every daily interaction with locals and passing strangers is out of the ordinary.

"The best conversations I have are with the *camino* pilgrims," Michael tells me. "They are inquisitive seekers, after or before a great adventure, and have interesting personal histories, which is what drove them to the journey in the first place." Perhaps it is the courage they discovered when they dared to leave their life behind and set out on a journey.

It appears that on the banks of the Minho, some amongst us search for a sense of freedom and other possibilities. As a man who has come here in old age, I feel that living as a foreigner has revived me. "The wandering man becomes a primitive man in so many ways, in the same way that the nomad is more primitive than the farmer. But the longing to get onto the other side of everything already settled, this makes me, and everybody like me, a road sign to the future," wrote Herman Hesse in his essay *Wandering*. Michael is happy to have opened his gates to the wanderers. From the river of pilgrims, a narrow channel is diverted into his courtyard.

This is how the Polish pilgrim Luka came into Michael's house. He is a young man with strawberry blonde hair, a beard and a moustache. He grew up away from his father and does not possess any happy childhood memories as his family moved from place to place. He worked on a secluded farm in Portugal for several months for a mad artist whose house was a pigsty. The site was contaminated and smelled of racism and slavery. There he met the Frenchman A., a shepherd, who after a while suggested they escape together for the purifying *camino*.

They set out on the road and walked for four hundred kilometres. A., who carried a twenty-five-kilo backpack, told Luka he felt as if he was flying, that something was waiting for him at the end of the road. When they arrived at Cerveira and stopped to rest, it dawned on them. "I rushed all the way to reach this paradise," said A. He immediately began searching for a house, and Luka, too, fell in love with this river town. "The weather is mild, sunny and rainy in good measure, and life and people here have remained simple, traditional; a way of life rarely found elsewhere," he tells me.

I pay him an hourly wage to help me clear a patch of land and some rubble at the back of the house. The forty-year-old avalanche from when the wall collapsed has grown into a wild mound with ivy and weeds. The skinny Luka is an efficient worker who can lift heavy rocks on his own, load them onto a wheelbarrow and stack them in the corner of the garden. He clears the debris while discussing Hebrew script, infinity, vegetation, survivalism and fire. His mind is full of wild thoughts, the apocalypse, prejudice, Catholicism and Communism.

We struggle together against the multi-tentacled giant plant which clings to the stone mound, its roots and branches so thick they have to be chopped off with an axe. We then wrestle with an ancient low stone wall until it is exposed.

Luka digs while talking about the end of the world. The Polish traveller believes we must prepare for catastrophe. There will be a global power outage and a stop to all modern life as we know it; we will have to live solely from the fruit of our labours. The Alto Minho seems to him to offer good shelter during chaotic times. In this, Luka is echoing generations of Alto Minhans who share similar feelings. Most of all, he likes to talk about fire, which is his true passion. He explains the different colours of flames and how they tell a story; how to utilize wood and other materials to achieve efficient combustion. Over the years, he has learned to make rocket stoves with his own hands from recycled materials, a sort of cooker that even makes use of the smoke. He shows me how to light the Salamander wood-burning stove, which António installed, but differently from how I was taught. He constructs a pyramid with the thickest branches on the bottom, thinner ones on top. He lays kindling and paper at its summit, and when he lights them, the fire spreads downwards.

He is a flame master, a traveller and a fire artisan like Franklin and Manuel are stonemasons. A constructive pyromaniac whose fire is internal combustion, primordial anger and childhood rage from Poland.

Only in proximity to flames does he calm down because he can direct the fire with complete control.

88

Both Isabel and Tiago have a vague recollection that Hansen's life came to a bitter end. I fail to locate a grave or tombstone with his name in the cemetery by his house. Nothing remains but his books in the local library and the abandoned house. If I could, I would hold a belated memorial service for him in Cerveira without a casket. I would have his nephew play Chopin on the glass harp, and someone make a speech about Hansen's musical talent, how he was one of the first outsiders to discover the beauty of Cerveira, and about his passion for aesthetics. Do I feel an affinity to Hansen because of the similar way in which chance has brought us, two foreign authors, to the same place on the banks of the Minho?

In the morning, the registry office is empty, and the official is very polite. I hand him the house documents obtained by Cristina the notary. The file is dated September 1999, thirty-six years after Hansen moved into the Red House. An English-speaking colleague volunteers to help; she diligently rummages through the files, locating a page missing until now, listing the chain of events before 1999.

It appears that a year after building the house, Hansen purchased N.'s share in the property. From that moment on, the whole place belonged to Hansen. People remember that N. was young, handsome and kind-hearted. He connected well with the locals and early on tied his destiny to a local woman, married her and left.

An entry dating December 1987 from a notary's office near Porto states that the sixty-nine-year-old Hansen transferred property rights for the house, garage and grounds *usufruto* to an António from Porto. The official explains that one of the conditions was that Hansen could continue to live on his estate until his death. The following entry date on the page is September 1999, when the entire property passed into the hands of António.

"This is probably when he died," the official remarks.

By the end of the twentieth century, Hansen was around eighty-one years old.

At noon, over lunch at the Dana snack bar in Cerveira, I show the documents to legal expert Tiago. He examines them as if reading a history book. He is a lawyer and a local who understands all too well the course of human actions, dry legal terms and sticky intrigues.

He clarifies the legal term *usufruto*, used to transfer a home or other property from parents to children while the former are still alive, to be enacted only after their deaths. The lawyer says that what is missing is the transfer document itself and an answer to the question of why the Dane gave his house to António. Rumour has it that one of the conditions was that Hansen be paid a monthly sum so he could lead the rest of his life in relative financial security.

Tiago notes the document's details and the address of the notary's office in the town of Póvoa de Varzim on the way to Porto. But when I get there, no other details are noted in the agreement to clarify the how and why of the transfer. All that remains is the rumour that Isabel and others heard that the new house owner did not fulfil his side of the deal. After a time, he failed to send the allowance, thus effectively sentencing Hansen, who had gone on his final journey, to die in poverty.

"When I passed this wonderful house as a child and looked at it from the river, I always imagined an interesting character living there," Tiago remarks sadly. The ending to the story of the beautiful Dane rattles him, as if a glorious past now completely erased somehow shakes the ground under his own feet. He accuses the deceased of folly, and we argue. I believe that Hansen was a man who started out with a difficult childhood but went on to live a full life, with many years of travels, friends and music, his aspirations fulfilled, books and success on television. I think of people he met along the way as described in his book, for example, James Dean, who was looking for work in Hollywood like him. Hansen was a man who led a humble life in India for periods at a time and lived for many years in the place he loved: Vila Nova de Cerveira.

I feel closer to Hansen's outlook on life than Tiago's, but the *vinho verde* softens our words, and we are amused, rather than upset, by the disagreement. At a nearby table, a man listens in to our enthusiastic conversation. Tiago quietly tells me that it is right for a stranger to listen in because "words are meaningful when they are thrown like a pebble into waters forming circles. The power of words is that they are absorbed and take on life." If so, at any moment we might see Hansen's dog walk past us, carrying round its neck the small basket containing fresh bread and a 1964 newspaper.

89

Luka and I are continuing our rubble-removing mission at the back of the house when suddenly I hear a commotion by the gate: clunks and screeches, several men talking all at once. I am not expecting anyone and no one usually comes by. But when I open the gate, I see two workers already unloading a rusty concrete mixer from a truck straight into my garden. After a year of interminable waiting for the roofers, this feels like a bizarre case of *déjà-vu*. But the boss in this case has appeared for a different reason and introduces himself: Manuel Cruz, here for the *calçada*.

I shake his hand in bewilderment. Manuel, the expert stonemason who promised to come but never showed up. Manuel, of whom I have despaired to the point of seeking out another stonemason, is finally here. He has come to pave the patio, flood-proof it, and create a layer of protection against the rampant vegetation that covered the soil when we first got here.

The uneven paving stones of the traditional *calçada* are found everywhere locally, including on old roads. They sink and fade from view when not adequately tended to; weeds grow between them. If weeds are not thoroughly uprooted, alluvium accumulates with the rains, and a thin layer of soil suffices to produce a jungle.

In the years since Marília's death, the courtyard has become overgrown and threatens to turn into woodland.

"If you don't want to weed between the paving stones, you can always scatter a sack of twenty-five kilos of salt," suggests Isabel's son. "By scattering salt, you prevent vegetation from growing." But salt is an imperfect solution because the water washes it away, taking it to places where you want flowers and shrubs to grow. Manuel intends to till the soil, which has not been turned since the digging of the septic tank, re-pave the inner courtyard, and fill the spaces with concrete so that no grass can grow and soil does not collect.

As Manuel's men unload their equipment - twenty sacks of cement, sand and small cobblestones - Luka carries on removing the debris from the area where I intend to plant a small, secluded space within the garden. I move between Luka and Manuel, who begins work immediately, kneeling and raking. When he finally gets up, he is gasping for air. Like his brother, he suffers from a lung disease caused by many years working with granite. He stretches before resuming his position, tilling and placing the stones. Beside him are his two Jorges.

One Jorge is heavyset and in possession of an immense belly, *gordo*, he admits. He speaks some French, and so becomes the official translator. Second Jorge is slimmer and more energetic. The *gordo* groans with each wheelbarrow shove as if about to burst, and the thin one hurries him along. They turn the radio up loud, then activate the mixer. Noisy discussions can be heard from their area of the yard as they rake all the leftover old paving stones. These stones carry the entire history of the house, the livestock and the hardships of time and the weather. When the boss leaves in his truck to a different site, the Jorges slow down as if hitting a sharp incline.

The role of the *gordo* lies in his weight. He is a crane and a bulldozer, pushing heavy rocks and swinging a crowbar. While the *gordo* pushes wheelbarrows, the skinny one builds the paved slope. Without machinery, they move a human-sized rock, uprooting it, and as it begins to roll down, directing it via smaller stones to its intended spot where it comes to rest. Manuel unloads square paving stones meant for the entrance to the animal pens as some form of terrace to blend in with the paved area.

Autumn is already at work as a master gilder. On sunny days, morning mists dissipate and disappear over the hills, giving way to bright light. Luka and I remove more rubble from the space between the renovated house and the former structure, and there seems to be no end to it; we dig and dig, reaching the depths. Only when we finish removing all the ivy branches and other fragments are three buried stone steps exposed. We also discover a large, smooth stone and a precise, man-made hole in its centre, on which the axis of an ancient gate once rested.

A damp creature is disturbed from its rest under the stone mound. It looks like a combination of an ancient lizard and a toad, coal-black with burning flames on it. "Salamander," says Luka. The flaming lizard was once associated with fire and believed to be born of it as it sometimes emerges from the woodpile where it has lain hidden when a fire is to be lit. It was blamed for the death of four thousand soldiers of Alexander the Great, who drank water from a pool where one was concealed. Luka regards the legendary creature with curiosity. When he releases it, the lizard scurries away and disappears between cracks in the wall.

Manuel's men have been at it for several days. During sunny weather, the Jorges work without their boss who is undergoing some medical tests. On rainy days, both melt away as if made of sugar. When Manuel silently returns from his tests, which he feels to be a stain on his industrious nature, the Jorges assist him. The skinny one constructs a curved stone wall for my small garden at the end of the *calçada* and together with the *gordo* installs a stone bench at the entrance to the ex-animal pens. The *gordo* sighs. The thinner one constantly scolds him as if in a failing marriage.

When Manuel returns, he kneels on the ground enacting an ancient ritual. He wears protection for his knees, measures and levels the surface of the sand he pours, builds a slope and then asks for pebbles from the Jorges according to exact sizes. He is a master of stone mosaics. He places a rock on the soft sand bed and then gently anchors it with light hammer blows securing it in place. Crawling and bending, stone by stone, the workmen encourage the jungle courtyard to take on its new-found neat appearance.

One day, towards the end of their project, the Jorges fail to show up, and Manuel appears unaccompanied. Using signs, I make him understand that I wish to work with him and be his water boy. He shakes my hand and instructs me to pour buckets of water from a keg filled with rainwater into the mixer, making sure to use what nature freely gives instead of municipal water. I view the experienced rural artisan as someone who could have lived a thousand years ago. So little has changed in his craft. He possesses a skilled eye in measuring surfaces, angles, waterline marks. He knows the precise spot where to place the stones and how to level them. He structures the pavement according to the design in his head, taking all positions and locations into account. The harmonious composition will serve the courtyard for many years to come.

Running out of some of the materials in the middle of the work, we rush in his truck to Nogueira, his village. Manuel proudly shows me the house he built with his own hands, the space outside and surrounding walls. The courtyard looks like an old, cluttered kibbutz garage: a bobcat, a tractor, trucks and mounds of materials, a cramped shed. With tremendous effort, we lift four wet sandbags into the truck, heavy as iron, and then, with difficulty, hoist up a small ground compactor with a petrol engine. Everything that was hoisted up is then unloaded in my backyard. Manuel pours the sand, lays down stones, chisels them a little and presses them together like a puzzle, sealing the in-between spaces with smaller pebbles. The ground is slowly being appropriated by the master.

This stocky, dynamic, wheezing man, who only speaks Portuguese, was born into a family of eleven children. To help his family, he dropped out of school as a child and went to work. In the old days, children were used as a workforce, and the practice prevailed locally until the second half of the twentieth century. Perhaps due to harsh childhood memories, Manuel has only one daughter and one son who were never forced to work but studied.

He is incredibly hard-working, and people who have recommended him told me that they like to watch him at work. He moves quietly, without music or speech, except occasionally shouting *"Luz!"*, light, when there is a power cut. I then rush to the machine to turn it off because the worn power cord of the mixer is lying on damp ground. When he returns from tests and I inquire after his health, he points to his throat and chest and dismisses the matter as if brushing off a pesky insect.

Work is the only medicine he happily takes.

Half the paving is complete. Then the entire yard. And after that, the area of small square stones in front of the old animal pens under the balcony. He turns on the concrete mixer which he had taken out into the street, pours buckets of water which I carry to him, cement from heavy sacks, sand and light pigment. He fills wheelbarrow after wheelbarrow and runs the liquid concrete over the stones. The concrete sinks, and Manuel goes over it with a broom to fill every nook and cranny. He compresses everything using the loud compactor and after a few hours washes the pavement with a pressure hose.

Before he leaves in the evening, Manuel breathlessly insists on hosing down the road in front of the house, clearing all traces of his work until darkness descends on the alley, and I forcibly push him towards his car:

"Go on Manuel, leave, thank you, *muito obrigado.*"

90

In the morning, the courtyard gate opens onto a shapely patio with its cobblestones and angles, a small stone bench and a round garden wall. Gilberto Carlos arrives, and his face brightens as if witnessing the end of a long journey. Thus conclude the labours of carpenters, stonemasons, builders, plumbers, electricians, insulators and window installers, the tardy and the punctual, the dodgers and the truth sayers. A blessing upon them all.

"And it grew into a real house," he says, almost surprised; according to his architectural credo, this means a structure that fulfils its inherent purpose through all its parts and materials.

Entering Casa Marília, the first thing to note is the wooden structure of the roof, its beams, and the way it rests its full weight on the concrete support, then the old stone walls, the polished wooden floor. Sunlight moves through the house at all hours, looking for openings. The light now touches on clean stone, fresh wood, red and yellow concrete floors and a blue tiled wall. It seems as if the porcelain birds could take off from the wall and fly to the ceiling at any moment.

"When you see the houses built by the Swiss architect Zumthor, you will understand what I am talking about," he says. "Zumthor was also a carpenter who understood wood so he could build houses with proper respect for natural materials. According to him, every material must convey its essential characteristics. One should not force a material to become what it is not." Gilberto tells me of the Japanese who once lived on islands without Archimedes' theories, stones or cement. How they learned to build everything from wood and other lightweight materials without theoretical physics. He enjoys discussing the history of architecture because it is a necessary distraction from headstrong clients, elusive carpenters and all the other irritations that get in the way of the proper use of materials. No frustrations, no liver problems.

Standing on the fabulous patio, Gilberto explains what an inner courtyard is to a house: when the gate shuts, it forms part of the house, an inner skylight room protected from strong winds and prying eyes, damp with rain and full of light, fresh air and birdsong. "Northern Portugal is cold and humid, sometimes hot, so houses are not built around the garden at the back; the balcony instead faces the patio. The storage rooms, wine cellar and exterior walls surround the patio as well."

I examine the house through his eyes, appreciating the patio and its old iron gate built by Franco and decorated by Orit. When it is shut, the yard is indeed hidden from strangers. I can get out of bed in what was the cow shed and stand in the fresh morning air surrounded by the chirping of birds as if I were alone in the world. I place the first flowerpot on the new patio and plant a wisteria seedling. With time it will climb the tight wires between the storage room roof and the balcony railings. I imagine heavy clusters of purple flowers. In a triangular corner left bare, near the entrance stairs from which Marília fell into her bedridden years, I plant a climber to cling to the stone wall. I put in a hibiscus bush with red flowers. Within days new leaves appear on everything I plant in the fertile soil.

As a finishing note, the silent electrician José Carlos Sousa arrives. The electrical arteries have already been put in place. He has come to install light-bulb sockets and extend the wiring to the storage rooms, studio, wine cellar and even the gate of the courtyard. He works all day quietly. After he leaves, and as darkness falls, I turn all the lights on, including the hidden arrangement in the ceiling, revealing the shape of an inverted boat. I go out into the yard, look at our illuminated house, and see the granite wall erected by Franco's father about one hundred and fifty years ago. It stands at the heart of our home, with all the different shades of its stones. Our granite stone wall.

91

As **always, after tremendous effort** comes a sense of emptiness. The entire house is filling with objects and furniture. Nights are quiet, the mornings full of plans, shopping and other to-do lists. I observe the wild green courtyard, our orchard. The debris has been cleared. A pit dug for a fishpond sprouts a cluster of weeds. It is five metres by three and sixty centimetres deep. Here between the red plum tree, the raspberry bush I planted, and the yellow apple tree is where the mound of rubble stood.

Seized by a desire for one last practical accomplishment, I search the web for instructional videos on building a fishpond. It is as simple as making home-made explosives; a matter of technical skills combined with many precautions. I weed and level the soil, remove stones so as not to injure the plastic sheets, tear holes so that water can percolate. I cushion the bottom with soft sand and old nylon, filling up some of the pit to fit the size of the thick plastic membrane I have purchased. I feel a simple joy at overcoming the obstacles through my actions and seeing a task to its end, as satisfying on a desert island as it is in a Portuguese village. This is the very same passion that Daniel Defoe described three hundred years ago in *Robinson Crusoe*, the sense of achievement in lifting a heavy rock or building a goldfish pond. Alone.

When the bobcat operator worked in the yard to clear the debris, he was like a robot moving his mechanical arms, driving back and forth, shovelling the soil. Forming a circle, he moved on an axis to dig the round pool with the elegance of an ice skater. Like this, he loaded all the rubble, pushing and pulling. And when the task was complete, he laid down two metal ramps, jumped into the bobcat and drove it onto the truck.

I stretch out the heavy plastic sheet alone, leaving its margins buried in the raised ground, placing stones along the edges. I collect colourful flat granite stones everywhere. I select the lovelier ones and set up stone banks for my pool. When the sides are finished, I pull out a hose and slowly fill the hole until it becomes a large eye looking up to the sky. It is a mirror reflecting the plum tree, the house wall, the clouds, a ray of sunshine and a flock of birds on a wire.

Only when the pond fills with water does our home seem complete. I enter my pool. Dipping my feet in the calm waters, I suddenly slip on the slick material underfoot, plunging into the water. I remain there lying, wet and peaceful, observing my palace and feeling as happy as the man who fell into a puddle in a story I wrote many years ago.

I am a stone, a star, a fish. Carefree.

At the village café, I find José Oliveira, the council worker, the petrol-powered scythe man. Mounted on an antique moped, he travels with his scythe. We communicate well through hand gestures, theatrics and growls. Within the hour, he leaves my estate with the tall grass trimmed, the fruit trees protruding from bare soil. The pears hang heavy and sweet like the breasts of a wetnurse. The apple tree drops its yellow fruits, and the pebbles cling to each other, forming a path by the water's edge.

Plop! A yellow apple falls into the water.

A startled bird takes off.

92

At THAT SPECTACULAR HOUR WHEN the light is dying, and as the municipal water pipe fills the pond, I see in the alley the man who sold us the house precisely one year before. It now seems like ancient history. Manoel Joaquim shuffles his feet, carrying the scars of a colonial war.

"Come, I will show you something." He draws me inside my courtyard, which he knows better than anyone. I point out the new pond, but the heart of this pragmatic man is not distracted by aesthetics. He sees the municipal pipe and, in broken French, says, "you know you have your own water system?" He leads me with his hand on my shoulder through the metal door of the storage room to the adjacent field and points to where three irrigation canals meet.

Two of them are overflowing with water coming down from the mountain, but one is blocked with debris beneath wild ivy. "If you unblock this, water will flow into your land."

I remember how he seemed when we first came to view the property: an elderly village man wearing a cap, resting on a bench by the fountain. Since that day, we have met numerous times, and I have grown to love my farmer neighbour, the old soldier from the terrible war in Guinea-Bissau, Maria's husband, who passes my house astride his tractor. Seventy-five years old and with a pacemaker, he is always hard at work, a chatty man who inspires warmth, like a French comedian from another time.

In the field, he points to the bottom of the external stone wall of our decrepit storage room and says, "This is where you will find the water passage to your plot." It is clogged with dirt, rubble and ivy roots seeking moisture. "Put your hand inside," he orders. I grope around blindly, finding a square opening dug into the ground at the bottom of the wall. He then approaches the fruit trees with the air of one who has fulfilled the sacred duty of passing on the ancient wisdom of water. He shows me the different fruits of the pear trees, one large with feminine curves and another smaller like an apple. By sinking his teeth into the fruit, he knows precisely when each tree was planted, the variety of fruit and how much everything cost. He installed the iron door to the shed himself, recycling an old door.

Standing by the concrete stairs where Marília fell down while cleaning, never to stand up again, Manuel recalls how she refused to be taken to the hospital in an ambulance as if she had been asked to get into a coffin. She lay in bed and did not complain, accepting it as part of the natural order of things, perhaps recalling her dying mother. Weeks before she died, when they offered to take her to a nursing home, she refused to abandon the village, and the fire brigade transported her bed up the alley to Manuel and Maria's house, to the same room where Manuel's own dying parents once lay.

Manuel now tells me that people from adjacent villages came to visit Marília even on her last day. And when he returned home and entered her room after the *padre* had left, she was breathing slowly and with a lucid mind asked to be dressed in the skirt and blouse she had prepared. She suddenly seemed to him as beautiful as a bride.

Now finished is the telling of the story, which began one year ago.

He pulls out a penknife from his dark jacket and cuts off a branch from the apple tree. He sharpens its end, revealing the green wood, then cutting into the centre of a thick branch, slips in the smaller one. "This is how you graft to make a better apple; you will need a good bandage here." He shows me how to tie it up around the tree wound.

The following day I go to work, clearing the blockage at the canal intersection in the field. I also clear the shorter canal, which extends to the storage room wall. I uproot the plants which disappear into the channel, thinking of Jean de Florette from Marcel Pagnol's Provençal novels. They recount the machinations of villagers in a mountainous, arid area above Marseille. The Alto Minho overflows with water and knows no shortages. Yet when I discover the blocked canal, I see myself as a Gérard Depardieu fighting to the death for my mountain spring.

The canal passes under the storage room crammed with old timber from the house. I dig all morning listening to the gurgling of cold water as it pulls away from the mountain. When the canal is clear of obstructions, I remove the stopper blocking the exit to the field and allow the water to rise up the cross-section until it reaches the top of the opening passage under my storage room; I run to the yard to its exit point and poke around with a long stick until it touches water. I cheer for the return of mountain water into Franco's plot of land.

I fall asleep alone in the refurbished cow shed, where sheep and pigs also lived and died. Early morning light filters through the window, softly waking the new occupant from his sleep. In the window alcove formed by Franklin, the flowerpots bloom. The water is flowing, the kitchen in order. I climb from the courtyard to the first floor and prepare a salad of pears from the tree, mozzarella, papaya, a local yellow mango and fresh mint from the yard. I season it with Portuguese olive oil, sea salt and fresh garlic.

Throughout the day, the sun revolves around the house, peeking through different windows each hour. At night a strong sea breeze blows, rattling a metal bucket and reminding me that winter is around the corner. The thick walls silence any noise, and my sleep is sound. Winter can wreak havoc outside; the animal rooms are a granite womb. Enveloped by the stones and a duvet, I wake up in the middle of the night, turn the lights on, read a little about different lives and listen to the sounds of silence. I fall asleep and wake up with daylight, opening the side door into the courtyard.

The peaceful autumn morning is filled with distant barking, cocks crowing and birdsong. I leave the door open and return to sleep in the fresh air. Day after day, I grow accustomed to the house, fitting it to my measurements. I spend much of my time in the kitchen, living room and studio area. At night when the new wood stove is burning, consuming timber from the old house, I sit by the round dining room table and feel that this home provides something warm and comforting like a familiar old coat.

Driving along the seven kilometres from the Candemil hills to Cerveira, I listen to the cicada-like song of the mechanical strimmers battling the weeds by the side of the road. Water continues to pour in a steady stream from the mountain. Elderly village women climb up the steep path with bouquets for the dead. A man and woman park their car by the side of the road, carefully stepping into the woods. The woman marches behind her husband, who is holding a heavy orange object. After they disappear into the thicket, I hear the sound of a chainsaw as they cut branches from their plot for firewood. Another neighbour hoes her patch of gigantic cabbages. Two municipal workers remove Jesus from the small display cabinet by the side of the road. They paint the small chamber, clean up the son of God and return him to his place.

And I am in mine.